The Phoenix Suburb

A South London Social History

Alan R. Warwick

The Norwood Society

First published, in the U.K. 1972 by The Blue Boar Press
Reprinted 1973
First edition re-printed in paperback by CPI Antony Rowe, Chippenham,
Wiltshire, and published by the Norwood Society.

To My Wife Joan
Who has shared it all with
me, including the historic
draughts of our Norwood home

Contents

Preface to this Edition

It has been 27 years since John Yaxley and I combined with eight other members of the Norwood Society to produce a second edition of Alan Warwick's excellent book on the history of Norwood. Because of the continuing demand the Norwood Society is publishing this softback copy of the original edition which stands on its own very considerable merits. It would be an understatement to say that a lot has happened in Norwood since Alan laid down his pen in 1971. There has certainly been a "stirring in the ashes", as Alan says in his last words. He also says in his preface: "The moment the pen has stopped writing something new happens".

It requires more than an additional chapter to record the past 37 years and one day this will be done in a separate book. John Yaxley's chapter in the Second Edition is now omitted and will surely be the first chapter in a future history.

The copyright of Alan's work passed on Joan Warwick's death in 1996 to their three children, John, Sally and Jasper and we are very grateful to them for their permission to publish this softback edition. Alan's book is dedicated to Joan. For 23 years after his death she worked unceasingly to carry on the work of the Norwood Society. We erected a commemorative plaque on their house in Beulah Hill.

Norwood changed as a suburb on 13th November 1936 when the Crystal Palace burned down. Alan's book records its history and the start of our efforts to "Preserve, Protect and Improve" this Phoenix Suburb. We in the Norwood Society continue this work and hope you enjoy the book. If you are moved to join us in any way or require more information, our website is www.norwoodsociety.co.uk.

July 2008

Leo Held
President
Norwood Society

Author's Preface

When one has lived in a South London suburb as long as I have, one has had to learn to come to terms with it. Failing that, one would have to go and live somewhere else.

Norwood has been variously described as Leafy Norwood, as the suburb built on seven hills (though I have never counted them), as a Hell-hole, as that place between Sydenham and Streatham, and as something akin to Sam Costa's famous "Croinge". However one regards it, to come to terms with Norwood one has to become insensitive to it, or acutely sensitive. I favoured the latter approach.

My earliest recollections of this southern suburb contain golden memories of going picnicking with my mother and brother in the nearby fields of wild flowers, and becoming acquainted with cows and donkeys and ponies. Those fields are now mostly transformed into rows of suburban houses or formal recreation grounds, but I remember them well. Then there were tranquil days at the Crystal Palace, when we had our picnic in the long grass, my mother shielded from the sun's glare by a parasol.

The Palace grounds were a source of special delight. I never failed to be impressed with the majestic flights of steps from the terraces and the pale statues standing rather mysteriously, as though in suspended animation, among the trees and fountains. To me the Palace grounds were as romantic and charged with magic as E. Nesbit's *The Enchanted Castle*, and had a profound effect on my imagination.

In fine weather balloons rose lazily from the Palace grounds and drifted over our garden on Beulah Hill. One day there was a great humming overhead – the first time I had ever heard a great humming overhead – and the *Nulli Secundus*, the first Army Airship, passed stupendously by with three little black silhouetted figures in the lattice-work gondola. That was a breathless moment. Norwood and the rest of South London was being given its first glimpse of a brave new world.

Later, the intrepid Grahame-White flew out of the Palace like a beautiful dragonfly, to be viewed with wonder and delight. It truly seemed in those halcyon days that positively everything worth while happened in this exciting suburb. Even the burning down of the Crystal Palace in 1936 was done in the grand manner, and left those who knew it to mourn its passing ever since.

It was after the war that I began searching for traces of a vanishing Norwood in the form of pictures and writings on the subject to augment my own memories. I found no histories later than about 1898, but by haunting second-hand bookshops I gradually amassed a considerable amount of casual literature bearing on the subject.

I began to visit libraries as well, and received splendid encouragement from such dedicated librarians as Miss Williams of the Minet Library, Mrs. Read of the historical library at Manor House, Lee, from the Croydon, Penge and Beckenham Libraries, and, of course, from the superb British Museum Reading Room. Mr. E. P. Winser, Librarian of the Science Museum Library, South Kensington, enthusiastically put into my hands a vast amount of contemporary information concerning the important ballooning and aviation days at the Crystal Palace. The Royal Aeronautical Society Library was equally a gold mine on this fascinating subject. From these I was able to glean a picture of the great ballooning days at the Crystal Palace, the final stages of which I had been a youthful spectator. The Church Commissioners provided me with some very human glimpses of the All Saints Parish, which were vastly helpful.

Such publications as *The Illustrated London News*, *The Times*, and many other periodicals, some now defunct, made long-forgotten events read as though they had only happened yesterday or last week. It is the curious vividness of the contemporary accounts, as for example the strange enquiry into the number of burials in All Saints graveyard, that caused me to quote rather than paraphrase where it seemed that the impact on the reader would be more graphic.

One embarks on a local history at one's peril! The moment the pen has stopped writing something new happens. The Greater London Council has now planned to wipe away the desolation that has for so long marred the eastern side of the Crystal Palace Parade, of which I make plaintive mention in chapter seven, and to develop it into fair parkland open to all from the Parade.

Whether a suburb is S.E. or S.W., or N. or E., or whatever, it represents a way of life with influences at work which fashion that suburb. It is those influences that in more recent years have prompted local communities to form their own preservation societies, so that they, as well as their stars – or local borough councillors – may to some degree shape their ends.

October, 1972   Alan R. Warwick

Vice-President
Norwood Society

Chapter One

A Suburb in the Making

Rocque's Survey of London, made between the years 1741 and 1745, extends on the south side as far as Mitcham and part of the vanished Croydon Common. The Survey stops short of the town of Croydon.

On this southern area the Survey presents a rural countryside composed of a mosaic of irregular-shaped fields, extensive woodland, common land, ancient highways and scattered hamlets, private estates, bridle-paths and streams. It is an orderly but haphazard countryside, sparsely populated. There is a sense of serenity and unhurried tranquility – a countryside unruffled by the coming Industrial Revolution, which before long, in conjunction with the inclosure of common land, was to change the rural image of South London into that of rows of suburban villas and shops.

One should not, however, hold the Inclosure Acts as being unduly responsible for the claustrophobic density of South London. In law, the term Inclosure signifies *Improving*.

The Inclosure Act of 1756, made in the reign of George II, was designed for the preservation of forests and the growth of timber for the requirements of the Navy. The Inclosure Act of 1773, made in the reign of George III, and entitled "An Act for the Better Cultivation, Improvement, and Regulation of the Common Arable Fields, Wastes, and Commons of Pasture in the Kingdom", was framed in order to secure a more abundant and less precarious supply of food for the people. The Inclosure Act of 1801, designed for the same important purpose, is described as "An Act Consolidating in one Act certain Provisions inserted in Acts of Inclosure." In all these great Inclosure Acts the welfare of the population at large was the first consideration.

This southern area surveyed by Rocque, half in Surrey, half in Kent, is dotted with such familiar names as Sydenham, Streatham (spelt Stretham), Penge, Elmers End (but here called Elms End), Beckenham, Mitcham, Dulwich, and two Knights Hills, fairly close to each other.

Two adjacent Knights Hills can be a source of confusion. One is at the southern end of West Norwood, rising up to the heights of Beulah Hill; the other is about three-quarters of a mile to the north, between Tulse Hill and Herne Hill, overlooking Brockwell Park. This duplication of names dates from the sixteenth century when two branches of the Knight family owned much land in Lambeth and Streatham.

Penge Green, shown on the Survey, is the oldest part of present-day Penge. A tavern called The Porcupine is clearly marked. Nobody living in Penge today seems to have heard of The Porcupine; its site would appear to be occupied by a public house called The Alexandra in Parish Lane, so there is probably a link between the two. The Crooked Billet is the oldest surviving public house; it is' 200 years old, and was not in existence at the time of the Rocque Survey.

Over the high ground to the north-west is shown The Horns tavern. It is near the foot of Knights Hill, and it was there that the waggoners stopped for refreshment and to water their horses before making the long haul up the steep hill. The licencee was a man named Catley, a retired hackney coachman, who was the undistinguished father of an outstanding daughter. Ann Catley became a celebrated actress and singer, a great beauty with a vivacious personality. A contemporary account says that she won all hearts by her breezy manner and air of camaraderie. She was bold, volatile and audacious. Ann Catley was very popular at Covent Garden, Vauxhall and

Marylebone Gardens; later she enslaved Dublin, so that even her hair style was copied. Her hair was cut straight across the forehead, in a style that the Victorians were to call a Piccadilly fringe, but in Ann's day was called "Catleyfying the hair". She was noted for her gift of exchanging repartee with the audience when she would step out of character in the part she was playing on the stage to sharpen her wits on someone in the pit, and then without pause return to the part she was playing.

At the top of Knights Hill, where the road meets Beulah Hill, was the Knights Hill Pound, where strayed horses and cattle were taken to await claim by their owners.

Rocque's Survey shows the Bree Kill Mill at Dulwich. The mill has gone, and its site is now occupied by Dulwich College. It stood near to the ornamental pond of that name at the intersection of College Road with Dulwich Common.

Hollow Comb Hill is an eastern promontory of Sydenham Hill, and in Rocque's Survey it overhangs Sydenham Wells which lies in the valley. Today Hollow Comb is a forgotten name, except that a house on that promontory has taken "Hollow Comb" for its name.

Sydenham Wells as a watering place no longer exists. Where it was is now occupied by St. Philip's Church at the southern edge of Wells Park. In its day Sydenham Wells was famous for its curative waters. George III paid it a visit. It is said that he arrived at the head of a troop of Life Guards, himself wearing an old blue military tunic which had belonged to a Captain and still bore the rank. George III had taken a fancy to the tunic and adopted it as his own – still displaying the rank of Captain! On his arrival at Sydenham Wells his Life Guards were posted around the perimeter, not so much to defend the King's person as to ensure him a day of peace and quiet, most of which he spent reclining in a chair.

Other names on the 1745 Survey have direct links with the present South London suburb. Bewlys Farm and the adjoining Bewly Wood are the predecessors of the romanticised version of "Beulah", which came into popular use in the early years of the nineteenth century in such names as Beulah Spa and Beulah Hill.

The name Norwood is not to be found on Rocque's Survey, though it was in common use. Instead, there is shown a great area of forest, about three miles across at its widest part, which bears the name NORTH WOOD in large letters. It sprawls diagonally across the Survey on a south-west/north-east axis, and is criss-crossed by tracks. Some of these can be identified with present day roads.

At its southern end the North Wood lies between Croydon Common to the east and Bewly's Farm and Mitcham to the west. Its northern end forms a wedge between Dulwich and Brockley. The northern tip is shown by Rocque to be already severed from the main mass of woods, and bears the peculiar name of Oak of Arnon.

Oak of Arnon can only be a corruption of Oak of Honor, the name that was bestowed on a famous oak tree under the shade of which, tradition has it, Queen Elizabeth I sat while picnicking one May Day. This special oak tree stood at the summit of what was afterwards called One Tree Hill, at Honor Oak. In the Lord Chamberlain's papers of the time is the entry: "On May Day the Queen went a-Maying to Sir Richard Buckley's at Lewisham, some three or four miles off Greenwich."

One Tree Hill has other claims to fame, for it is said that Boadicea, Queen of the Iceni, suffered defeat at the hands of Suetonius Paulinus, the Roman General, on the slopes of that same hill, and died of poison on Peckham Rye.

At the end of the eighteenth century the East India Company established a semaphore on the summit of the hill to signal the arrival of their ships in the Thames. When the Napoleonic invasion of England was threatened, the Admiralty requisitioned the semaphore. By 1790 the so-called Oak of Arnon wood had vanished, and the North Wood itself had shrunk to the limits of Norwood, Sydenham, Dulwich and Penge, and as far as Forest Hill.

The tree-clad slopes that ascend to the high Sydenham ridge are a tiny remnant of that once great wood. Those slopes form a noble and picturesque setting to the suburban land below. They should be admired and appreciated while there is yet time, for the rapacious urge is there to whittle away those last lovely vistas.

Why the North Wood, when it lies to the south of London? The Great North Wood was so called by the Anglo-Saxons to distinguish it from the Great South Wood that lay over the Weald of Kent and Surrey, Croydon lying between the two. From time immemorial that part of the North Wood within the parish of Croydon has belonged to the See of Canterbury. In Domesday Book it says that Archbishop Lanfranc holds in demesne Croindene. The part of the Great North Wood within the parish of Croydon, and a peculiar to Canterbury, was given for the Archbishop's pleasure, for his hunting, for fuel and pannage for 200 swine. The fact that no ancient buildings have been found within the wide Norwood area speaks of its original wild, primaeval state. The name Norwood itself is, obviously, a contraction of North Wood.

Daniel Defoe in his account of the great plague of London in 1665 notes how fugitives from the pestilence fled to the woods of Norwood. There, utterly shunned by the locals for fear of infection, they were left to die of starvation. It is frequently said that the field which lies at the foot of Gipsy Hill, where seven roads meet, is a plague pit, though it seems very large considering how sparse the population was at that time.

There are many early instances of the use of the name Norwood. When the revenues of the Archbishop of Canterbury were seized by Oliver Cromwell, it was stated that "in the woods of Norwood such extreme waste was at this time committed that there remained but 9,200 oaken pollards and 80 timber trees."

In Tudor times the North Wood stretched from Honor Oak to Tooting, and still retained much of its primaeval character. As a refuge for fugitives from the law it was conveniently near London, and for that reason it was not a healthy place for the unwary traveller. It was nevertheless valuable property. In the reign of Henry VIII the forest consisted chiefly of oaks, the timber of which was much used in the Deptford dockyard.

Sir Francis Drake's ship *The Pelican,* afterwards renamed *The Golden Hind,* was built from oak timbers taken from that part of the forest called Great Stake Pit Coppice. The coppice was in the possession of the Archbishop and occupied that area of land approximately bounded by Beulah Hill, Crown Dale, Central Hill and Church Road, in Upper Norwood.

A truncated oak tree that stands by the footpath at the lowest point in Hermitage Road is probably the last surviving fellow of the oaks that went into the building of Drake's ship. Up to the early years of the present century there was a twin oak tree that stood on the other side of the road. They made a magnificent and noble pair in their mature beauty, their boughs meeting across the road. But despite their beauty, one was felled when the houses were built nearby, and the other was drastically lopped of its splendid limbs.

Drake's other ship, *The Revenge* (500 tons, 46 guns) was also Norwood bred. Its oak timbers came from that part of the North Wood where the Crystal Palace Park lies.

The River Effra had its source in the Great Stake Pit Coppice. It emerged as a spring near the junction of Highfield Hill and Harold Road, whence, fortified by another stream from Church Road, it flowed in an open brook through the valley, crossing at the lowest point of Hermitage Road, and then via Elder Road to West Norwood and Dulwich. Its course then took it to Herne Hill (Island Green), Brixton (Brixtow Causeway), Kennington and Vauxhall, where it joined the Thames. Today there is no visible sign of the Effra in Norwood, but there is a circular grating in the middle of Hermitage Road from which one can hear the sound of rushing water of the stream, now piped underground. It does not emerge until it reaches the gardens of Belair in Dulwich, where it appears in the form of a long ornamental lake in the grounds. Other ornamental waters in Dulwich, including the Dulwich Park lake, are also manifestations of the lost river. Herne Hill, when the Effra was an open stream, was once known as Heron Hill.

Norwood was a beauty spot in the eighteenth century. The poet James Thomson, author of *The Seasons,* enchanted by Norwood's woods, wrote his *Hymn to Solitude:*

"Oh let me pierce thy secret cell
And in thy deep recesses dwell,
Perhaps from Norwood's oak-clad hill,
Where meditation has her fill.
I just may cast my careless eyes
Where London's spiry turrets rise;
Think on its crimes, its cares, its pain,
And shield me in the woods again."

There was in ancient times a boundary tree of great size called the Vicar's Oak. It stood at the high point in Norwood where four parishes met. The parishes were Lambeth, Croydon, Camberwell and a detached portion of Battersea. This part of Battersea comprised the district of Penge, which until the year 1855 paid tithes and taxes to Battersea. Though seven miles from Battersea it had been part of that parish for a thousand years. The Saxon King Eadwig (AD 955–959) granted certain lands in Battersea to his theign Lyfing: "Hereto belongeth the wood that is called Penge, seven miles, seven furlongs and seven feet round about."

William the Conqueror granted Battersea to the Abbot of Westminster in exchange for the Regalia of King Edward the Confessor, which had previously been deposited in the Abbey for safe keeping. Penge was specifically included by William in the transaction for obtaining the Regalia by the words: "Moreover I have also conceded to them all the hunting of the wood Penceat."

The ancient meeting point of the four parishes, once marked by the boundary tree, is at the junction of Anerley Hill, Church Road, Westow Hill and Crystal Palace Parade. It is the present boundary point of the London Boroughs of Lambeth, Croydon, Bromley and Southwark.

The Vicar's Oak was in a flourishing condition in the reign of Queen Elizabeth I. John Aubrey in his *Natural History and Antiquities of the County of Surrey,* published in 1719, wrote: "In this Parish lies the great Wood call'd *Norwood*, belonging to the See of Canterbury, wherein was an antient, remarkable Tree, call'd *Vicar's Oak,* where four Parishes meet in a Point. This Wood wholly consists of Oaks. There was one oak that had *Misselto,* a Timber Tree, which was felled about 1678. Some Persons cut this Misselto, for some Apothecaries in *London,* and sold them a Quantity for Ten shillings, each time, and left only one Branch remaining, for more to sprout. One fell lame shortly after. Soon after, each of the others lost an Eye, and he that fell'd the Tree, about 1678 (tho' warned of these Misfortunes of the other Men) would, notwithstanding, adventure to do it, and shortly after broke his leg; as if the *Hamadryades* had resolved to take an ample Revenge for the Injury done to that sacred and venerable Oak."

Aubrey goes on to say: "It is a common Notion, that a strange Noise proceeds from a falling Oak, so loud, so to be heard at half a Mile distant, as if it were the Genius of the Oak lamenting. It has been not unusually observed, that to cut Oak Wood is unfortunate."

Exactly when the Vicar's Oak was felled is not known. The tree was standing in 1647, but it was probably cut down a few years later, though why so important a boundary tree was permitted to be felled is not known. The Vicar's Oak may indeed have been the "Timber Tree" described by Aubrey, that bore mistletoe and was felled about 1678.

Such was the fame and significance of the tree that the name "Vicar's Oak" survived as a place name well into the middle years of the nineteenth century. The son of the first curate at All Saints Church, the Revd. Rupert Montague Browne, said that when he lived on Beulah Hill in the 1860s, the older Upper Norwood inhabitants sometimes spoke of Church Road as Vicar's Oak Road.

Vicar's Oak Road is indeed an intriguing alternative name, though it does not appear on any old map or plan of the neighbourhood. A map of 1810 gives the name New Road. A plan of 1824 of the Proposed District Chapelry of All Saints, Norwood merely marks the road as "to Sydenham". Built as a Chapel of Ease in 1828, All Saints was constituted the parish church in 1845. It was then, it would seem, that the road was named Church Road, though on a map of 1860 or thereabouts the road is merely shown, unnamed, as on the crest of Isabel Hill. Vicar's Oak Road would nevertheless seem to have been a reasonable name for identification, for it led straight as an arrow to that historic boundary point.

From ancient times parish boundaries were carefully preserved, and their principal points and boundary lines methodically perambulated every two years or so in Rogation Week.

"On Ascension Day" says Sir John Hawkins in *History of Music*, "it is the custom of the inhabitants of parishes, with their officers, to perambulate, in order to perpetuate the memories of their boundaries, and to impress the remembrance thereof in the minds of young persons, especially boys."

Concerning the perambulation of Croydon parish, which would take two to three days to complete, it was so arranged that the party led by the vicar or curate would reach the Vicar's Oak on Holy Thursday. A service was appointed to be read at the principal boundary points, consisting of the 103rd and 104th Psalms and the Homily of Thanksgiving, the Vicar being directed to "muster at certain convenient places and inculcate this and such like sentences, 'Cursed be he which translateth the bounds and doles of his neighbour'. "

Accompanying the Vicar were the churchwardens, the beadle, choir men, choir boys and other "honest men" of the parish. With the first warmth of spring in the air, such perambulations were festive occasions. It was only the advent of the modern Ordnance Survey that rendered these unnecessary. The parish choir boys, being the youngest members, were an important part of the perambulations. They had to be shown precisely the extent of the boundaries, so that they in their turn could pass on the exact information. Hence the custom of inflicting on the choir boys some sort of beating at the key point of the perambulations the better to instil in their young and impressionable minds the precise extent of the boundaries. An old man of 85 once affirmed that he could always remember each point where he had been beaten. He remembered his perambulations without rancour, and had in his turn cheerfully helped to whack his successors. There did not appear to be any law by which the observance of the custom could be enforced.

There were rewards as well as beatings. For example, in 1661 it is recorded that the sum of £3 8s. was spent by Battersea "for a dynner for the parish agoeing the bounds of the Parish of Penge." By 1733 the cost had gone up. "In going ye bounds of ye Parish to Penge in Procession £17 18s." The following is a list of moneys spent in beating the Croydon bounds:

1583	When we went our perambulation at Vicar's Oke in Rogation week ..	2s 6d
	Item for drinking the same day ..	6d
1584	In going our perambulation to Vicar's Oke—churchwardens and other honest men of the parishe	2s 6d
1586	For making honest men drinke when we went to Vicar's Oke in perambulation	2s 6d
1589	When we went our perambulation to Vicar's Oke to make the parishoners drynke	5s 0d
1592	When we came from Vicar's Oke perambulation	4s 0d
1594	For going to Vicar's Oke drinkinge ..	4s 0d
1597	At the King's Head when we came from the Vicar's Oke	6s 0d
1610	Bread and bear [beer] at Vicar's Oke for the procession	9s 0d
1612	For a kilderkin of beer and other charges spent on the parishoners at the Vicar's Oke	6s 6d

1625	At the perambulation	£1 10s 2d
	Item for carrying the provisions to the Oke	2s 6d
1634	When we went to the bounds of the parish	13s 0d
	When we went to the Vicar's Oke ..	12s 0d
1635	At the perambulation to Vicar's Oke ..	£3 8s 6d
1704	Paid for 100lbs. of cheese at the Vicar's Oke	8s 0d
1716	By going a presesioning	£4 0s 0d

The processional banners of Croydon Parish Church were often carried during the perambulations, though according to Prideaux, on *Churchwardens,* "in consequence of the Popish abuses arising from feasting, processions and superstitions, during these boundary journeys, Queen Elizabeth forbade processions, but retained the useful and innocent part of the perambulations."

The Croydon perambulators were sometimes spoken of as the Archbishop's men, the Archbishop being the Lord of the Manor of Croydon. The boundary between Croydon and Lambeth extended from High Cross to Vicar's Oak; thàt is to say, from the Streatham Common end of Crown Lane, Crown Dale, Central Hill, and Westow Hill to Vicar's Oak. At High Cross the Croydon men were met by the Lambeth men, also on their perambulations. The Lambeth contingent were sometimes known as the King's men (or Queen's men), the Monarch being the Lord of the Manor of Lambeth. The purpose of the confrontation was to see that neither side strayed over the centre of the road into the other's parish. Thus, the two groups would march side by side to the Vicar's Oak.

At the Vicar's Oak it was the custom of the Archbishop's men to cut crosses in the bark of the tree on the side facing Croydon. After the gospel was read, there followed the customary refreshment. After this, the Vicar of Croydon and his band would strike down Gravel Hill by way of a track called Gravelly Way, which today is Anerley Hill. The Vicar kept on his right a coppice called Ridgewood. At a point where today the railway line from Crystal Palace to Norwood Junction passes under Anerley Road, stood an ancient boundary tree known as Elder Oak, or Deadman's Oak. After the usual formal observance at the Elder Oak, the Croydon perambulators bore to the right in a southerly direction along the lower end of a wood called Gravelly Hill Coppice, following approximately the line of the present railway, where they reached another boundary mark. This was an oak tree that stood on the bank of a ditch called Bishop's Ditch that ran in a south easterly direction and was a boundary ditch dividing Croydon from Penge.

The Elder Oak was cut down in about 1540, an act which was regarded by the Croydon men as "Ill done in that it was a boundary tree", for under it the Croydon vicar had many times read the gospel and they had cut their crosses on the side of the trunk facing Croydon.

It became increasingly evident that the area of land occupied by Ridgewood Coppice and Gravelly Hill Coppice was a disputed area. Today that area contains Cintra Park, Belvedere Road and Hamlet Road – a considerable slice of land. Friction between the Croydon men and Penge men had grown over the years. Thus, the Penge men on beating their bounds made it their practice to travel up the western side of Gravelly Hill Coppice and Ridgewood Coppice, by that implying that the coppices were in the Manor of Battersea. But in fact only the young men and boys followed the difficult route on the west side of the woods; the old men were content to take the easy way up Gravelly Hill (Anerley Hill).

Matters came to a head in the second year of the reign of Queen Elizabeth I. In 1560 the Vicar of Croydon was Mr. Richard Finch, a man of not very determined character. Having arrived at the Vicar's Oak on his Rogationtide perambulation, for some reason he did not then proceed down Gravelly Hill. One wonders, was he dissuaded by Penge men? Instead, he walked along the top of the hill, that part of Church Road which extends as far as Belvedere Road, though in Mr.

Finch's time it was only a woodland track. He was making for a stile at the upper end of Gravelly Hill Coppice. His purpose was to climb over the stile and descend by a pathway to the Elder Oak, leaving Ridgewood Coppice on his left. But on reaching the stile the Vicar and his followers were halted by the Penge men who told him he was trespassing.

Denied access to the Elder Oak, Mr. Finch meekly asked permission to pass down the side of the coppice so as to gain the Bishop's Ditch. This the Penge men allowed him to do, but that meant leaving a large area of woodland on his left in the hands of Penge.

Not surprisingly, when he learned about it the Archbishop was extremely annoyed, and Sir Nicholas Heron of Addiscombe, who had accompanied Mr. Finch on the perambulation, was held responsible. Sir Nicholas's reply to this was a blunt, "Let the Lords righte their owne causes. We will trouble ourselves no more about ytt."

In preparation for the next perambulation, the Archbishop gave the Vicar a detailed guide concerning the precise Croydon boundaries. Accordingly, Mr. Finch proceeded from the Vicar's Oak down Gravelly Way, keeping the threatened Ridgewood Coppice on his right hand, and arrived at the point where the Elder Oak had formerly stood. But there he was defeated in his purpose; the track through the lower end of Gravelly Hill Coppice was now overgrown and impassable. The Vicar reluctantly retraced his steps to the Vicar's Oak, and walked once more along the brow of the hill to the far side of the coppice, and then down the hill to the Bishop's Ditch.

Queen Elizabeth was Lady of the Manor of Battersea. This was a result of the Dissolution of the Monasteries in 1540, when Henry VIII had taken the Manor from the Abbots of Westminster. Elizabeth had let the Manor to a Mr. Henry Roydon as tenant. Mr. Roydon had felled a considerable amount of wood in Ridgewood Coppice, claimed by the Archbishop as part of Norwood and a parcel of the Manor of Croydon.

Archbishop Parker ordered 20 loads of the felled wood to be taken to Croydon Palace. This brought matters to a head. An action of trespass was brought against the Archbishop's men who had removed the wood, though in fact it became a legal battle between the Queen and Archbishop Grindal, who had recently succeeded Parker as Archbishop and Lord of the Manor of Croydon.

The legal argument turned largely on the boundary dividing Croydon from Battersea, and this drew attention to the respective routes taken by the parishioners of Croydon and Battersea on their perambulations. Mr. Finch's failure to keep firmly to the ancient boundary between Croydon and Penge in the end cost the Archbishop the action. The case was decided against him, and Croydon lost for evermore an important slice of land in Upper Norwood.

A curious legacy of that Elizabethan dispute is to be found in the present boundary line between Croydon and Penge at that point. The present boundary line follows Church Road from the top of Anerley Hill to Belvedere Road, at the White Hart angle of the triangle. It then passes along Lansdowne Place and down Fox Hill. Instead, however, of following the centre of the roadway as is usually the case where a road follows the boundary, it will be seen from the Ordnance Survey that in this instance the boundary line hugs the building line of the shops and walls and fences along the inside of the pavement on the Penge side. Thus the entire roadway and *both* pavements are within the Croydon boundary, whereas the boundary between Croydon and Lambeth uncompromisingly follows the centre of the road.

Tracing that broken dotted boundary line along Church Road and down Fox Hill, it is almost as though one can follow the reluctant footprints of the Revd. Richard Finch, walking as close as he dared to the disputed property. The present anomaly is that the properties on that stretch of Church Road, Lansdowne Place and Fox Hill within the Borough of Bromley have no roadway of their own, and vehicles such as

Bromley's dust carts must there use Croydon's roadway to service Bromley ratepayers!

In such a manner as this the pattern of Norwood was slowly fashioned and in time took its present shape. Rocque's Survey shows that while Penge and Sydenham and Streatham and Dulwich had recognisable features, Norwood was mostly without form and void of almost everything but hills and woodland. Nevertheless, the present shape of the suburb is to some extent the outcome of the perambulations of a Vicar in the reign of Queen Elizabeth I who was not sufficiently resolute.

The rural remoteness of Norwood persisted until the early years of the nineteenth century. Evelyn the diarist, when riding from Tunbridge Wells to London in 1652, was set on by two men close to the Vicar's Oak. Evelyn was dragged off his horse, tied to a tree and robbed. After two hours he freed himself and found his horse not far away. He immediately rode to the nearest magistrate; the robbers were captured, and Evelyn recovered most of his property.

Nearly eighty years later conditions were much the same. A newspaper of 1728 reported that "Two footpads who lately robbed Mr. Raddle in Norwood have been taken and committed by the Justice to the County Gaol." Another newspaper, of 1754, contains a grimmer report. "On Tuesday last a man genteely dressed was found hanging from a tree in Norwood with his head almost off, and both hands cut off, and no money in his pockets."

By 1800 Norwood had been described as a hamlet with a score of farm houses and cottages scattered about the lanes which intersected the woods. The only means of communication with the outside world was the carrier's cart, which started off daily from the village that had begun to grow up in the Triangle. The first public house in Upper Norwood, The Woodman, made its appearance on Westow Hill, its front windows looking out over London, the cross on the Dome of St. Paul's Cathedral exactly level with the step into the public house.

By 1820 Norwood had taken on the character of a delightful suburb, but it was still remote. A Dr. Leese, who lived on Central Hill, on winter nights used to fire a pistol at an open window to let people know he had firearms in the house.

At that time there was a considerable expanse of pasture land between Upper and Lower Norwood, while Upper Norwood was still surrounded on the south and east by thick woods. Houses were beginning to appear at wide intervals, and there were not half a dozen shops in the neighbourhood.

Bread was supplied from Streatham, and an Irish woman, Peggy O'Neale, mother of the famous prize-fighter Ned O'Neale, brought fish to sell from door to door. She carried her fish in a flat basket poised on her head, and decked her neck and shoulders with a handkerchief of yellow silk. She was immensely proud of her son's pugilistic prowess, and would sit on anybody's doorstep just to talk about him.

When Ned retired from the ring, he purchased the goodwill of the Rose and Crown tavern at the crossroads leading from Norwood to Streatham, at the top of Knights Hill.

Like Hampstead Heath, the heights of Norwood were the holiday playground of the cockney tripper. Traditional pastimes die hard. Fortune-telling by the gypsies was still one of the attractions. The Thames Watermen after the Dogget Coat and Badge Race used to repair to the White Hart public house at the Westow Street–Church Road corner to celebrate the annual event.

A popular amusement was that known as Tumbling. Men and girls linked their arms in a row and started to race down the steep slopes. Many of course fell and, with shouts of laughter, rolled over and over down the hill.

It was a frolic not without danger. A notice appeared in the Press dated 1827: "An inquest held at The Woodman, Norwood, on the body of J. W. Weightman. It appeared that the deceased had fallen upon his face and cut the temporal artery, while amusing himself with racing downhill with some ladies."

Another attraction was The Jolly Sailor at the foot of South Norwood Hill, its large tea gardens running down to the canal with its pleasant boating facilities.

Tea gardens abounded in Norwood. There were the Windmill tea gardens in Westow Hill, near to the Norwood windmill. The foundations of the old windmill lie behind Squire's Printing Works, close by the Royal Albert public house. Skittles were played there. There were tea gardens attached to the White Swan and to the White Hart. The entrance to the White Hart tea gardens was through the enormous jaws of a whale. Within the gardens were arbours all around and a bowling green in the centre. Waiters from the White Hart dashed to and fro with tea and refreshments. The White Hart itself was a single storey wooden structure with trees and posts and chains in front. Beneath the trees were seats and tables, while pails of water and supplies of hay were there for the horses. There was also a pump from which, in large barrels on wheels, water was supplied to the local inhabitants at so much a pail.

So idyllic a spot as Norwood could not fail to attract people of means as a place in which to live. It rose clear of the smoke of London that lay in the valley. Church Road had two or three handsome detached villas and a little wooden cottage. The rest was fields, over which a footpath led to Beulah Hill. The footpath was closed during hay-making, but the meadows were very popular with the visitors and invalids that came to Norwood, and with the growing number of residents. On fine summer days many people could be seen reading or doing needlework, and children playing. Across the fields were the Beulah Spa Gardens. Further along Beulah Hill were strawberry gardens.

Even by 1849 the whole area was thinly populated. A Mr. Leach was fond of wandering about the district gathering wild flowers, ferns and berries. In November of that year he set off with his basket to gather specimens. Afterwards he was traced as far as Anerley, but was never seen or heard of again, despite the most thorough search. His wife who lived for another 30 years never knew whether she was a widow or not.

It was the coming of the Crystal Palace in 1854 that was to bring the greatest change to Upper Norwood and to some degree obliterate its past. The place lost much of its natural beauty due to uncontrolled building. The Great North Wood seemed to melt away into the shadows of other days like a pale ghost in the face of Victorian go, go, go!

Nevertheless, the North Wood remains a subtly pervading presence in Norwood. The hills are still wooded to a degree that seems to impress many who come from less wooded parts. "When I think of Norwood," one visitor said nostalgically, "I always think of the trees dripping over the pavements!" Something of the spirit of the Old North Wood is obviously still there.

On April 13th, 1953, a lady was turning over earth in a flowerbed in her garden on Beulah Hill when she uncovered a leather bag. It was quite rotten and, at the touch of the trowel, out from it spilled a little heap of gold and silver coins. The silver was black, but the gold gleamed yellow. There were 14 gold nobles and 124 silver groats, all of the reign of Edward III, King of England between the years 1327 and 1377.

Most of the coins were in mint condition, and they had lain undisturbed on Beulah Hill for 600 years. Suddenly, in that suburban garden past and present touched hands as 600 years rolled back and the treasure that had lain in the North Wood yielded itself up in Norwood.

The one riddle remains. What was it made someone 600 years ago bury a small fortune at that point in the Great North Wood? Was he being pursued by enemies as he fled through the forest? Had he desperately hidden the money to save it from falling into other hands? Perhaps, after he had hidden it, he had been overtaken and slain. Perhaps he had escaped, but could never again return to the place, or perhaps he could never find the place where he had hidden the money.

The Beulah Hill Treasure Trove, as it is named in the British Museum records, will in that respect always remain a mystery. But at that moment of turning over the soil it was as if fingers had met across the gap of time. The place was the same; only time and circumstances had changed. That is history; that is a tiny part of the process of a suburb in the making.

Chapter Two

Colliers, Smugglers and Gypsies

From early times until the last years of the eighteenth century the southern slopes of Beulah Hill overlooking Thornton Heath and Croydon were where much of the smoky trade of the Croydon charcoal burners, or colliers as they were termed, was carried on. The Croydon colliers were a breed of men who supplied the fuel needs of the City of London for its domestic heating and cooking. Croydon was the earliest and most important colliery of the City, producing the bulk of the charcoal which was the staple fuel of London from medieval times.

Pit coal was practically unknown. What was termed sea coal, that is to say coal found on the Northumbrian shore, washed up from exposed coal seams on the sea bed, was largely forbidden. According to Stowe, in 1273 sea coal was prohibited from being used in or near London, as being prejudicial to human health. Much later, King James I strongly objected to the burning of coal, on the grounds of pollution and damage to the lungs. London depended on charcoal, much of which was manufactured on the Beulah slopes. Ducarel, writing in 1783, describes Croydon as being a town "surrounded by hills well covered with wood, whereof great store of charcoal is made."

In the laudable process of keeping medieval and later London a smokeless zone, it is evident that, in consequence of the great number of colliers' damped fires, Croydon itself was far from being a smokeless zone. Prevailing winds carried much of the smoke into Croydon, and the consequent smog and grime settling on the town was a Croydon characteristic. "Black as a Croydon collyer", and "The unchanging Croydon Complexyone" were descriptive terms used in Elizabethan and Jacobean comedy. A play appeared in London entitled "Grimes, the Collyer of Croydon".

Charcoal burning in the form carried out on the wooded Norwood slopes is an industry that has almost passed into extinction, but in its heyday was a trade of some magnitude which followed a seasonal pattern.

In the autumn the colliers moved out to the North Wood, with its oaks and a plentiful supply of water provided by the many streams and ponds. Water was a necessary adjunct to the process of making charcoal. The name Collier's Water Lane at Thornton Heath, close under the Beulah slopes, is a reflection of this.

The charcoal burners' autumn routine was to cut their sticks and branches and leave them stacked to dry out so as to be ready for use the following spring, when the colliers would return to the Norwood hills to camp out all the summer. Then they would construct their huge slow fires, or kilns, damp them down with water, and so convert the sticks of wood into charcoal. When the process was complete, the fires would be put out, and holes driven into the kiln at various points to let out the imprisoned gases. Finally, the kiln would be dismantled and the staves of charcoal taken out and tied in bundles for market.

It appears, however, that the Norwood and Croydon colliers did not usually sell their wares direct to the inhabitants of the City of London. They were met on the way by what we would call middlemen, who bought their staves of charcoal at the lowest price they could get and sold them in London at the highest.

Out of this charcoal manufacture Elizabethan Croydon acquired a reputation for dirt and grime and squalor that would make a modern Croydonian blush. A contemporary observer wrote: "The streets were deep hollow ways and very dirty, the houses generally with wooden steps into them, and darkened by large trees growing before them, and the inhabitants in general were smiths and collyers."

The Archbishop's Palace itself was surrounded by trout streams and vineyards, and was well fitted to give the Archbishop a pleasant retreat from his duties in London. Nevertheless, at certain times of the year he must have suffered much from the industry of the colliers. John Bennington in 1862 describes a feud that existed between a certain collier, Francis Grimes, and Archbishop Grindal in the reign of Queen Elizabeth I. The story goes that the Archbishop was in his study one day when Grimes was damping down his kilns on the Beulah slopes, and that heavy smoke pervaded the palace and grounds.

"Good Master Chamberlain," roared the Archbishop, who was fully aware of the source of the smoke, "what means this smother? Is good Croydon town ablaze?" He thereupon dispatched his chamberlain with a peremptory message to the collier to abate the nuisance.

Francis Grimes's reply was to the effect that the good people of London – meaning the Lord Mayor, Sheriffs and Aldermen – required the charcoal to cook their banquets, and was reputed to have added, "How can I direct the smoke? God blows the wind whither he wills it to go. Sometimes it goes over into Kent, sometimes into London, and sometimes it goes over Croydon. If my Lord Archbishop will show me the way by which I can direct the smoke, I will say paternosters for the welfare of the souls of himself and his family."

With this unsatisfactory reply, the Archbishop instituted a law suit against the master collier in the London Courts, but he lost his case. Charcoal manufacture went on as before, to the advantage of the wealthy burghers of the City and to the intermittent discomfort of the more sensitive residents of Croydon.

Grimes (or Grim) the Collyer of Croydone was a traditional figure, a character somewhat akin to the chimney sweep of later days. His rough, scarecrow appearance, weather-beaten skin grimed with smoke and his red-rimmed eyes gave him a certain picturesqueness as he stalked through Norwood and the North

Wood. His hardy independence and toughness caused him to be respected, though not particularly liked. The fact remains that the gently nurtured citizens of London who valued their creature comforts and fine cooking could not do without him and his wares, though in the stage dramas of the Tudors and Stuarts he was commonly presented as the personification of vice.

A comedy entitled "Grim, the Collyer of Croydone, or the Divell and his Dame" was performed before Queen Elizabeth in 1577. In his play "Quip for an Upstart Courtier", written in 1592, Robert Greene brings in the following lines: " 'Marry,' quoth he that looked like Lucifer, 'though I am black I am not the Divell – but, indeede, a collyer of Croydene.' "

Seventy years later, in 1662, a comedy was published entitled "Grim, the Collier of Croydon, or the Devil and his Dame, with the Devil and St. Dunstan". Observe again the identification of the Croydon collier with the Prince of Darkness.

In former days Collier's Water Lane stretched from Thornton Heath Pond to Thornton Heath railway station. In October 1895 a small and very ancient cottage which stood by the station was pulled down. Its gable bore the date 1590. In the garden behind the cottage was a cairn of stones on which was a small wooden cross bearing the legend: *In Memoriam, Francis Grimes, Collyer.*

Tradition had it that there once lived in the cottage a collier whose baptismal name was Francis. Probably Grimes was merely indicative of his trade, just as Jack Tar is a sobriquet for a sailor. The cairn was a memorial, not a grave.

Incidentally, there is further history attached to the cottage. Its greatest fame was that of having been for a time the residence of the original John Gilpin. The Gilpin family appeared to have been connected with Croydon for many generations. In the earlier Croydon Parish Church, which was destroyed by fire, was an old chalice bearing the inscription, "The gift of Mr. John Gilpin of Croydon".

Tradition also has it that at one time the cottage was a resort of the highwayman Dick Turpin, whose aunt lived there. There was a secret staircase that led to the roof, which could provide an easy way of escape from the constables, if so needed. It was from this cottage that Dick Turpin and his gang made a number of their raids.

It is not known with certainty when the charcoal trade ceased on the Norwood hills. In the year 1784 Ducarel, who was the first published historian of Croydon, wrote: "Croydon is surrounded by hills well covered with wood, whereof great store of charcoal is made." *The Ambulator,* published in 1782, gives the same information, but in all subsequent editions the reference to charcoal is omitted, which suggests that by that time the trade had virtually ceased.

The earlier name of Spa Hill was Leather Bottle Lane, a name with a slightly sinister ring about it, suggesting the leather bottles for containing spirits carried by horsemen of those days. Leather Bottle Lane, too, was one of the ways into the fastnesses of the North Wood, and was said to be much used by smugglers.

Thomas Frost, a Croydon journalist of the last century, wrote his *Reminiscences of a Country Journalist* in 1886. "We are apt to be misled perhaps", he said, "to associate the smuggling of the eighteenth century and the early part of the nineteenth century exclusively with creeks and 'gaps' on the coast, forgetting that the contraband goods had to be distributed over the whole country. There were members of my mother's family living less than 20 years ago [circa 1866] who remembered deceased relatives who had been engaged in the forwarding branch of the contraband trade in Surrey and Kent; and I remember being one day, about 30 years ago [circa 1856], at the house of a spinster aunt at Norwood, when a bottle of Hollands was placed on the table with the remark, 'This was smuggled by old Will Fox. It is the last bottle!'

"The said Will, whose bones, with those of many more of the Foxes,* Sharpes and Ayreses, rest in Beckenham churchyard, was engaged in the inland smuggling trade at the beginning of the nineteenth century.

* Fox Hill, off Church Road, is named after the Fox Family, who had a farm there.

"Spirits and tea, silks and laces, upon all of which very heavy customs duties were then levied, were the chief commodities of the 'free trade' of those long bygone days. The agents on the coast knew when a sloop or lugger in that trade was expected to arrive, and were on the lookout, provided with well-understood signals . . . . Under cover of darkness, the casks, chests, or bales were removed in carts or by means of packhorses . . . . The green lanes were continuous at that time to the Thames below Greenwich, or through the woods between Croydon and Camberwell to Southwark. Along these byways strings of packhorses, laden with smuggled goods, could pass for miles without attracting observation, or seen only by those whom fear or self interest rendered silent.

"Smuggled goods had, within the recollection of persons then living, passed by night along what was then called Back Lane, now Park Lane, on the east side of Croydon, within five minutes walk of the main street, . . . then across Croydon Common and along the green lanes of Norwood."

Those were indeed the days, both in Croydon and Norwood; the rule was to "turn your face to the wall when the gentlemen ride by". Nor was all danger over when the North Wood was gained. Sometimes the customs men would be lying in wait. Cutlasses were more than once drawn and blood spilt.

There was a mansion in the region of Norwood in 1846 that was known as Smugglers' Hall. Frost records that it had been built by a silk-mercer who had made a large fortune in the contraband silk trade at the time when customs duties, so heavy as to be almost prohibitive, were levied on the production of the looms of Lyons.

At the beginning of the nineteenth century, Norwood, where not covered with oak woods, was largely a furze-clad waste with patches of cultivated land. The inhabitants for the most part were farmers and labourers with almost as large a shifting population of gypsies, who pitched their tents in Norwood and Penge. According to Frost, the gypsies who frequented the woods and green lanes were not held in such disrepute as in some of the other localities, perhaps from the circumstances of the Lees and Coopers being reputed rich. He says:

"Stories were current in my boyhood of Adam Lee – hanged with his son Thomas at Horsemonger Lane Gaol for an alleged robbery with violence at Hersham, between Esher and Walton – having his coat buttons made of guineas and his vest buttons of seven-shilling pieces, and giving his daughter a peck measure of gold coins as her dowry."

An old master baker named Theobald told Frost that in the 1840s he and Adam Lee played the violin at farmhouses around Norwood and Streatham when a dance was given on the occasion of a birthday or a wedding, while an old woman, believed to be the mother of Gypsy Cooper, of pugilistic renown, was for many years allowed to tell the fortunes of those who crossed her palm with a piece of silver in the Beulah Spa gardens.

In the latter years of the eighteenth century gypsies camped in large numbers during the summer months upon the waste land bordering the lanes of Norwood and Penge. The men made clothes-pegs and wooden skewers, and these were hawked through the neighbouring villages and hamlets by brown-faced boys and girls. The men themselves travelled round with the treadle-wheel and fire-basket of the itinerant tinker and knife-grinder. Others dealt in horses.

As recently as the year 1853 gypsy encampments could be found near White Horse Farm on the northern verges of Croydon Common. Thomas Frost remembered his father's story of a fright he got one night when accompanied by John Skelton Chapman, master of Archbishop Whitgift's School.

"It must have been about the year 1812, at which time there were not more than two houses between the top of Leather Bottle Lane and White Horse Farm. The two men had crossed the brook and were close to the waste, when the moon shone out suddenly from the clouds which had obscured it, and showed the rushy strip of common-land covered with tents, little tilted carts, and tinkers' barrows. Chapman took to his heels at the sight, and my father, catching his panic, followed, both leaping the low hedge and running at their utmost speed across the green pastures bordering the north side of Croydon Common."

That the gypsies in the surroundings of Norwood were a secretive, closely-knit community is illustrated by an experience which befell an Upper Norwood medical practitioner, Dr. Gardiner, in the early 1800s. One evening he received an urgent call from a young gypsy, who asked him to come at once to attend his wife who was in labour and in much pain. On the gypsy's face was the strain of anxiety and keenest solicitude, which at once told the doctor that this was not a ruse to get him out of the house, but a call for medical help. Dr. Gardiner collected his bag and at once proceeded with the gypsy to the camp in the Penge woods.

It was growing dark when they entered the wood, and there the gypsy stopped and said, "Give me your handkerchief. There are reasons why you must not know the way to our tents. But it will be only for a few minutes."

Having no alternative but to comply, Dr. Gardiner took out his handkerchief and submitted to being blindfolded. Then, holding on to the gypsy's velveteen coat tails, he stumbled through the tangle of undergrowth. At last they entered a closer atmosphere. The handkerchief was removed, and the doctor found himself in a gypsy's dome-shaped tent.

A young gypsy woman was lying on a bed of freshly-cut bracken, and two women of the tribe were crouching by her with anxious looks.

An hour later Dr. Gardiner left the tent, having delivered the gypsy woman of a baby boy. Once more he submitted to being blindfolded, and was led out of the wood by a different way. On reaching the road the blindfold was removed.

The gypsy held out a guinea piece. The doctor waved it on one side. "No, no", he said, "give it to your wife."

"She won't want for a guinea while I have one", replied the gypsy. "But if you won't take it, all I can say is that I hope I may find another way of repaying my debt to you. If ever you get into any trouble with our people, you have only to say that you are a friend of Ned Righteous, and you will be all right." Then, with a brief farewell, the gypsy disappeared into the darkness, and Dr. Gardiner proceeded home.

A year or so later the doctor was riding along the wooded lanes making his calls when some gypsies sprang out of the bushes, seized the horse's bridle and demanded money.

Dr. Gardiner, though very doubtful as to its effectiveness, retorted that he was a friend of Ned Righteous, and expected to be allowed to move freely through the woods. The gypsies were nonplussed at this, but said that it was a trick, and they would soon find out if it were so.

One of them gave an owl hoot. This was answered by a similar signal, and in a few minutes Ned Righteous appeared. The gypsy at once recognised the doctor and greeted him.

At the sound of Dr. Gardiner's name, the gypsies instantly released his bridle. "If we'd known who you were", one of them said, "we would not have touched you. You saved Ned's child and his wife as well, and your name is remembered for that in all the tents of the Romany."

It has been said that if you look into the eyes of a Norwood local you look into the eyes of a gypsy. After the Croydon and Lambeth Inclosure Acts in the first years of the nineteenth century dislodged the gypsies from their traditional Norwood camping grounds, many abandoned their tribal ways and merged into the local communities to become labourers, agricultural workers and artisans, and married into local families.

This was to be the great parting from gypsy tradition and way of life. That they had been a well-established community on the Norwood heights in the seventeenth century is shown by an entry in Pepys diary dated 11th August, 1668. "This afternoon my wife and Mercer and Deb went with Pelling to see the gypsies at Lambeth and had their fortunes told; but what they did I did not enquire."

In the registers of Camberwell is an item relating to the marriage of Robert Hern and Elizabeth Bozwell, described as the "King and Queen of the Jepsies". Quite the most famous of the Norwood gypsies was Margaret Finch, who died on 24th

October, 1740, at the age of 108 years. After travelling around for many years she came to live in Norwood on the Lambeth side, near the lower end of Gipsy Hill.

During her lifetime she was the Queen of the Gypsies; and a strange woman she must have been. There is a portrait of her drawn from life in 1739 by John Straeche, which shows her in a crouched attitude, smoking a pipe. Her two dogs are beside her, and in front of her is a pewter beer tankard. That, it would seem, was her characteristic attitude, for it is recorded that by her constant habit of sitting with her chin resting on her knees the sinews became so contracted that she could not extend herself or change her position. No doubt it was an acute arthritic state.

When she died it was found impossible to straighten out the limbs, and so the body of the old Queen was placed in her customary attitude in a square coffin. The hearse, followed by two coaches of gypsy mourners, proceeded to Beckenham Parish Church. There a sermon was preached by the vicar, after which the interment took place in the churchyard. Such was the fame of Margaret Finch that her funeral drew a vast concourse of spectators who followed the coffin to Beckenham in a long line of carriages. A considerable number of those who came were people of quality who had no doubt visited her from time to time to have their fortunes told. The expense of the funeral was paid for by the publicans of Norwood, whom Queen Margaret had indirectly benefited by the attraction of her fortune telling.

The successor to Queen Margaret was her niece Bridget, who also lived in Norwood. When Bridget died on 6th August, 1768, she was buried in the old College burial ground in Dulwich Village. This, as in the case of her predecessor, was carried out with great ceremony, in which she was described as "Old Bridget, Queen of the Gypsies".

She in turn was succeeded by her niece Margaret, granddaughter of Margaret Finch, which represented an interesting example of the preservation of the matriarchal line. The Norwood Gypsy Queens lived, unlike the rest of the tribe, in a house, which was always known as the Gypsy House. It was situated at a point north of the present railway line to Gipsy Hill station, in an angle formed by Gipsy Hill and Gipsy Road. Margaret's granddaughter was living in the Gypsy House in the year 1800. It was pulled down some years afterwards, in about 1808.

The title of Queen was purely titular. According to a contemporary report, the Gypsy Queen received no sort of homage from the members of the tribe, the only visible distinction at Norwood being that she lived in a house contrary to the Romany custom. (Purists claim that the spelling of "Gipsy", as in Gipsy Hill and Gipsy Road, is incorrect, and that "Gypsy" is the true adaptation of the word "Egyptian", from which it is derived.)

That the gypsies were famous in their day is shown by the fact that a pantomime produced at Covent Garden in 1777 was entitled "The Norwood Gypsies". When the poet Byron was a boy at Dr. Glennie's school in Lordship Lane he used often to visit the gypsies in Dulwich Wood. A report in *The Times,* describing a visit by Queen Victoria to Scotland, said: "Outside Dunbar a gypsy encampment was passed, in which is Queen Reynolds, sovereign of the gypsies of Norwood Park." For the occasion the gypsies had erected a platform on which was seated Queen Reynolds, wearing a dark purple dress trimmed with white lace. By her side stood a woman wearing a yellow handkerchief on her head and a crimson shawl over her shoulders. The two men on the platform wore red coats and white vests.

Despite their popularity with certain sections of society, the Norwood gypsies were far from popular in official circles on account of their depredations and light fingers. Farmers and commercial travellers suffered from the gypsies' pilferings and robberies, and formed an association for their own protection and control of gypsies. The surrounding villages undoubtedly suffered considerably from their attentions, whereby the gypsies hastened their own expulsion from their ancient Norwood retreat.

An Act of Parliament ordered them to be dealt with under the Vagrant Act. Instructions were given to the chief constable in

1797 to go with his men one Sunday and make a seizure of the band.

He purchased two suits of livery, in which he dressed two of his officers; two others disguised themselves as gentlemen of leisure and fashion. The chief constable and a number of other policemen unobtrusively stationed themselves at a strategic point on Gipsy Hill. In due course up drove a coach with the two "noblemen" attended by the two "footmen" and, as was expected, they were soon surrounded by the gypsies, who were looking for rich pickings. Instead, the police arrived on the scene, and after a short struggle eight of the gypsies were hauled off to Horsemonger Lane Gaol.

That surprise attack was followed by another, which was made by twenty police officers early one morning. They stole up and threw down the tents and carried off the occupants in hackney coaches which had been brought up for the occasion.

Other raids took place, and those, coupled with the inclosure of the common land, decisively broke the gypsies' ancient hold on that area of Norwood. The defeated gypsies were presented with the alternative of leaving the district or living in houses and conforming to the laws and customs of ordinary citizens. Many adopted the latter, and became integrated with the local population.

Nevertheless, old customs and old habits die hard. Even as late as 1866, when the foundation stone of Christ Church, Gipsy Hill was being laid among the surrounding brickfields that had replaced the woods, the hill was still a rendezvous of gypsies who had retained their nomad way of life. The camp fires of the Romany could still be seen flickering in the night. The surroundings were not safe to walk or ride through after darkness had set in.

On the Croydon side the same elimination of gypsies was slowly taking place. Thomas Frost wrote: "I have not seen any considerable company of the swarthy race since 1839, when I had the privilege of being the only house-dweller in a large party of both sexes assembled at the Greyhound Inn at Streatham.

"There was about that time, and for some years afterwards, a gypsy named Stevens who with his two dark-eyed daughters used to go the round of the south of England fairs with a refreshment and dancing booth, having for his sign a green bough. Naturally, all the gypsies who frequented the fair to buy or sell a horse, or preside over the exercises of the votaries of Aunt Sally, resorted to Stevens' booth; but a far larger number of persons visited it from curiosity, as one of the sights of the fair. I have only a dim recollection of Stevens, but I have heard of him spoken as a quiet well-conducted man, and that the late Nelson Lee, who had a good opinion of the gypsy race, was in the habit of giving him and his party an occasional free admission to his portable theatre – a treat which afforded them the greatest delight."

Nelson Lee was a pioneer in the presentation of traditional pantomime, and in the early days of the Crystal Palace the theatre that was inside the glass building was run by him.

The descent from All Saints Church to South Norwood was in the old days called Beggars' Hill, and was covered with thick woods of oak and hazel. Gypsy camps would be set up silently and secretly, so that the next day the hillside would be dotted with their tents, and then as secretly and silently they would depart. Strolling players would come with their canvas theatre to the foot of Beggars' Hill, and sometimes a circus troupe would set up their ring under the open sky. But by the time Beggars' Hill had taken on the better sounding name of South Norwood Hill, the last of the gypsies had vanished. They, too, had become integrated with the local population, or had gone off into the deeper countryside.

Chapter Three

Mary Nesbitt

The Hon. Augustus John Hervey, R.N., Vice-Admiral of the Blue, Colonel of Marines, and Commander-in-Chief of His Majesty's ships in the Mediterranean, became the third Earl of Bristol on the death of his uncle in 1775. He was of the aristocratic family of Herveys, of whom Lady Mary Wortley Montague said that mankind was divided into three species – Men, Women and Herveys.

In the same year that he became Earl of Bristol, Augustus Hervey set up house at Norwood with a young widow named Mary Nesbitt. His wife, whom he had secretly married, and who had since left him, was the somewhat notorious Elizabeth Chudleigh, who became the bigamous Duchess of Kingston. Hervey had come out to Norwood on many occasions for riding and sport, and had found a pleasant cottage in a sheltered position against a background of woods. The cottage is shown on maps of the period as being not far from a gravel pit in the valley through which the tiny Effra flows. The gravel pit lay near to the roadway which today is Central Hill, at the point where it forms a junction with Crown Dale and Elder Road.

Sir John Stanley, later to become Lord Stanley of Alderley, visited the house a number of times. He wrote in his Journal: "Lord Bristol in his rides had been struck with the picturesque and peaceful character of the woody recess in which the cottage stood, divided by a space of cleared land, enclosed from Norwood Common. He purchased the place, and obtained from the Archbishop of Canterbury a grant of several acres at that time covered with wood, so that there were meadows and pasture fields, a garden and pleasure grounds of nearly half a mile in length, all within a ring fence. The common was covered with gorse, and extended from the crown of Norwood Hill towards the west, to the Dulwich Road on the south, crossing a valley to cultivated fields, with only here and there a dwelling on them."

Hervey greatly enlarged the cottage, converting it into a sizeable country house. He added stables and made the gravel pit into an ornamental lake, his supply of water being drawn from the Effra, which flowed through his property. And thus, this man of the world, a brave and experienced and typically haughty aristocratic seaman, possessed of a town house in St. James's Square and an estate in Lincolnshire, devised a pleasant retreat from the artificiality of Georgian London society, in tune with the then fashionable Romantic revival.

The ornamental lake has long gone, as has the stream, which is now piped underground. The stables were finally pulled down in the early 1960s, yet the view through the large iron gates, which stand at the lower end of the high wall in Central Hill, offers a fine prospect of the house.

Today the building houses the junior school for girls of the Virgo Fidelis Convent. There have been alterations and additions, but the house is essentially as Hervey knew it.

Mary Nesbitt was Hervey's mistress, in consequence of the extreme difficulty of obtaining a divorce in those days. Hervey remained married to Elizabeth Chudleigh to the end of his days, but it is evident that had he been free to marry again he would have married Mary Nesbitt. When he died, at the age of 55, he left her his Norwood property and all other property and money not entailed, describing her in his will as his "dear, valuable, and best friend."

Augustus Hervey and Elizabeth Chudleigh had been married secretly in 1742, at a time when he was a young Naval Lieutenant and she was a Maid of Honour to the Princess of Wales, a post which required her to be celebate.

While Hervey was serving with the Fleet, and was away from England for as long as two years at a time, his wife was distinguishing herself in various ways, not least when she made her appearance at the Venetian Ambassador's Ball in the year 1749. It was a masquerade, and Elizabeth came as Iphigenia, in which, so an account had it, she "appeared almost in the unadorned simplicity of primitive nature. Whether to demonstrate how nearly she was allied to her ancestress, Eve, before the fall; or, whether from a religious veneration of the custom which prevailed in Eden; whatever was her motive certain it is, that she was everything but naked, and yet, like our first parents, she was not ashamed."

That celebrated 18th century blue-stocking, Elizabeth Montague, wrote afterwards to her sister at Bath: "Miss Chudleigh's dress or undress was remarkable. She was Iphigenia for the sacrifice, but so naked, the High Priest might easily inspect the entrails of the victim. The Maids of Honour, not maids of the strictest, were so offended they would not speak to her." Horace Walpole said, "You would have taken her for Andromeda."

The Duke of Kingston, who had recently commanded a squadron of light horse at Culloden, fell in love with Elizabeth, and she, regarding him as a better catch than her secret husband, succeeded in abstracting and destroying the register of her marriage to Hervey, and bigamously married Kingston. When she was presented at Court as the Duchess of Kingston, Hervey amused himself by turning up to see his "widow" being presented!

Hervey served in the Mediterranean under the ill-starred Admiral Byng. When Byng was defeated at the indecisive battle of Mahon, which led to his recall to England, and after a court-martial, to be shot on the quarter-deck of H.M.S. *Monarch* at Portsmouth, the man who stuck to him through thick and thin was Hervey. He remained the unfortunate Admiral's warmest defender up to the moment of his judicial murder, which had been perpetrated *pour encourager les autres.*

In his will Admiral Byng left to his "worthy and sincere friend", Augustus Hervey, "my French clock ornamented with Dresden flowers which I desire he will accept as a small token of our friendship."

Admiral Byng dispatched the clock to Hervey a few days before he was executed, with the words engraved on the clock, "May Time serve you better than he has served me." Hervey brought the clock to Norwood, and it remained in the house until the death of Mary Nesbitt in 1835.

One of Hervey's great exploits was at the siege of Havannah in 1761, when he played a distinguished part in leading his men in a land assault by which he captured Moro Castle. This finally broke the Spanish power in America. Hervey brought home the great bell of Moro Castle, and this he hung over the stables at Norwood, where the historic trophy could serve, if needed, as an alarm bell.

Hervey died at the age of 55 on the 22nd December, 1779 of "gout in the stomach". He left all that he possessed to Mrs. Nesbitt, outside of family entail. He left her his Norwood property, an estate in Lincolnshire, the family papers, and, it is recorded, the deer in the park at Ickworth, the family seat of the Herveys.

Heir to the Earldom was Augustus Hervey's younger brother, the Bishop of Derry. Horace Walpole wrote of the event that Hervey "leaves a Duchess-Countess and an Earl-Bishop!"

The owner of the house at Norwood was now Mrs. Mary Nesbitt, and it is quite evident that she became increasingly a woman of great influence, who knew many people in high places, and had many interests. Nevertheless, she remained all her life somewhat of an enigma, a woman who moved behind the scenes, deeply involved in foreign policy and a Secret Agent for the Government. Many great people came to see her at Norwood, and the King himself, George III, on various occasions held Privy Council meetings with his Ministers in her house.

The one-time ballroom on the first floor, with its massive oak floor, is much as it was when Mrs. Nesbitt was the châtelaine.

The sisters of the Virgo Fidelis School still speak of that magnificent room with considerable reverence as "The Privy Council Chamber", and show it with pride. May it long be preserved in its present form!

Mary Nesbitt's early reputation and background remain elusive, and a series of question marks. Certain articles, such as appeared in *The Town and Country Magazine* and *The Letters of Junius,* claimed that she had started as a common prostitute. At the same time, it should be pointed out that as a young woman she had married a banker named Nesbitt, who died soon afterwards. Nesbitt had relations named de Crespigny who lived at Camberwell – de Crespigny Park is a road named after the family – and despite scurrilous press comments which were such a feature of that period, it is notable that members of the de Crespigny family were visitors to the Norwood house, and were in her social circle.

Lord Stanley of Alderley first came into contact with Lord Bristol and Mrs. Nesbitt while he was a schoolboy at Loughborough House, an expensive school for the sons of wealthy and aristocratic families. The school was an old nobleman's mansion, with fine grounds and a walled fruit garden, where Loughborough Junction now stands. The boys used to take their walks over Stockwell Common. Stanley's friend at the school was young Augustus Hervey, a natural son of Hervey and a Miss Kitty Hunter. Lord Bristol and Mrs. Nesbitt used frequently to visit the school and were very kind to the boys. Young Augustus, says Stanley, was mothered charmingly by Mrs. Nesbitt. Later, when Stanley was at school at Greenwich, Lord Bristol and Mrs. Nesbitt used to call to visit him and beg a day's holiday for him.

When Lord Bristol died Mrs. Nesbitt became guardian to the boy. In the terms of Augustus Hervey's will she was to allow young Augustus £300 during his minority, and £400 afterwards.

"Poor Augustus Hervey", wrote Stanley in his Journal, "he was a noble-spirited lad, warm in his youthful friendship for me, and for the few years it lasted. He had the character of a

Hervey; impetuous, eager, clever, and fascinating. He went to sea when he was twelve. On an exchange of very few shots with the French fleet besieging Gibraltar, one struck him in the chest."

Stanley's first visit to Norwood House, as Mrs. Nesbitt's house was named, took place in 1789. "I was at Streatham, where my brother was at a school kept by the Reverend Reynolds Davies. 'Do you remember' he said to me, 'a lady who, with Lord Bristol, whenever his son, Augustus Hervey was sent out of school, used always to send for you at the same time? A Mrs. Nesbitt: she is living not far from here.'

"I remember her well . . . . The day after my conversation with Mr. Davies, I mounted my horse, and was soon at Mrs. Nesbitt's door. I found her in a long boudoir, working at a tambour frame – her best-looking days all passed by, and her grey hair tucked up under a close French cap. The moment she heard my name she got up and threw her arms round me, crying out, 'can it be you, the friend of Augustus?'

"After this I visited her often, dining, and sometimes passing two or three days at Norwood. It was at her house that I made acquaintance with George Rose, Lord Mulgrave, Mr. Townshend, an East India director, the daughters of Lord Chancellor Thurlow, and Mr. Crespigny, a relation of her husband, Mr. Nesbitt, dead long before, and some few others."

George Rose was at that time Secretary to the Treasury, and later a Privy Councillor. At one time or another he had held many distinguished posts in the Government. He was a close friend of Mrs. Nesbitt's, and secret affairs of State were arranged between them.

An entry in Stanley's Journal of 1808 touches more particularly on the political background of Mrs. Nesbitt. It is an entry which colours so much of her background in European affairs.

"August 1808: I rode down to Norwood and found Mrs. Nesbitt very glad to see me. She was in the midst of bricklayers, plasterers, etc. The whole house was undergoing thorough repair. She contrived, however, to give me an excellent dinner, venison to eat, and Burgundy to drink. She is very little altered in person, from what she was 12 years ago . . . .

"She related many of her adventures when she was in Germany and Switzerland, and brought to my mind one circumstance which I had forgotten. When I was in Paris with her, she was visited by many great ladies, and I remember two being in the room when I came to her with the news of the Hotel de Castres being stripped of its furniture by the mob. One was Madame de Chateaureux the wife of the general and colonel of the Swiss regiment of that name. The other was Madame de Beauharnais, *alias* the Empress Josephine. Mrs. Nesbitt has the most curious kind of connection with the world that ever any woman had."

The Morning Chronicle of 25th September, 1797 had a leading article on Mrs. Nesbitt, which points clearly to her importance in European politics. Her involvement with matters of British diplomacy concerning the French Royalists after the French Revolution of 1793, and after the Directory of 1795, is obvious.

"This celebrated woman has become the topic of universal conversation from the mention which Citizen Noel makes of her transactions in Germany, and she is likely to suffer a great deal of impertinent slander on account of the allusion to her name. It certainly is no discredit to the sex that an accomplished woman is capable of playing a part so conspicuous and interesting to the state of Nations, as that which Mrs. Nesbitt has lately performed. During the last twenty years, we will venture to say that no just reproach can be thrown on her *moral* conduct. The allusions made to her acquaintance with Mr. Rose [Secretary to the Treasury 1782-1801] are illiberal. Her intimacy with many of the most distinguished characters of the age – with Lord Thurlow and others, was no more than the society of kindred minds. An intelligent woman in the decline of years, possessing the charms of conversation, unrestrained by prudery, and endowed with elegant talents improved by knowledge of the world, drew around her a select circle of friends, and made her retirement to Norwood desirable to the Politician and the Scholar from its intellectual and unembarrassed

Politics. We abhor the idea of pursuing political hostilities into private life; we sincerely believe that Mr. Rose cultivated the acquaintance of Mrs. Nesbitt from the attraction of her mind, and he introduced his young family to her house that they might form their manners under so perfect a model.

"Such has been the situation of Mrs. Nesbitt for the last twenty years. With an independent fortune of between £2,000 and £3,000 a year; debarred to a great degree from the female world by early events of her history; surrounded by men of the first distinction, it was no wonder that a woman so endowed, and so successful, should be induced to turn her talents to political intrigue. Her marriage *à-la-main-gauche* with a German Prince introduced her to the best society at the Court of Germany, and in all diplomatic circles she was considered as a woman of infinite address, and of profound discernment. Our readers are not ignorant of the nature of a German marriage *à-la-main-gauche*. The pride of Royalty will not permit a Prince to marry a woman of inferior rank otherwise than with the left hand. This, without elevating the lady to the blood royal, reserves her character unstained, and she is received into society with respect. The connections that she formed in the Empire and in Switzerland, her knowledge of the languages, the symmetry of her person which made it easy for her to assume the male habit, and the confidence reposed in her by Ministers pointed her out as a proper agent; and on the 5th of August, 1795 she left England, and has ever since resided in various parts of the Continent. It is not easy to develop the course she has pursued, and until it shall be declared infamous for Courts to employ secret agents, it surely cannot be imputed to her as a crime that her accomplishments entitled her to the appointment.

"We know that public curiosity will not be satisfied until we shall tear off the mask from the early periods of her history. And yet nothing can be more base and detestable in morality than such an exposure. Let the generosity of the sex decide on the question . . . . Mrs. Nesbitt has had to combat through life with the prejudice which her first connection excited, and the woman whom the dreadful pen of Junius consigned to an immortality of disgrace could only rise superior to the Memorial by extraordinary exertions – yet this she had effected. She has acquired an elevation in life which she has preserved with dignity because she has acted in good fortune with moderation. She has used her influence with the great in favour of the unfortunate, and many deserving men owe their present situation in public life to the patronage of this lady.

"We certainly do not know that she was employed abroad. As a woman of easy fortune she could chuse her place of residence; and was too independent to assign motives for her conduct. This, however, is obvious, that known as she is to all the diplomatic circle of Europe, the accusation of M. Noel will be implicitly believed, and the British Court will stand convicted of the charge of undermining a Government with which they professed openly to treat upon candid terms."

The barb in *The Morning Chronicle* leader is of a political nature, being principally directed against Pitt's Government, which was seeking to overthrow the French Directory in favour of restoring the Royalist regime. The M. Noel referred to in the leader was, of course, a member of the Directory, and he would hardly be in favour of Mrs. Nesbitt's activities on behalf of the British Government. *The Morning Chronicle,* being pro-Directory, would inevitably take such a line with Mrs. Nesbitt, as the following examples from its columns show.

"Mrs. Nesbitt's well-known talents, her connection here, her residence at the Hague, will be used as arguments of her agency, and though this clever woman may have merely retired to the Continent for motives not difficult to explain, her journeys to Pyrmont and Brandenberg, and finally her visit to Switzerland will subject the British Court to suspicions that they were not unconcerned spectators of the Royalist Conspiracy."

The idea of bribing the Members of the French Legislature originated with Mr. Rose, claimed the newspaper. It was also hinted that when Mrs. Nesbitt left Norwood House for one of her trips on the Continent, dressed either as a man or a woman, she would be well-equipped with British gold for that purpose.

"Mr. Pitt will gain some character with the fair sex from his late intrigue with Mrs. Nesbitt . . . . Ministers are so very prudent that they are determined to keep well with all parties concerned in French politics. They send Lord Malmesbury to Lisle to show their respect for the Republic; and with proper attention to the character of Kings and Courts, they depute a lady to manage their intrigues with Louis XVIII . . . .

"The Lady, who had been of so much conversation on account of her diplomatic celebrity was visited by Mr. Rose and other great politicians [at her house in Norwood] for the charms of her conversation . . . .

"Ministers certainly deserve the praise of perseverence in their hostility to the French Government . . . . Undismayed by disappointment, they still be in afresh to weave their dirty web, and if Camille Jordan is defeated, Mrs. Nesbitt is still indefatigable in her exertions for the *advancement of religion* and the *cause* of Kings . . . . Mr. Pitt has no intention of employing Mrs. Nesbitt in the Home Department. He never makes use of the agency of the ladies but in Foreign Affairs.

"The figure which Madam de Stael has lately made in Paris is now satisfactorily explained. The Directory, aware that they were assailed by the arts of Mrs. Nesbitt, saw that it was necessary to have a lady on their side, too. *Opposite* forces thus destroying each other, the Republic for this time is saved."

Gossip for ever followed this remarkable and often mystery woman who, when she was at home, lived so naturally and simply in her Norwood house with its delightful background of woods. But always there were the comings and goings of the great in the land, not excepting the King himself!

Concerning the rumour in *The Morning Chronicle* of Mrs. Nesbitt's marriage to a German Prince, there is an interesting echo to be found in a letter from Maria Josepha Stanley, wife of J. T. Stanley, afterwards Lord Stanley of Alderley, written to her sister.

"You have surely heard talk of Mrs. Nesbitt. She makes a conspicuous figure, you see, in the late revolution in Paris. The best beloved is at the moment writing to her; if papa still takes in *The Morning Chronicle* you will have seen a very fair account of her, except that I do not believe she married the Duke of Wurtemburg; she refused him once, actually, however."

And so Mary Nesbitt flits from Norwood to the Continent and back again, a woman of intrigue at Government level, a woman who found enemies and strong enduring friends. It is believed that Mrs. Nesbitt, who certainly knew Madame Tussaud in Paris, aided her when she was first released by the French Government and was permitted to come to England. Mrs. Nesbitt, so it is said (though I have not been able to substantiate the story), found Madame Tussaud a house not far from her own on Central Hill, namely Effingham Lodge, that stands midway between Harold Road and Rockmount Road. And it is from there that Madame Tussaud is supposed to have started out on her tour of Britain with her waxworks.

Mary Nesbitt became a considerable landowner in Norwood, as the Enclosure Acts of both Croydon and Lambeth show. She died abroad in about 1835 at the age of ninety. The house at Norwood was sold and was converted into the Park Hotel, which remained a fashionable resort until 1848.

A Memorandum by Stanley, on revisiting Norwood in about 1845, gives a last glimpse of the house as it was in that day, still haunted, as it were, by the ghost of Mrs. Nesbitt and those who came to see her there.

"After a passing away of fifty-six years, it was not without pleasure that I found myself in the haunt of my early days, with almost everything within the fences unchanged but for the growth of trees. The wild common had, however, vanished. It was parcelled out in the fields and gardens, and covered for the greater part with houses. My pleasure was indeed tempered with remembrances of the friend with whom in the same place I had spent many days of bright sunshine of my life. The woods, the fields, the garden, formerly so well known to me, were so little changed that Time, as to them, seemed to have had his wings clipped, or been lying down asleep.

"But where were all I had beheld when my former 'I' had existed? The owner and the visitors of the place? If the woods asked, I could only answer in Echo's words, 'Where are they?' And then the house, no longer the quiet home of one, but an hotel, open to all comers, and though many of the rooms I had wandered over were the same, all the well-remembered books and furniture which had been in them had been removed and scattered. My eyes had fallen on new pictures or vacancy, where I had been accustomed to see full length portraits by Gainsborough of Lord Bristol (died 1779) and Mulgrave; and the portrait of my school-fellow, Augustus Hervey, and of Mrs. Nesbitt herself in the beauty of her youth. The clock was gone that Admiral Byng sent to Lord Bristol a few days before he was shot, with the words, 'May Time serve you better than he has served me,' and I missed the great bell which had been brought away from the Moro Castle by Lord Bristol when the sailors of his ship stormed it, and placed by him over the Norwood stables."

The portrait of Mrs. Nesbitt "in the beauty of her youth", by Sir Joshua Reynolds, was given to Lord Stanley, and hung in the Green Drawing-room at Alderley until after the Great War, when it went to America, and hangs to this day in the Smith College and Museum, Northampton, Massachusetts. In this lovely portrait she is depicted as Circe.

Chapter Four

Canal and Railway

Norwood Lake, adjacent to South Norwood Hill and Beaulieu Woods, tree-lined, and for much of the year enhanced by the flash and curve of yacht sails, is a stretch of water of some beauty, a rendezvous for anglers, yachtsmen, bird-watchers, occasionally ice-skaters and, in earlier years, a popular bathing place.

The lake is indeed a link with the past. It is more than 170 years old, and is a relic of the old Croydon Canal. In its day, the canal was a waterway of charm, a resort of boaters, strollers, anglers, skaters and bathers. Picnic parties resorted to its wooded fringes and the gardens that ran down to the tow-path. Horse-drawn barges with their assorted loads moved from lock to lock in leisurely procession.

Norwood Lake was formed as a reservoir for the canal. There was a similar reservoir on Sydenham Common, which has long been filled in. Their function was to keep the highest levels of the canal filled with water. There was also a pumping station at the Croydon end of the canal.

The Croydon Canal was first mooted at the close of the eighteenth century by a group of gentlemen living in and near Croydon, who were conscious of the need for opening up new lines of communication between Croydon and London. There were times in winter when the roads were almost impassable. The old system of pack horses was already a thing of the past and had been superceded by so-called fly-vans, which crawled along the bad roads at 2 miles per hour. A committee was formed, which included Lord William Russell, Lord Auckland, Lord Gwyder and Sir John Frederick. The purpose of the canal would be to bring coal and general merchandise to Croydon, and return with agricultural produce, lime, chalk, flint, fuller's earth and timber. There was also a scheme to supply water to Croydon, Norwood, Sydenham, Dulwich and Streatham.

Croydon at the end of the eighteenth century had a population of approximately 7,000. Norwood was a village in the woods, and the whole length of the canal would be through sylvan surroundings. The Croydon Canal was authorised by Act of Parliament in 1801. It was 9¼ miles long, and its route from West Croydon to the point where it linked up with the Grand Surrey Canal at New Cross was via South Norwood, Penge Woods, Sydenham, Forest Hill and Brockley. The terminal basin at West Croydon was where today is West Croydon station. The Croydon Canal Company was empowered to raise by subscription £50,000 in shares of £100 each; and if that sum should be found insufficient, then £30,000 by additional shares or by mortgage; and in order to repay the subscribers, the Company was authorised to charge 3d per ton per mile on timber, stone, coal, bricks, tiles, and other goods, and three halfpence on chalk, clay, lime, dung, and such articles.

The celebrated engineer John Rennie built the canal. He had advised a longer and more circuitous route, via Woodside and Lewisham, which would have generally followed a lower and more even level, requiring fewer lock gates. As it was, for some not very clear reason, it was taken over the high ground of Forest Hill. From New Cross to Forest Hill there were no fewer than 26 locks. After that there was a level stretch of 5½ miles to Selhurst, followed by two locks. These two locks were required to carry the canal over the river Graveney.

The total rise from New Cross was 167 feet, and during times of great water shortage the canal authorities were hard put to it to keep the highest levels full of water. At times it was not possible, and then for a while the canal would be unnavigable at the top level.

The Croydon Canal was formally opened on 22nd October, 1809. A contemporary newspaper account of the occasion was as follows: "On Monday last the navigation of this canal from the Thames to the town of Croydon was opened. The proprietors assembled to celebrate so interesting an event. They met at Sydenham, about five miles from Croydon, and there embarked on one of the Company's barges, which was handsomely decorated with flags. At the moment of the barge moving forward an excellent band played 'God Save the King', and a salute of twenty-one guns was fired.

"The proprietors' barge then advanced, followed by a great many other barges loaded, some with coals, others with stone and corn. The zeal and exhilaration of the traders would not let them suffer their barges, loaded as they were, to be destitute of decoration; accordingly they all hoisted flags or streamers and whatever should testify their joy that their speculations of a profitable traffic were now realised. After passing a wharf erected at Penge Common, by John Scott, Esq., by means of which the towns of Beckenham, Bromley, and a considerable part of Kent are accommodated with coals, manure, and all articles of merchandise at a greatly reduced rate of carriage, the gay fleet of barges entered Penge Forest; the canal passes through this forest in a part so elevated that it affords the most extensive prospects, comprehending Beckenham and several beautiful villages and seats, Shooters Hill, Addington Hills, Banstead Downs, and numerous other picturesque objects in the counties of Kent and Surrey. The proprietors found their calculation of profit irresistibly interrupted by the rich prospects breaking upon them from time to time by openings among the trees, and as they passed along they were deprived of this grand scenery only by another and no less gratification, that of finding themselves gliding through the deepest recesses of the forest, where nothing met the eye but the elegant windings of the clear and still canal, its borders adorned by a profusion of trees of which the beauty was heightened by the tints of autumn.

"The anxious inhabitants of Croydon met this interesting procession some miles from their town, and hailed it with loud and repeated cheers. When the proprietors neared the basin of Croydon, they saw it surrounded by thousands of persons, assembled to greet with thanks and applause those by whose patriotic perseverance so important a work had been accomplished. It is impossible to describe adequately the scene which presented itself to the feelings which prevailed when the proprietors' Barge was entering the basin, at which instant the band was playing 'God Save the King', the guns were firing, the bells of the churches were ringing and this immense concourse of delighted persons were hailing, by universal and hearty and long continued shouts, the dawn of their commerce and prosperity. The proprietors walked from West Croydon to The Greyhound, accompanied by music, and preceded by the workmen who marched in order, with their tools on their shoulders, enjoying the consciousness of having finished a canal which is allowed to be one of the tightest and best constructed in England."

Croydon undoubtedly regarded the occasion as a red letter day with the prospects of greatly increased trade, so it may be assumed that this contemporary account was not exaggerated, despite the slight overstatement that "the bells of the churches were ringing", when, in fact, at that date there was but one church, the parish church of St. John the Baptist.

At The Greyhound celebration banquet it was reported in a speech that circumstances were highly favourable for the extension of the Croydon Canal to Portsmouth, and the toast was given, "The Union of the River Thames and the English Channel through the Croydon Canal."

There was indeed a scheme afoot for extending the Croydon Canal to Portsmouth, inspired by the war with France. John Rennie surveyed a scheme for a canal with 41 locks and a formidable 4½-mile tunnel through Merstham Hill. The canal would then go via Crawley and Pulborough, making use of the River Arun for 1¼ miles, to Chichester, Havant and Portsmouth, terminating by the dockyard.

This would have been a militarily strategic canal, enabling incoming merchantmen to unload their cargoes at Portsmouth, instead of having to run the gauntlet of French privateers and men-o'-war in the narrows of the Channel while making their way to the mouth of the Thames. There were, however, strong opponents to such a massive scheme, which would have entailed that 4½-mile tunnel with all its inherent problems. With the defeat of Napoleon at Waterloo in 1815 the plan was finally abandoned. There was also looming ahead the prospect of railways and steam taking over the function of the canals.

During the days of the Croydon Canal's prosperity heavy merchandise was delivered at the West Croydon basin, and barges were loaded and unloaded at the extensive wharves that fronted the warehouses. Later, business on the canal declined, although during its existence it had been extremely advantageous to the trading interests of the town.

In one respect, the canal was always a success. It was throughout its existence a popular pleasure resort and an unfailing attraction to those who lived in the vicinity. The wooded surroundings of Penge was a favourite picnic region. The Canal Company sold angling licences at a guinea each. In his *Recollections of Croydon,* William Page described the Croydon Canal as being a source of delight to the inhabitants, whether they were angler, bather, skater, boatman or pedestrian. They all paid tribute to its charms. Some fine jack were caught in its waters, and there was good fishing for dace, perch and roach. When the ice was firm the skater came to enjoy a run to Brockley. Boats could be hired, and parties were made up to row to Forest Hill through beautiful countryside, with scarcely a house to be seen on the journey. Teas were to be had in the extensive gardens of the Dartmouth Arms tavern. The walks on the banks or towing path could not be surpassed in the neighbourhood. Norwood and its grand woods were on one side, and wide, well-cultivated fields on the other. At Penge Reach the canal widened, and the journey through Penge Woods passed through country as picturesque and romantic as an American backwater. The country was varied, and the activities on the water, barges passing and repassing, boating parties, anglers on the banks, all added to the charm and attraction. The gardens of the Jolly Sailor tavern at South Norwood, where teas were served, were visited by family parties where they would watch the various craft passing to and fro.

At the point where the canal crossed Portland Road at the bottom of South Norwood Hill, where the railway bridge is today, there was a low swing bridge, which was opened to let the barges through by a canal employee known as Old Grumble. Oarsmen on the canal used to shoot the bridge, rather than wait for Old Grumble, lying flat on their backs as their boat carried them under with only a few inches to spare.

There was a famous rival to the Croydon Canal in the transport of goods to and from Croydon. The "Grand" Surrey Iron Railway had the distinction of being the first public railway in the world, all previous railways having been privately owned by collieries and other industrial ventures. The Surrey Iron Railway was authorised by Act of Parliament in 1801, a couple of months before the authorisation of the Croydon Canal, and was opened on 26th July, 1803. It followed the line of the River Wandle, and linked Croydon with the Thames at Wandsworth. It approached Croydon from Mitcham, and terminated at West Croydon.

The railway was operated by horses or mules, one horse or mule being able to draw six trucks. The smooth wheel running on a smooth rail surface produced some startling results. A wager was won that a horse could draw 36 tons for 6 miles along the road, and the horse could draw that weight from a dead pull, as well as take it round the occasional windings of the iron road.

The two systems of transport, horses pulling trucks on the railway, and horses pulling barges on the canal, were close rivals in competition for the carriage of Croydon's trade.

On completion of the Surrey Iron Railway, a new company was formed to build a continuation of the railway from Croydon to Godstone via Merstham, with a branch to Reigate. The proposed extension to Reigate was never carried out, and the line stopped at Godstone. It was opened to the public on 24th July, 1805.

The rival concerns of railway and canal were, of course, cutting each other's throats, and neither was a financial success. Times, too, were soon to change. The steam locomotive was being developed, and was taking over. The success of George Stephenson's locomotive, the *Rocket,* which on its trials averaged 14 miles per hour, and on occasion reached 30 miles per hour, was altering the whole concept of travel. Minor canals and railways were being absorbed by the new railway companies, despite one dogged champion of the horse asserting: "Does anybody in possession of his senses expect that this snorting, spluttering, hideous iron machine, belching forth smoke and steam can ever accomplish such a draught as is easily undertaken by the horse on the Croydon Iron Road?"

In August 1836 the Croydon Canal was closed and drained of its water. The London and Croydon Railway, constituted by Act of Parliament, had purchased it at a price favourable to the canal company, and now adapted the greater portion of the canal bed for its permanent way, which represented a useful saving in costs. But with the passing of the canal, South London lost one of its most charming and tranquil features. Gone was the gleaming waterway through the green woodland, with its anglers, its summer picnic and boating parties that gave such holiday character to a district so pleasing in its rural calm. The Norwood Lake is the last gleam of that vanished thread of water, which, designed for commerce, was also a pleasure resort.

The London and Croydon Railway was opened on 1st June 1839, by the Lord Mayor of London. The iron horse took over, the steel rails having adopted the bed of the canal, except that there was a sharp curve in the canal at Anerley. Permission had been given by the owner of the adjoining land for the railway to continue on a straight course over his property without payment, in return for a station being built there. The story is that when the landowner, a Scotsman named Sanderson, was asked the name of the place, his reply was that his was the *annerley* (only) *hoose* there. So the station was duly named Annerley (later to be spelt Anerley). A Bradshaw of the time, under the station name "Annerley", added the note: "But there is no place of that name."

The loop of canal by Anerley station remained full of water, and was, apparently, well stocked with fish, and the railway advertised day tickets enabling passengers to alight there and fish. There was a railway advertisement to the effect that "Marquees are Erected in the Wood, close to the Anerley station and Parties using the railway will be permitted to angle in the adjacent canal, which abounds in fish."

All that remains today of that piece of the canal is a stretch of ornamental water in Betts Park, between Anerley Road and Weighton Road, immediately behind Seymour Villas. But any sense of the old canal is quite lost.

The London and Croydon Railway formed a junction with the London and Greenwich Railway at Corbett's Lane, and had its terminus at the Bricklayers' Arms Station, near London Bridge. Southward from Corbett's Lane, the railway proceeded to New Cross, and climbed the long slope up to Forest Hill. As there was no village of Forest Hill, the station was named after the local tavern, the Dartmouth Arms. Only much later was the name of the station changed to Forest Hill.

Not far from the present Norwood Junction Station is the Jolly Sailor, a public house standing at the foot of South Norwood Hill. In those days, the earlier building had as a tavern sign the capering figure of a sailor with a pot of beer in one hand. It stood over the entrance porch. The first railway station, which was nearer to the public house than the present Norwood Junction station, was named the Jolly Sailor. The railway station at West Croydon occupied the site of the old canal basin and wharves. A stretch of canal tow-path can be seen beside the railway, from Spurgeon's Bridge where it crosses the line near West Croydon.

It was quickly established that the steam locomotive, with its smoke and steam and hot cinders, was the most practical form of locomotion to date. In the year 1845, however, the London and Croydon Railway took a jump in the dark by adopting an experimental form of rail transport which, if successful, would make for more comfortable and cheaper travel.

In the rapidly expanding railway age, various methods were being tried out to find cheaper running costs and greater passenger comfort. One of these was the entirely novel "atmospheric" system, which was designed to do away with the locomotive altogether. In one sense, it was on the same principle as present day electrification where the power is picked up from a conductor rail or overhead cable, but instead of electric power, atmospheric power was picked up from a conductor pipe. In each method, the source of power remains stationary, while the power itself is delivered direct to the moving train.

With the atmospheric railway a continuous pipe, 15 inches in diameter in the case of the London and Croydon Railway, was laid between the running rails. This continuous pipe, firmly anchored to the sleepers embedded in the ground, looked rather like a water main, except that along the top of the iron pipe was a continuous slot. The slot was sealed along its entire length by leather flaps, fixed along one side but free on the other. This leather flap or valve could be opened as required and then pressed back into place.

The purpose of the slot was to allow the free passage of a strong iron rod or plough. This plough joined the underside of the railway coach framework with a piston that fitted tightly but smoothly inside the pipe. The piston could slide along inside the pipe while remaining airtight. If air were exhausted from the pipe in front of the piston, normal atmospheric pressure behind the piston would force it forward, taking the train with it. The leather flap valve, pressed firmly down by outside atmospheric pressure, would only lift to admit the passage of the iron plough, and would then be restored to its former sealed position. The leather flap would be kept supple and airtight by a mixture of tallow and wax.

The pipe itself was connected to pumping stations at 3-mile intervals, where powerful air pumps were installed. These would exhaust the air from the tube in front of the train, the other end being left open. Starting and stopping the train was effected by manipulating the brakes. The driver of the train was, in effect, the brakeman.

Considerable speeds were obtained by this system, up to sixty miles an hour, and it was freely suggested that speeds up to 100 miles per hour would soon be attained as a practical proposition. In fact, it was claimed that a train had travelled from Forest Hill to Croydon, which is 5½ miles, in 2 minutes, 47 seconds, including starting and pulling up. This showed an average speed of more than 100 miles an hour. One gentleman who was in the habit of travelling by atmospheric described it as very similar to falling from a height; it fairly took your breath away! The motion was very regular and smooth, with not half the rattle and jar there was on a train drawn by a loco-motive.

The atmospheric principle could take trains up gradients where the driving wheels of the conventional locomotive would slip impotently, and the wear on the running rails would be vastly reduced. It could take curves at speed without danger of jumping the metals because the leading coach was locked by the piston in the tube. Also, it was impossible to have collisions between trains, because no two trains could operate on the same stretch of line at the same time.

William Cubitt, Engineer of the London and Croydon Rail-way, gave the atmospheric principle such a glowing recom-mendation that it was installed on a special experimental track from Forest Hill to West Croydon. Pumping stations were installed at Forest Hill, Norwood, and West Croydon.

Since the atmospheric track was laid on the east side of the conventional track, a problem had to be overcome at South Norwood. It was there that the line to Brighton and Dover branched from the West Croydon line, and the experimental track with its 15-inch pipe had to cross it. This was done by what was then termed "a flying leap", which consisted of a massive timber viaduct with a gradient of 1 in 50 to carry the atmos-pheric track over the Brighton line. The flying leap had the distinction of being the first railway flyover ever to be employed in railway engineering. During tests at the Norwood flyover, atmospheric trains were successfully started from rest and took the gradient with ease.

Pumping stations at Forest Hill, Norwood and Croydon were given the most careful aesthetic consideration in the matter of their outward appearance. That was because of the proximity of gentlemen's residences and fine estates. The pumping stations were given an Early English Gothic appearance, and looked vaguely like churches with tall chimneys. The chimneys were somewhat disguised to look like bell towers. They were called "stalks" by the engineers, and were necessary for providing a draught for the boiler fires, and for carrying away smoke and steam as well as the exhausted air from the vacuum pipe. The Forest Hill "stalk" was 120 feet in height.

The *Pictorial Times* of August, 1845, published an article on the subject. "The engine houses are the most beautiful things of their kind that have ever been erected in this country. They are the work of Mr. W. H. Breakspear the Architect, and his object has been to show that the most uncouth forms may be so decorated as to become ornaments to the landscape . . . . But a chimney being a most unsightly object, and many of them being wanted on the course of the atmospheric line, to the certain annoyance of the gentlemen through whose grounds the railway would pass, it was determined that they should receive at the hands of the builder such an amount of architectural direction as would make them objects of interest rather than eyesores."

Still, despite the decoration, there were many complaints about the smoke and smell from the chimneys of these pumping stations. The ordinary public, on the other hand, enjoyed their atmospheric rides on account of their speed, their silence, their easy motion, their freedom from smoke nuisance, and above all their initial cheapness. Travel was free from 27th October, 1845 to 19th February, 1846. After that time, the train service from Forest Hill to Croydon became entirely atmospheric, and fares were charged. It was also planned to extend the atmospheric line to New Cross, and beyond Croydon to Epsom.

The silence of the atmospheric service had its own problems, and people were in frequent danger of being run down. At some of the stations the passengers from the steam trains had to cross the atmospheric track, and the silent approach of the atmospheric train led to some narrow escapes.

There were teething troubles. In wet weather, when the metals were slippery, brakes would not bite, and sometimes a train would run a considerable distance beyond the platform before coming to a standstill. With a conventional train that would not have been of much consequence; the locomotive would merely back the train to the platform, but with the atmospheric there was no such backing possible, and the passengers had to alight as best they could and walk back.

A defect of a much more serious nature emerged, and occurred in the longitudinal valve. The problem lay in the use of leather for the valve. The summer of 1846 was one of great heat, and the compound of tallow and wax with which the leather was anointed became too soft for the valve to perform its function properly. Air leaks occurred whereby power was lost to work the train.

To some extent this was remedied by altering the compound, but other problems affecting the leather emerged. Rain would wash the lubricating compound out of the leather, and when the leather dried it would become hard and brittle, and fail to function. In winter, frost made the leather stiff and incapable of closing properly. Worst of all, there was a fatal affinity between the leather and the iron with which it was in contact. The iron attacked the leather by extracting the tannin, and so decomposed it that it broke to shreds. Rats, too, had a fondness for the compound designed to keep the leather flexible. They would invade the track nightly, devouring the leather.

When the pumps were started up in the morning, rats would be sucked through the pipe into the pumping station. To combat this, the engine room men placed open sacks over the inlet, to catch the rats as they poured in.

One of the severest indignities suffered by the Croydon atmospheric railway was when a train, due to the leaks in the valve, failed to get over the flying leap at Norwood. When that happened the train was uncoupled in the middle, and the front half would stagger over the top of the hump. There it would be brought to a standstill while a stout rope was attached to it and to the other half of the train at the foot of the gradient. Then the train would be started up, and the front half, on the descending slope, would be able to haul the other half up the gradient, and the two halves of the train would continue their journey to West Croydon a rope's length apart!

There were other unfortunate occasions when the male passengers were invited to alight from the train and help push it. On several occasions the train then went on its way, leaving the passengers behind!

Had rubber or plastic compounds as we know them been available in those days, the story of the atmospheric experiment might have had a different ending, with trains to Brighton in 30 minutes. As it was, the problem remained unsolved.

On 27th July, 1846, the London and Croydon Railway amalgamated with the London and Brighton Railway, to form the London, Brighton and South Coast Railway, which dispensed with the atmospheric experiment. The physical remains of the whole imaginative scheme were sold for scrap, and an idea that was far ahead of its time passed into the limbo of forgotten things.

Chapter Five

The Beulah Spa

On the southward sloping ground lying between Beulah Hill, Spa Hill and Grange Road may still be traced the shadowy outline of the remains of the once famous Beulah Spa – the Royal Beulah Spa and Gardens, as it styled itself when Queen Victoria came to the throne. What there is left today is little enough. There are a few indistinct paths and an overgrown carriageway amid a semicircle of trees. This belt of trees protects the site from the north and east, embracing a bowl-like contour of land which was once a centre of gaiety and fashion and gala events.

The peculiar qualities which made the Beulah Spa a popular health and pleasure resort for Londoners were the spring of chalybeate water, the idyllic setting in which the medicinal spring was embowered, and its nearness to London.

The origin of the curative spring is lost in the years, but the quality of the water was locally known and appreciated a hundred years or more before the Beulah Spa was so named and the spring made popular. While Dr. Samuel Johnson was visiting the Thrales at Streatham Park, and sampling the waters of Streatham Wells during his perambulations over Streatham and Lime Commons, the Norwood locals and Norwood Gypsies had, in a more rough and ready manner, long resorted to drinking from the spring at Upper Norwood. It lay a few yards to the east of Leather Bottle Lane, now Spa Hill.

It was not until the development of Norwood as a residential area began to take place, following the Croydon Inclosure Acts (1797–1801), that the Beulah Spa came into prominence and found a place in the hierarchy of the pleasure gardens of the eighteenth and early nineteenth centuries. It was, indeed, the last of the pleasure gardens to be opened in the outskirts of London, and very little art was required to make it into such an ideal resort.

Spas and gardens were a feature of social life in and around London at that period. Streatham and Dulwich and Sydenham Wells had long been popular, and Beulah Hill was rich in mineral springs. There were in the earliest years of the nine-teenth century several houses on Beulah Hill with wells in their gardens, from which chalybeate water was obtained. Springfield, a large estate on the corner of Beulah Hill and Biggin Hill, was one of them, as its name so clearly denotes. The house was pulled down in 1910, and the estate split up, and all that is left to mark it is the magnificent cedar of Lebanon tree, which can be seen behind a modern villa. The spring itself has been long filled in. Charles Dickens knew Springfield well, for he was a frequent guest of the family, and hearsay has it that he wrote much of his novel *David Copperfield* beneath the spreading boughs of that cedar tree. David Copperfield and Dora are firmly enshrined in the district.

In the early years of the nineteenth century John Davidson Smith became the owner of the Manor of Whitehorse, and caused Grange Road to be cut through Bewlye Coppice. He also developed and exploited the medicinal properties of the Beulah Spa spring. He showed himself to be a man of vision. The buildings and grounds of the Spa were designed and carried out by the well-known architect of the day, Decimus Burton. The lower end of Grange Road, where it joins Whitehorse Road, was for many years named Decimus Burton Road.

An octagon-shaped building with arcades on either side, occupying the central position of the Beulah Spa, formed the refreshment room, reading room, and confectionery. The building was thatched. Immediately opposite was an orchestra in which a military band played daily. In the grounds was a camera obscura, a maze or wilderness, a circus ring, a rosary, an upper and lower lake, woodland walks, arbours, and an archery ground. The chalybeate spring was, of course, the central feature of the Spa, incongruously shrouded – as we would think today – in what looked like an Indian wigwam. There were lawns and a dancing platform. In accordance with the taste of the time, the general effect was consciously artificial.

A brochure by Dr. George Hume Weatherhead, in 1832, described the Spa as lying "embosomed in a wood of oaks, open to the south-west, whose dense foliage shelters and protects it, and is now the sole vestige of the former haunts of the gypsies."

The Beulah Spa gardens were opened by the Countess of Essex on 1st August, 1831. The first advertisement of the Spa, which appeared at the same time, gives a clear indication of the social habits and tastes of the times. "Visitors to this fashionable place of summer resort, which is now open every day, will find every convenience there for the enjoyment of a variety of cheerful, elegant, and healthful recreation and amusement amidst landscape scenery of the most splendid description. The gardens contain a most superb variety of floricultural specimens. A new archery ground is in every way to the convenience and enjoyment of this fashionable and healthful recreation. Bows and arrows are provided for the use of visitors. Picnic and gypsy parties are catered for. A brass and quadrille band is in daily attendance. The Beulah Saline Water is forwarded to all parts of the Kingdom at 2/- a gallon."

In the official guide, the Beulah Spa was stated to be seven miles from the Southwark end of London Bridge, the road passing through Newington, Walworth, the populous parish of Camberwell, celebrated for its annual fair, and also for its embowered walk of nearly half a mile in length, called the Grove, through the beautiful villas of Denmark Hill, Herne Hill, and Knight's Hill, to the turnpike gate near the Church, where the road is divided, that on the left running in a straight line to the entrance gate of the Beulah Spa Grounds.

Norwood itself was described in the guide as "a village situated on the outskirts of an extensive wood, and long famed for the salubrity of its air, and the beauty of its surrounding scenery, with smiling villas and blooming flower-gardens." It added that "the ancient allurement of Norwood – fortunes told by the nut-brown Gypsy with 'shuffled card and geometric lore' – had passed away, and an attraction more adapted to the well-being and mode of thinking of the present age had arisen." Despite this last assertion, the Beulah Spa was not above including Gypsy fortune-tellers among its regular attractions.

The present overgrown carriageway was then Sylvan Road, the property of the estate, and attached to the Spa. It was described as "extending for a mile and a half, winding round the flank of the hill, and is a delightful ride for invalids taking horse or carriage exercise."

"On the right of the entrance", said the brochure, "is the Rustic Lodge, a combination of the Gothic and Elizabethan styles of cottage architecture. Mr. Decimus Burton, the talented designer of this and other rustic edifices that adorn the grounds, has given to this building specimens of all the varieties of gable, dripstone, portico and bay window."

It was also ornate, with a thatched roof. The lodge is still there, though no longer has it a thatched roof, and is now a private dwelling, standing prominently at the top of Spa Hill at the entrance to The Lawns. It is not greatly changed from its original appearance, and one can see how it commanded the entrance to the Spa gardens.

The charge levied for entering the Spa grounds varied according to the degree of entertainment that was being provided, but was usually one shilling, or two shillings and sixpence on gala occasions. An annual season ticket cost one and a half guineas, a family season ticket, three guineas.

The coach ran daily from the Silver Cross Hotel, Charing Cross, to the Beulah Spa, at 11 a.m., 2 p.m., and 5 p.m. The fare was 1s. 3d. outside, and 2s. 6d. inside. The threepenny post delivered letters three times a day and carried letters to London twice a day.

A guide book to the tea and pleasure gardens of London of that era describes the amusements to be obtained there as "innocent, the indulgence temperate, while a suitable mixture of female society renders them both gay and pleasing."

The visitor on entering the Beulah Spa was provided with a bottle of Spa water, if he desired it. "On stepping out of the Lodge", said the brochure, "an extensive prospect presents itself; the bright, grassy fields, divided by dark green hedges, the feeding cattle, and the landscape stretching itself to the dark blue hills that distantly bound the horizon, create within the bosom of the emancipated citizen sensations of pleasure and delight. Descending the winding path, and passing a small lawn tastefully laid out, we arrive at the Octagon Reading Room, a rustic building used for refreshment and reading room, on the left of which is the Spa Well under a thatched roof, built in the form of an Indian Wigwam."

The Spa water rose about fourteen feet from the spring, and was encircled and contained in a chamber or grotto of rockwork, with a fairly narrow orifice at the top, about two feet across. The water was raised in an urn-shaped glass vessel, terminating with a cock of the same material, and having a stout rim and cross-handle of silver. To this handle was attached a thick worsted rope, passing over a pulley, and the vessel would be lowered into the well and filled with water. This was described as being beautifully transparent and sparkling, innumerable bubbles of fixed air rising to the surface when allowed to stand. Its taste was distinctly bitter, without being at all disagreeable, leaving on the palate the peculiar flavour of its predominant saline ingredient, the sulphur of magnesia. It was considered to be one of the purest and strongest of the saline spas in the country.

Professor Faraday analysed a pint of Spa water and gave the following figures:

	Grains
Sulphate of Magnesia	61.35
Chloride of Sodium	17.74
Muriate of Magnesia	9.28
Carbonate of Lime	7.80
Carbonate of Soda	1.90
	98.07
Carbonic Acid Gas	7.6 cubic inches

A military band was advertised during the season as constantly attending and performing from 11 a.m. until dusk. The smooth grass plot in front of the orchestra building "affords ample space for those who are inclined to 'trip it on the light fantastic toe' to the sound of their dulcet harmonies."

There was also a rosary, in the centre of which was a beautiful grass plot surrounded by rose-bushes, and closely mown for dancing. Close by was what was called the Wilderness, a series of tortuous paths, formed by rows of trees whose foliage becoming thickly entangled would render any attempt to pass into the neighbouring path futile. The point to be gained was the seat in the centre of this maze.

Adjacent was the Archery Ground, a large meadow with butts, targets and an attendant in Lincoln green to supply bows and arrows. In an adjoining field a marquee was provided for the accommodation of those parties who brought their own refreshment with them. No refreshment was allowed to be taken in the grounds, but this arrangement enabled them to enjoy a "rustic picnic". Not far away was a camera obscura, "on the disk of which is depicted a mimic picture of the subjacent scenery". At the lower end of the grounds was a lake ornamented with a rustic bridge; in the grounds were seats on which to relax and admire the view. One of the most constant visitors was the Countess of Essex, who had a house on nearby Central Hill. It was said that she so monopolised a certain seat that it earned for itself the name of "Lady Essex's Seat".

A Guide to The Beulah Spa, published in 1834, recommended the visitor, having rambled through the wilderness and woods, to repose upon the seats and enjoy the beauties of the surrounding scenery. "The ancient archiepiscopal town of Croydon lies at his feet; the Banstead Downs, in all their beauteous variety of fallow field and grassy meadow, are in the distance; further yet the scarcely perceptible towers of Windsor Castle give variety to the landscape; and the extreme distance is bounded by the dark blue outline of the Surrey and Hampshire Hills.

"Turning to the left you enjoy a view of Addiscombe Place, the seminary for Cadets of the Honourable East India Company, of Shirley, formerly the sporting-seat of John Maberley, Esq., M.P., and of the Addington Hills, clothed with heaths; and the seat of his Grace the Archbishop of Canterbury, when the prospect deepening in extent stretches as far as Knockholt Beeches, near Sevenoaks, and winding round comprehends the tall spire of Beckenham Church, piercing through the dense woods which surround it, Shooter's Hill, Blackheath, and the villages that intervene."

Dancing, brass bands, fireworks, fortune-telling, a Beulah minstrel, and the pleasures of food and drink formed a good part of the entertainment. One of the principal fortune-tellers was a Mrs. Cooper, a descendent of the Gypsy Queen, Margaret Finch. Mrs. Cooper had sixteen children, and she named them all after flowers, such as Daisy, Heliotrope, Rose, Mignonette.

The Beulah Minstrel sang love ballads, as he strolled at will about the gardens. For this service he expected to be rewarded with silver. If any visitor, so serenaded, tendered less than a silver coin, it was returned with a bow. At the height of the Spa's popularity, the Beulah Minstrel was a dark-complexioned young man, with ample cloak, turban hat and guitar. He sang love-lyrics on the Beulah Spa lawns, and quite turned the heads of all the young ladies by his handsome appearance. It transpired that he was a young man of good family, named Charles Cochrane. Later, he married a rich widow, and occupied himself with the welfare of the London poor. He subscribed largely to charitable societies, and instituted a corps of street cleaners.

An interesting side of the early popularity of the Beulah Spa was a serious proposal for developing the high ground over-looking the Spa into what might be described as a mini-Bath, with a fine crescent of Regency terrace houses dominating the crest of the hill. This crescent would have been close to All Saints Church, on the opposite side of Beulah Hill, and facing the valley. The idea is illustrated by a contemporary engraving, but it never materialised. The whole concept was termed "the New Town of Beulah", and was based on "the increasing popularity of the place, demanding the erection of suitable residences for such as wish to render this beautiful spot a place of permanent abode".

In 1833, Madame Vestris, a popular actress of the day, put on at the Olympic Theatre a farce by Charles Dance called *The Beulah Spa*. It was a typical, popular, light-weight piece of the period, in which Madame Vestris took the lead. In it she goes with a party of friends to the Beulah Spa, she disguised as a minstrel, while another of the party goes as a gypsy and tells fortunes.

The Spa was in great favour as a venue in which to hold charity fêtes. On the occasion of one *fête champêtre*, in July 1834, there were 3,000 people present. This was in aid of the funds of the Blenheim Free Dispensary and Infirmary. *The Illustrated London News,* covering the event, said: "In this forest pleasaunce the gay company assembled in groups, whilst the band of the Royal Artillery played an excellent selection of pieces; and a fancy fair was held beneath the rustic arcade. Towards evening an elegant *déjeuner* was served to 200 guests in a pavilion in the dell; the carte by Messrs. Pursell, Cornhill. The *fête* concluded with waltzes, polkas, &c; and the party broke up with the pleasant reflection of having numbered in the day's enjoyment 'the luxury of doing good'."

It seems evident that Thackeray visited the Beulah Spa on at least one of these fêtes, for he introduced a skit on such an event in a humorous account of a hairdresser and his family who come into a fortune, and try to lead the fashionable life of those times. They visit the Beulah Spa on the occasion of a fête in aid of the Washerwomen's Orphans Home. The cartoonist, George Cruikshank, illustrated this fictional occasion exquisitely, under the title *JULY – Down at Beulah,* in which Mr. Orlando Crump and the Baron Chicot de Punter are rivals for the hand of Jemima Ann. The sketch shows a scene of fisticuffs at the Beulah Spa between the two rivals in the presence of an enthusiastic audience, and the affecting collapse of Jemima Ann.

The original pen and ink and wash sketch used to hang in the saloon bar of the old Beulah Spa tavern, at the top of Spa Hill. With the transplant of the tavern to the present building, the sketch was lost to public view. The present Beulah Spa tavern stands on the site of the old Beulah Spa Hotel, which was contemporary with the Spa gardens, though not part of them. It had its own supply of spa water for many years. It was pulled down in 1936, and the present public house was built.

The celebrated opera singer, Grisi, was amongst those who sang at a concert given on the occasion of a fête at the Beulah Spa for the Freemasons' Girls School, under the patronage of Queen Adelaide, in 1839.

In the classic comedy, *Our Boys,* the immortal Butterman, alluding to the pleasures of youth at a time when "the Continent was a sealed book to them as wasn't wealthy", observes that "they seldom went further than White Condick Gardens or Beulah Spor."

Marshal Soult, hero of France in the Napoleonic wars, came as ambassador to England for the Coronation of Queen Victoria. Soult was received with warmth by his erstwhile military opponent Wellington, and by the nation with enthusiasm. A fête was held in Soult's honour at the Beulah Spa, which he attended, and it is recorded that the visitors' carriages extended from All Saints Church to Crown Lane, a length of a mile and a quarter.

Prior to the opening of the London and Croydon Railway, the Beulah Spa announced that, in honour of the historic occasion, Mr. J. W. Hoar would be making a grand ascent from the gardens in his new Montgolfier balloon of enormous proportions. Mr. Hoar had drawn some attention to himself by announcing that he intended to lead a team of aeronauts on a scientific balloon voyage over darkest Africa.

There was some speculation as to the outcome of the proposed ascent from the Beulah Spa gardens. Mr. Hoar's previous appearance had been at the Surrey Zoological Gardens with a Montgolfier balloon 130 feet high, with a capacity of 170,000 cubic feet. In honour of the Queen's birthday he had named the balloon *The Queen's Royal Aerostat*. Unfortunately, the Royal Aerostat had signally failed to become airborne. Large crowds which had assembled in the Surrey Gardens had become restive as the hours passed by without any sign of ascent, despite much activity. There was much stamping of feet from the Walworth crowds, and shouts of "Let it off". When at last a large notice was held up to announce that the balloon could not ascend, there were angry shouts of "Hoax", and bottles and stones began to fly. At the hands of the crowd the balloon collapsed and was torns to shreds. Mr. Hoar had by then made a discreet departure.

The indefatigable Mr. Hoar had now built an even bigger Montgolfier, and this had been set up in the Beulah Spa gardens to do honour to the London and Croydon Railway. It was an impressive sight, but once more the aerial display turned out to be a non-event of equal magnitude. Again the crowd became vocal and hostile; once more Mr. Hoar had to beat a hasty retreat.

For the sake of the record, Mr. Hoar's final appearance on the public scene was shortly after he had built a still bigger balloon of 215,000 cubic feet capacity, with which, he announced, he would make an ascent from Notting Hill racecourse. The Montgolfier remained doggedly earthbound, and after that no more was heard of Mr. Hoar or his proposed scientific balloon trip to Africa.

Balloon ascents and balloon displays of various sorts were frequently featured at the Beulah Spa. A poster advertising fêtes to be held on the 18th and 21st August, 1854 read as follows:

ROYAL BEULAH SPA
NORWOOD

It is intended that these LAST FÊTES of the Present Season shall be divested of all apparent sameness with preceding ones – so in the

ILLUMINATION

of the Gardens – while the Brilliancy and Superbness of former Galas will be in the abstract retained, the mode of display will be novel and striking, embracing most particularly that part in which THOUSANDS OF SPARKLING LAMPS hung in various appropriate DEVICES, some suspended from branches of Trees, others Exhibited in Designs – will produce an effect which may admit the expressive designation of

THE GLOW-WORM'S FESTIVAL

Derby's Giant Montgolfier Balloon
will ascend
And when at a GREAT ALTITUDE
will DISCHARGE
A Magnificent Display of Fireworks
ILLUMINATING
The HORIZON to a large EXTENT

Dancing in the Monster Pavilion
to a FULL MILITARY BAND
ADMISSION—ONE SHILLING
Children half price
Doors open at 1   Fireworks at 9

The Duke of Gloucester, brother of William IV, visited the Spa to try the waters for his liver's sake. The celebrated Mr. Fitzherbert and the Earl and Countess of Munster were constant attenders, when the Spa was a fashionable rendezvous for the *beau monde*.

By 1845, the glories of the Beulah Spa had faded considerably, and from then on, until its final extinction in 1856 – two years after the Crystal Palace opened in Norwood – it waxed and waned in popularity, and gradually sank into a languid and desolate condition. A *Punch* correspondent visited the grounds in September 1845. His account was penetrating. "We entered a lodge in the Swiss style; and here a gentleman demanded a shilling from us before we were free of the Spa gardens. They are beautiful. The prettiest lawns, the prettiest flowers, rocks, grottoes, bridges, shrubberies, hermitages, kiosks, and what not; and charming bowers wherein a man might repose by the lady of his heart, and, methinks, be supremely happy. But the company we saw were: three trumpeters dressed in green, blowing 'Suoni la tromba' out of a canvas arbour, a most melancholy obligato, a snuffy little old gentleman with two grandsons, one a Bluecoat boy. His yellow stockings glittered like buttercups on the sunshiny grass; a professional gypsy in a dark walk; two pretty servant-maids carrying a small basket and on the look out for their masters and mistresses, who were straying in some part of their Elysium.

"When the trumpeters had done, a poor wizened Italian dressed in a hat and peacock's feathers – very like the monkey that accompanies the barrel organs – came up and began warbling, in rather a sweet feeble voice, the most seedy old love song. There was something ludicrously sad in that honest creature's face. He didn't mind being laughed at, but joined himself quite good humouredly in the jocularity. . . . Then we strayed through shrubberies and rose gardens until we came to the archery ground. Targets were set up; just for all the world as in *Ivanhoe* – and a fellow in Lincoln green came forward and invited us to the butts. . . . The odious fellow in Lincoln green sneered all the while. 'It isn't the harrows that's bad,' said he, sardonically, laughing at our complaints, *'they're* good enough to shoot with'. . . . Rather to his discomforture, we called upon him to do so. He levelled his arrow, he bent and twiddled with his bow, previous to stringing it; he lifted up to the sight mark and brought it down, he put himself in an attitude so prodigiously correct that we thought that the bull's eye might shut up at once. . . . At last, whizz, the arrow went.

"It missed. The old humbug could no more shoot than we could. He took twelve shots at the target and didn't hit once. . . . And so we left the archery ground with the most undisguised contempt. No new company had arrived at the Spa during our brief absence. The little old man was still sunning and snuffing himself on the bench. The Bluecoat boy and his companion were still clambering over rustic archways. The two servant-maids had found Master and Missus and were spreading out a cloth in an arbour. . . . The band began to blow when this banquet was served – and the poor minstrel came up, leering and grinning with his guitar, ready to perform for them. They and we were the only guests of the place – the solitude was intense. We left them there, of a gorgeous afternoon, drinking tea and eating shrimps in the sunshine."

The Beulah Spa lasted until 1856, having changed hands several times, but by then the taste and style of pleasures of the people were altering. The Great Exhibition of 1851 in Hyde Park was producing a faster tempo. The Crystal Palace came and settled in Norwood in 1854. The Beulah Spa could not survive with so sophisticated a rival at close quarters, and it passed into limbo. The grounds and buildings were sold by auction in 1858, and part of the land was built over.

A Norwood resident, Mrs. Elizabeth Louisa Dee, lived in Leather Bottle Lane in 1858. "We used to get over a ditch at the bottom of our garden into the Spa Grounds, which at that time were all in ruins, the beautiful rosary running wild, the camera obscura table falling to pieces. My husband took a piece of it, polished it, then drew the outline of Sir Charles Napier's bust from a picture published in *Bow Bells* (Sir Charles was very popular then, just after the Crimean War). After polishing it and getting it ready, my husband carved it out and put it in a frame."

In 1903, Mr. Alfred Stanley Foord, the author and historian, visited the Beulah Spa grounds, which were by then reduced in size from 25 acres to 6½ and were called The Lawns. He remarked that parts of the garden were still in their original form, and the famous well was full of water and in good repair. The Indian wigwam had long disappeared, and the orifice to the well was protected by a wooden cover, almost flush with the surrounding lawn. The octagonal reading room, somewhat overgrown with ivy, was in good shape. The lake still glistened in the lower part of the grounds.

In 1946 my wife and I visited the forlorn remains of the Beulah Spa grounds. Everywhere was unkempt and deserted, and the years of war had hastened the disintegration. It was a place of ghosts. We cast round to try to find trace of the well itself.

In the tangle of briers we located the foundations and ruins of the octagon. Trees and bushes were growing haphazard where the building had once stood. I took a compass bearing, and walked backwards through the rank grass, and all but stepped into the dark open well. It was quite hidden in the grass, and a trap for the unwary.

It was exactly as described in the records. There was the circular rockwork enclosure through which the glass vessel with the silver handle had been lowered and raised so many thousand times, bringing to the surface its medicinal waters. From that orifice the best houses in London had been supplied with the curative water, delivered in a daily service at the price of two shillings a gallon.

There it lay at our feet, forgotten and furtive, half-concealed in the long grass. It was quite full of water, dark and still. We dipped cautious fingers into the Spa water, and tasted it. It was bitter, and almost certainly no longer wholesome. We tugged some of the grass from the rockwork opening, and photographed it. And then we left it to the loneliness and memories of an Upper Norwood of a hundred years and more ago.

The next time we visited the place, the well had gone. That unique monument of Norwood's lively past was no more. The top layers of the rockwork and masonry had been broken away and the well chamber filled in with rubble and earth. All that remained was an oozy patch among the tall weeds.

Chapter Six

The Parish of All Saints

Populations everywhere at the end of the eighteenth century began to increase rapidly. At the termination of the Napoleonic wars, with the victory of Waterloo in 1815, the Church of England made a serious effort to provide for the population growth in her ancient parishes. That was the era of Church expansion in many parts, including South London. The Norwood woods were still thickly timbered, indigenous population was sparse, and Londoners became increasingly attracted to the fresh air and beautiful views of the Norwood hills.

Following a Vestry meeting early in April 1825, the Revd. J. C. Lockwood, Vicar of Croydon, made application to the Church Building Commission for the subdivision of the parish as was made possible by an Act of Parliament passed in the 58th year of the reign of George III for the building and promoting of building of additional churches in populous areas.

"The Humble Petition of the Vicar, Churchwardens and undersigned inhabitants of the Parish of Croydon in the County of Surrey, a Peculiar of his Grace the Archbishop of Canterbury, and within the Diocese of Winchester:

"According to the Census made in 1821, amounted to 9,254, but at this present time amounts to nearly or quite 11,000, of which the District of Norwood contains upwards of 1,400.

"The Petitioners desire two chapels should be erected, one on Croydon Common, and the other at Norwood. The Chapel at Norwood to be purchased and erected by the parishioners.

"The inhabitants of the said Parish are willing to purchase and erect the Chapel at Norwood at their own expense if your honourable Board will be pleased to afford them the means of erecting the other near the Common.

Petitioners humbly pray.
12th April, 1825
(Signed) J. C. Lockwood, Minister"

Concerning the proposed chapel at Norwood, the Committee appointed by the Vestry recommended that the Norwood chapel should contain accommodation for 800 persons, to be built at the south-west corner of a field belonging to His Grace the Archbishop of Canterbury, in lease to Lord Auckland, situated at the angle of the roads leading to Camberwell and Sydenham. A plan dated 27th September, 1805 shows the area of ground in the fork of the two roads, which today is occupied by All Saints churchyard. It is described in the plan as arable land, lately common, and a part of Lackcorn. The name Lackcorn designated the entire field belonging to the Archbishop, and adjoining the Great Stake Pit Coppice, also in the ownership of the Archbishop. Lackcorn and the Coppice together occupied almost the entire length on the north-east side of the roadway now called Beulah Hill.

It was proposed that the cost of building the chapel on Beaulieu Hill was to be effected by raising a loan from the Commissioners, and repaying the interest and principal over a number of years. The Norwood chapel would cost about £4,000 exclusive of the site and cost of enclosing it.

It was resolved "that an absolute necessity exists for the parish to purchase a New Burial Ground . . . a burial ground will be provided at Norwood and another near the Common which will probably be sufficient for the wants of the parish for many years to come."

In response to this petition, the Church Building Commissioners asked for details of any manufactories, mines, etc., in the area. The reply was that there were bleaching grounds and a silk factory, also there were soldiers' barracks in the parish, and the East India Company's Military College at Addiscombe.

Plans were advertised for, and the plan submitted by Mr. James Savage was chosen for the Norwood chapel. In May 1826 he was directed to lay the plan and design for the Norwood chapel with all possible expedition before the Commissioners for their approval.

Nevertheless, there were considerable delays. For one thing, the site had to be acquired. The land was the Archbishop's freehold, but was on lease to a local resident, Lord Auckland (after whom the present Auckland Road is named). Lord Auckland's agent suggested £40 as a compensation for his Lordship's interest as lessee of the land, and the offer was accepted.

A complication then arose. A sub-lessee in possession, Mr. Hamilton, demanded £300 for his interest in the land. His demand was thought to be preposterous, and finally Mr. Hamilton was paid £83. 15s. By July 1827 it was discovered that a Mr. Birkett was the rightful claimant to the land as sub-lessee, and that Mr. Hamilton's claim was not valid. It would seem that the money was recovered from Mr. Hamilton, and Mr. Birkett was paid £72. Mr. Perryman, a tenant in possession, was paid £10 for crops on the land. The Executors of Lord Auckland, who had recently died, were paid £51. 5s. The Archbishop of Canterbury gave the Freehold and Reversion to the parish.

The intended chapel was to be Gothic, of the period of Henry III. The accommodation, allowing 20 inches for adults and 14 inches for children, would give a total of 1200 persons, all adults.

On the ground floor there were to be 88 pews containing 164 seats, and 256 open seats. There were to be two galleries containing 48 pews holding 336 seats, and also 144 open seats.

Estimated cost of the chapel was £6,632. The smallness of the sum allowed had obliged the architect, Mr. Savage, to specify the facing bricks of Second Marles, and to divest the design of some details.

The Foundation Stone of the Norwood chapel was laid by the Hon. Mrs. Carey, wife of Admiral Carey, afterwards Viscount Falkland. The exact date is uncertain. According to a Mrs. Gilbert, the first stone was laid on November 27th, 1827. According to the researches made by the late Canon Taylor, Vicar of All Saints in the early years of the present century, the date was November 12th. There is, however, a letter in existence from the Ecclesiastical Commissioners to Canon Taylor which says: "It appears from papers in the Ecclesiastical Commissioners' possession that the church was consecrated on the 30th December, 1829. The first stone was laid on the 8th November, 1827."

The same letter adds: "Croydon was at that time reckoned to belong to the Diocese of Winchester but under the peculiar jurisdiction of the Archbishop of Canterbury." Thus, the final solution to this academic speculation as to the date of laying the first stone may lie in the Surrey Registry of the Diocese of Winchester.

The chapel was consecrated by the Archbishop of Canterbury as a Chapel of Ease in the Parish of Croydon. The living was vested in the gift of the Archbishop.

It was built of grey brick, and has been rather slightingly described as a poor adaptation of the styles of the fourteenth and fifteenth centuries. It has also been described as George IV Gothic, Victorian Gothic, and cardboard Gothic, of spindle proportions, the fane dignified and fairly proportioned, tower and spire not uninteresting. Canon Taylor claimed that the tower and spire, added in 1841, are the best parts of the building, and the spire very graceful. "Indeed," said the Canon, "those who would view it aright should visit it by pale moonlight."

The position of the church is excellent, and charmingly set in its graveyard. It stands at a height of 378 feet above sea level, and is a landmark to the country around, though somewhat dwarfed by the television mast close by. It is claimed that the steeple can be seen from Harrow on a clear day.

A form signed by the Vicar of Croydon on March 30th, 1828, stated that All Saints Chapel would hold 1,000 people, with 600 letting seats, the letting of which was to constitute the living of the officiating curate. All Offices were to be performed in the chapel, to which a burial ground was attached, except that of the solemnisation of marriage.

At the same time the Parish of Croydon was being sore pressed by tradesmen for money owing in the building of St. James's Chapel and All Saints Chapel. A letter from Thomas Penfold, Solicitor to the Vestry, addressed to the Secretary to the Church Commissioners on May 3rd, 1830, puts the matter bluntly:

"Sir,

I am directed by the Parish Committee again earnestly to entreat His Majesty's Commissioners will be pleased to take into immediate consideration the outstanding demands of the Tradesmen on account of St. James's Chapel at Croydon. The applications for payment are now become so urgent, and indeed threatening, that the Committee begin to be personally alarmed for the consequences, and they have no means of discharging these outstanding claims but from the balance of the £6,500 agreed to be advanced by His Majesty's Commissioners to the Parish aid of building the two Chapels.

"The Committee are informed that the whole cost of building Norwood Chapel has been ascertained and therefore in reference to your letter of the 8th August last they trust the Commissioners can now tell what surplus will remain to be paid over to the Parish. At all events the Committee hope the Board will be able to order them an immediate remittance so as to enable them to pay at least a percentage to the different contractors, some of whom it is understood are labouring under the most distressing inconvenience by their accounts remaining so long unsettled."

The Revd. Edmund Harden, M.A., was the Curate-in-Charge of All Saints Chapel. The Baptism and Burial Register was started in 1830. During 1830 there were 44 baptisms and 15 burials. Between the years 1830 and 1838 three people were buried, being found drowned in the Croydon Canal.

The congregation at All Saints Chapel was a mixed one. Artisans and semi-skilled workers predominated. There were plumbers, carpenters, cabinet-makers, carters, coal-dealers, iron-dealers, smiths, leather-dyers, printers, gun-makers, gardeners, saddlers, grocers and fishmongers.

The burial register records very few people dying at an advanced age. Most of the entries in the first fifteen years are for middle-aged or even young men and women. There is also evidence of a high infant mortality rate. This is very marked in the year 1838, when out of a total of 91 burial certificates, 72 were for very young children, many under 6 months of age, and all from the nearby Norwood Infant Poor House, which later became the Central London District School.

From 1830 to 1839 there were only four certificates for people who had died over the age of 80.

Permission for the solemnisation of matrimony was granted by the Archbishop of Canterbury in 1839. Most people could not sign their own names in the early years. Women, particularly, seldom signed other than with a cross. No profession other than that of "spinster" was given for the women. The age of persons married was given as "full age" or "under age," not in figures. By 1843, women were stated to be minors rather than "under age."

By 1845 the population of Upper Norwood in the Parish of Croydon had risen to 3,085. This led to the setting up of All Saints as a Parish Church, which was done in ritual form and picturesque language in an application by H.M. Commissioners for building new churches: "To the Queen in Council: By leave humbly to represent to your Majesty that having taken into consideration all the circumstances attending the Parish of Croydon in the county of Surrey and Deanery of Croydon the peculiar and immediate Jurisdiction of the Cathedral and Metropolitical Church of Christ Canterbury and locally situated within the Diocese of Winchester, it appears to them to be expedient that a particular district should be assigned to the Consecrated Church called All Saints Church at Norwood." Then followed a detailed and precise description of the extent of the boundaries of the new parish, which were very much wider than they are today. It was then stated that "Bans of Marriage should be Published, and that Marriages, Baptisms, Churchings and Burials should be solemnized and performed in the said Church called All Saints and that the fees arising therefrom should belong and be paid to the present Vicar of Croydon during his Incumbency of that Vicarage but that from and after his avoidances thereof the said fees should be received by and belong to the Minister of the said Church called All Saints Church."

The Commissioners then stated "That the consent of the Right Honourable and Most Reverend William Lord Arch Bishop of Canterbury to whose peculiar Jurisdiction the said Parish of Croydon is subject and of the Right Reverend Charles Richards Lord Bishop of Winchester within whose Diocese the said Parish of Croydon locally situate have been obtained . . . .

"Your Majesty's Council therefore humbly pray that Your Majesty will be graciously pleased to take the premises into Your Royal consideration, and to make such Order in respect thereto as to Your Majesty in Your Royal Wisdom shall seem meet."

All Saints became the earliest constituted Parish in Croydon after the Mother Parish, although the Chapel of St. James at Croydon Common had actually been consecrated a few months previously to All Saints.

Mr. Harden became the first Vicar of All Saints, having been Curate-in-Charge of the Chapel of Ease since its inception. At a meeting of the Minister and Householders on August 23rd, 1845 in the schoolroom adjoining, Mr. Harden arranged for the appointment of Church Wardens, and this was duly done. In 1846 no householders turned up and the same Church Wardens were re-elected in default. The same thing happened in 1847. After that the matter became more regularised.

Mr. Harden died in 1856. The Revd. Rupert Montague Browne, Curate at All Saints, said of him that "Mr. Harden was a much respected, kindly man, who died rather tragically of angina after eating ice pudding at a wedding breakfast, to which feast he had unhappily hurried."

The Revd. James Watson succeeded Mr. Harden, and held office until 1894. His incumbency lasted throughout the time when the parish was at its most wealthy and influential, Norwood having become attractive to rich people and the affluent middle class. The advent of the Crystal Palace in 1854 was the cause of swift local developments.

That part of the parish between Central Hill and Beulah Hill, before 1854, was fields in which stood a few cottages, and through which the Effra stream meandered. Then came the New Town housing estate, which helped to house the tradesmen and artisans of every kind that poured into the district.

Baptisms, marriages and deaths went up steeply in the All Saints parish. In 1854 it would appear that the new workers in the district may have brought infection with them, for on four burial certificates at All Saints in that year cholera was shown as the cause of death. There may well have been more than four cholera deaths, for it has been said that many victims of the epidemic were buried in a common grave in the middle of the churchyard. That is uncertain.

In 1880 the Archdeacon of Croydon, on one of his visitations, complained of the neglected state of the churchyard, particularly in the middle where the gravestones were falling to pieces. Mr. Watson remedied the matter by having all the dilapidated gravestones, including, presumably, any memorials there may have been to the cholera victims, taken away, and trees planted. This accounts for the apparently vacant space in the churchyard.

In 1859 Mr. Watson wrote to the Church Estate Commissioners, seeking to enlarge All Saints Church. He wrote:

"In consequence of the near proximity of the Crystal Palace, and the great facilities of access afforded by the various railways, freehold property in Norwood has in the last few years become very greatly enhanced in value, and land which has hitherto been used for agricultural purposes only, has now become eligible for building-sites. The greater portion of the most valuable land in Norwood is in the hands of the Church Estates Commissioners, and very large sums are being and will be realised on this account, through the granting of leases for building of 99 years.

"The effect of these measures has been that a large increase of the population has been already, and for some years will probably continue to be, brought into the neighbourhood . . . . The cost of providing the additional Church accommodation, thus rendered necessary, ought not to fall on the present inhabitants of Norwood only. A portion of the proceeds of the land itself might be fairly looked for to aid the residents in supplying the religious wants of the new population. The private land-owner, and other resident inhabitants are willing to bear their share of the burden . . . .

"I beg therefore to make an application to the Church Estate Commissioners for a grant of £1,000, one half of the estimated expense of the undertaking . . . ."

The Church Estate Commissioners wrote back pointing out that they held no property in Norwood, and that the property belonged to the Archbishop of Canterbury. Accordingly, a similar letter was addressed to the Archbishop, asking for approximately £1,000, the landowners, occupiers and others having raised the sum of £1,016. The letter concluded, "that as your Grace, in right of your See, is the largest Proprietor of lands within the District – and as the Norwood estates of Your See are being improved by building leases in progress, whereby the population of the District is being augmented – Your Memorialists venture to solicit your aid, out of rents and profits of your property at Norwood . . . ."

The Archbishop wrote in his own hand at the foot of Mr. Watson's letter: "I am desirous that the sum of £250 should be contributed, out of the rents of the property of the See, towards the object stated in this Memorial . . . ." and sent it to the Commissioners.

The Ecclesiastical Commissioners in their turn resolved "That the Appl. be informed that the Commissioners will be prepared to approve a gift by his Grace as a Landowner of a donation not exceeding £200 towards the designed object."

It seems that the Vicar and Churchwardens and Congregation had no difficulty in raising the rest of the money, and a Faculty for Altering and Enlarging the Church of All Saints, Norwood, was obtained on 4th April, 1860. By the proposed alterations about 250 additional sittings would be obtained, and the church, as thus enlarged, would contain 1,250 sittings, of which 650 would be free. The church was enlarged accordingly, and the work was completed by June 1863.

Contemporary records give one a clear picture of this nineteenth century parish church. In the mid-years of the century it was definitely evangelical, without surpliced or chancel choir. The choir, which was crinoline and side whiskers, sat below the organist in the west gallery, where the organ was placed. It is reported that the singing was good and hearty, the music being congregational. The font was placed in the centre of the nave, down which were wooden benches with backs, for the poorer members of the congregation, and these were "free." The pews in those days were high, though not of oak; they had doors with fastenings, and the occupants of the pews were thus shielded from the inspection of their neighbours, though not from the occupants of the north and south galleries, who could gaze down upon them. There were high red hassocks on which to kneel. Brass square-topped gas standards, with blue and white colouring in their interstices, decorated and illuminated the chancel. These vied with the ladies' pretty Leghorn straw hats trimmed with poppies, oats and corn flowers, popular at the time.

For many years Miss Letts, the ground-floor pew-opener, in shawl and scuttle-shaped bonnet, and grey curls, rosy-cheeked, and with eyes sparkling, was an institution in herself. She was active and nimble, and would proceed the "quality" to their pews, and fasten them in with a click. It would be her work to find strangers seats in the church, and bring glasses of water to those who might suddenly be feeling faint. She also brought hot water to temper the rigours of the Font at baptisms.

Upstairs, doing gallery work, was Anne Wright, with her spiritual type of face and silver hair, and, so it was said, as deaf as a post!

Mr. Penny was the gravedigger and local postman. Not only did he walk 10 or 12 miles a day, he also helped to bury 600 people. By the year 1860 the churchyard was long full and becoming overcrowded. He was a man of prodigious energy and toughness. He lived to a great age, attaining his nineties, and died in the early years of the present century. There was also a uniformed parish beadle, with cocked hat, gold lace and staff, who lent great presence to the occasions. Regrettably, he died one Christmas after a surfeit of Christmas boxes of an alcoholic nature.

Among the distinguished worshippers at All Saints was Admiral Carey, whose wife had laid the first stone of the church. He was very much of the old school, and would go to church wearing a blue coat with gilt buttons and a black silk stock. He was a notable figure with his silver hair and curled side-whiskers. He was the Hon. Plantagenet Pierrepoint Carey, later to become on the death of his brother the 11th Viscount Falkland. He lived at Falkland Park at the top of South Norwood Hill.

The considerable grounds have long been built over, the name being commemorated in Falkland Park Avenue. The present Spurgeon's College is housed in the mansion that was his, and at the corner of South Norwood Hill and Grange Hill still stands the house that was the Lodge at the entrance gates.

Admiral Carey was related to the famous Carey family who lived at Torquay. It was reported with awe by his laundry-woman that he wore two white shirts each day, and changed his tablecloth daily. Arriving at All Saints Church he would walk up the aisle proceeded by Miss Letts, and followed by his man-servant holding his bible, prayer book and hymn book, which he would hand to his master before the pew door clicked shut. The servant would then retire to his own place in one of the galleries, to collect the books once more from his master at the end of the service.

A second Admiral – and professionally far more distinguished – was Admiral Robert Fitzroy, the celebrated hydrographer and meteorologist. He lived on Church Road during the last years of his life.

Admiral Fitzroy was the youngest son of General Charles Fitzroy, and grandson of the third Duke of Grafton. His mother was Lady Anne Stuart, eldest daughter of the first Marquis of Londonderry.

Fitzroy was born 5th July, 1805, and entering the Royal Navy at an early age, he eventually became Vice-Admiral. One of his most important commands was that of H.M.S. *Beagle*, and in the years 1828-31 Fitzroy surveyed the coasts of Patagonia and Tierra del Fuego. He commanded the *Beagle* during her famous voyage around the world in 1831-36 with Charles Darwin as official naturalist to the Government.

In 1843 Admiral Fitzroy was appointed Governor and Commander-in-Chief of New Zealand, where he became unpopular with the white settlers by trying to conserve the rights of the Maoris and to see that they had a fair deal. The white settlers succeeded in securing Fitzroy's recall to England in 1845.

He was then appointed chief of the newly formed Meteorological Department of the Board of Trade. While in that office he initiated many valuable investigations into the subject, devising the system of weather forecasts and storm warnings which have developed into the present daily weather forecasts.

Admiral Fitzroy's last years were utterly devoted to the Lifeboat Institution. Sadly, the work overstrained his health and he died by his own hand in his house on Church Road in 1865, and was buried in All Saints churchyard.

One can see the gravestone close by the West Door. It is distinguished by the meteorological instruments carved on it. The verse from the Book of Ecclesiastes on the footstone had previously been thought of as a mere poetic imagery. It reads:

"The wind goeth towards the south, and turneth about
unto the north; it whirleth about continually, and the wind
returneth again according to his circuits."

Admiral Fitzroy had shown it to be a scientific fact.

The present Fitzroy Gardens, off Church Road, and near
to the house in which he lived, commemorate the name of that
famous man.

The middle and later years of the nineteenth century saw in
All Saints a church that mirrored the comfortable, well-kept
and dignified homes of the richer element of the congregation.
On Sunday morning carriage would follow carriage closely up to
the West Door and set down their occupants with all the animation and bustle of arrivals at the theatre or opera, to the sound of
horses' hooves, the crunch of wheels on gravel, and the banging
of doors and jingling of harness on departure.

In the early months of 1869 a curious and somewhat macabre
chapter in the history of All Saints arose, and became widely
talked about. It had been known for a long time that the
churchyard was full up and was getting overcrowded. Contro-
versy had it that it was becoming a real danger, surrounded as it
was by houses of affluent parishioners. The church had been
built on what was practically meadow land, almost opposite the
Beulah Wood, on its south side plantations of firs and other
trees, a few cottages down hill in the distance. But now the
crowded condition of the churchyard with built-up surroundings was described by local doctors and others as scandalous.

A handwritten note, signed by Mr. J. J. Welch of Beaulieu,
Upper Norwood, was like a first broadside. It enquired "as to
whom the custody of the Church Yard is vested in, and whether
we cannot compel the Vicar to open it for the purpose of assisting
an enquiry desired by Dr. Hetley one of the Churchwardens and
two or three of the parishioners."

A reply to this enquiry was made by a firm of Solicitors. It
read: "All Saints, Norwood. The Vicar has the freehold of the
Churchyard. The Churchwardens have the care and repairing
of it. The Vicar's title is subject to the interest of the

parishioners in the burial ground. If the Churchwardens want to enter for the purpose of performing their duty in connection with the Churchyard they have, we presume, a right to do so. But we doubt whether they can break up the surface or enter the Churchyard for such a purpose, without the Incumbent's consent.

"We are not clear however as to whether you mean opening the ground *soil* by the expression 'opening the Churchyard'."

From then on things moved rapidly, and a Commissioner appointed by the Home Office came on the scene and instituted an enquiry. A leader in the *Norwood News* 10th April, 1869, commented on the enquiry.

"Our readers will doubtless be surprised to learn that three thousand and twenty-five corpses have been buried in the small space of ground comprising All Saints churchyard, and knowing the fact they will wonder at the pertinacity with which the proposition to cease opening fresh graves is opposed. Several gentlemen residing in the immediate neighbourhood of the churchyard at first asked that a time might be defined for discontinuing further interments, but now, finding the number of burials to be so much greater than they had supposed to be the case, they ask that it should be at once closed except as to burials in family graves and vaults, which they expressly state they have no desire to see closed. They are opposed by the Vicar, and also by the grave-digger and all his assistants past and present, and the statements made to the Commissioner who has conducted the Enquiry that has been held upon the subject have been framed evidently quite at random as regards the facts, and dictated only by a desire to keep the churchyard open. However, passing that, and without commenting upon the childish obstructiveness that has been practiced, we would only remark that after the discrepancy that has been found to exist between the facts as alleged by the opposition and facts as they exist, it is important to ascertain the exact accuracy of the plan that has been prepared of the churchyard . . . ."

The enquiry itself brought some remarkable facts to light, and might well be described as the Scandal of the Burial Ground! A

Dr. Holland, appointed Commissioner by the Home Office, was placed in charge of the Enquiry, which was held in the All Saints schoolroom, adjoining the church. The Enquiry itself concerned the propriety, or rather the necessity, of limiting the number of future interments to be permitted in the churchyard annexed to All Saints Church.

It was reported that at the enquiry the burial register book currently in use was produced, and the previous one was asked for. After some hesitation on the part of the Vicar, the Revd. James Watson, Dr. Hetley said that he thought it was very important that the previous book was immediately produced.

The second book was then produced, and upon examination it was found that 3,025 corpses had been buried in the churchyard, and not about 1,900 as had been stated by Mr. Watson. Mr. Hassard stated that the number of square feet in the churchyard was 43,100; and taking each grave space at 31½ square feet, that would give 1,368 grave spaces in the whole churchyard, so that, Mr. Hassard pointed out, there was already an average of two and a half dead bodies buried over the whole of the churchyard.

Mr. Heathorn, upon sanitary grounds, suggested the entire closing of the churchyard against all future interments. He said that water had been found in several of the graves; that therefore rapid decomposition must ensue, the emanations from which, permeating through the soil to the surface, must be highly injurious. Dr. Rutter stated that the water from a well close to the churchyard had been found too impure even to water the roads with, and had therefore to be closed.

It was agreed that a trench should be dug through what was claimed to be virgin ground, to find out if the soil was actually wet, and also to see whether the ground through which it passed was occupied by corpses. Several difficulties were raised by the Vicar with regard to the proposed trench, namely, the expense, the difficulty of finding wood to bank up the sides, the scarcity of sufficient skilled and valuable labour, the disturbance of the appearance of the churchyard and the necessity of a clear understanding as to the responsibility to the

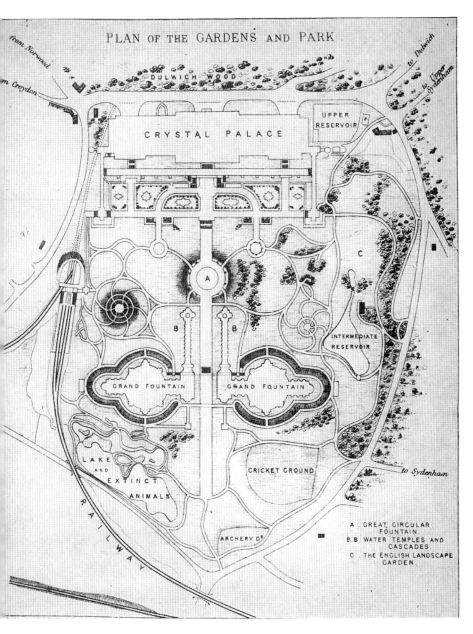

1. Plan of the Crystal Palace, Gardens and Park as laid out by Paxton, and showing the pattern of water displays.

2. Nave looking north. Photograph by Philip Delamotte. A full picture record was made of the construction work.

3. The Crystal Palace Parade, *circa* 1900, showing the main and south transepts.   4. Paxton (with scroll) in the open colonnade.

5. Paxton, 1851. Plans of the Palace by his left arm, the Hyde Park Exhibition over his right shoulder. South London next!

6. Augustus Hervey, Third Earl of Bristol.

7. Mary Nesbitt as *Circe*, by Joshua Reynolds.

8. Charcoal burners camped on the Beulah slopes. The Croydon Colliers provided charcoal for the City of London.

9. The Norwood House where Mary Nesbitt lived. Today it is a girls' school – Virgo Fidelis, Central Hill.

10. New Year's Eve party in the model of the iguanodon, December 1853.

11. Education for Colonial life at the Crystal Palace, 1876!

12. Waterhouse Hawkins' extinct animals studio, Crystal Palace.

13. The Royal Crystal Palace Hotel, 1853. Paxton stayed there.

14. The White Hart, 1868. Its tea gardens were very popular.

15. The Croydon Canal near Sydenham, 1815. A holiday spot.

16. Fox's Farm, Norwood, 1823. View down Fox Hill.

17. The Crystal Palace, showing the south nave and Osler's Crystal Fountain.

18. The Palace, 1854. The Parade is not yet made up.

19. The Crystal Palace before the north transept was destroyed by fire, 1866.

20. The Village. Westow Hill, *circa* 1898. Still a Victorian shopping street.

21. The Village. Principal shops in Westow Street in 1860.

22. The Village. F.A. Cup Final at the Crystal Palace, *circa* 1900.

23. The Village. Westow Street decorated for Royalty, 1888.

24. Post-war desolation. By 1950 time and vandalism had wrecked the deserted gardens of the Crystal Palace.

25. The remarkable vaulted subway under the Crystal Palace Parade.

gravedigger for the outlay necessary. Mr. Welch agreed on behalf of the memorialists in the matter to pay all expenses, and Dr. Hetley agreed to be liable to the gravedigger.

When the trench was dug it was inspected by the Home Office Commissioner, and it seemed evident that no burials had taken place in the ground through which the trench had been dug, but the soil was very wet, and it was stated by a gentleman residing nearby that he and his family had seen men baling out water from this trench.

The Commissioner, at the resumed enquiry in the school-room, said that the soil was of a nature to render it very objectionable for the purpose of interment. The Commissioner then expressed his disappointment to find that the statements repeatedly made to him by the gravedigger that there were no graves more than 20 feet from a drain were quite inaccurate. The Commissioner then read a memorial that had been handed to him, which said:

"Your memorialists submit that the evidence which has at length been obtained, by the production of the burial register, has disclosed a state of things worse than they had anticipated; a state of things so bad indeed as to demand, for the protection of public health, that urgent measures be at once adopted.

"Your memorialists regret very much to be obliged to draw your attention to the very great discrepancy in the evidence given at your examinations, between the number of deaths per annum and amount of burials, and those numbers which actually have occurred. Your memorialists further painfully feel that such discrepancy in the figures could only have arisen from a desire on the part of the Vicar to obstruct their investigation.

"For instance, it was publicly stated that the number of interments which had taken place up to that time (Nov. 16th) was 1,900 – 1,500 being registered in one book, and 400 in another; the fact being, as now ascertained from your examination of the registers, that the number of burials to the present has been no less than 3,025.

"It was also publicly stated that the number of interments had increased from 60 per annum in 1863, to now about 90. It turns out, however, from the books that the number of burials for the year 1868 amounted to 137.

"The great excess of actual over alleged interments, and of the actual over the alleged present number of deaths, will probably account for the systematic obstructions which your memorialists have met with throughout the course of the enquiry, and the pertinacity with which the burial registers have been withheld from them, and indeed now produced only on compulsion.

"The trench sunk in the churchyard shows the substratum to be dense impervious clay (as your memorialists have always stated but which has been hitherto flatly denied) – quite unsuited for the purpose of interment; it being well known that earth of this description fails to absorb the products of decomposition, even after periods of 40 or 50 years.

"Your memorialists wish to draw attention to the plan of the churchyard lately made, which professes to show grave spaces available for future interment which do not in reality exist. Your memorialists have requested from the Incumbent the loan of this plan in order to prepare evidence on that point, but have not been able to obtain it from him.

"The space occupied by graves in this burial-ground, assuming $31\frac{1}{2}$ square feet as the average area of a grave space (being the mean between an adult and an infant grave), will show that the entire churchyard which has been used for the purposes of interment must be covered with tiers of corpses averaging $2\frac{1}{2}$ bodies deep.

"Taking into consideration the systematic violation of the law, in neglecting to provide a plan of the churchyard, and a register of graves and in burying corpses within 20 feet of the outer wall of the church, which has been going on since the special order of 1863; and further taking into consideration the crowded condition of the burial ground and the nature of the soil, your memorialists think it only reasonable now to ask that no new grave shall for the future be opened in this churchyard.

"That a list of those persons who have family graves be at once ascertained and such graves be indicated on the plan of the churchyard as those only in which interments are for the future to take place in consequence of the discrepancies already alluded to, and that such plan of the churchyard shall be at stated times open to the inspection of parishioners."

The Memorial was signed by Dr. Butter, Dr. Guthrie, Mr. Peek, Mr. J. J. Welch, Mr. Gray and Mr. Hassard.

Mr. Watson said that the figure of 1,900 quoted by him as the total number of interments at the time was then stated to be merely a vague guess, and that he had so expressed himself at the time. This, however, was not the case, as Mr. Watson's figures were accepted as a close approximation to the fact in the absence of the burial register.

The Commissioner admitted that the soil was a very objectionable one to bury in. Mr. Gray pointed out the extreme danger of opening graves prematurely and the great evil therefore of constant interments in so impervious a soil as this appeared to be.

With regard to the production of the plan of the churchyard, some difficulty was raised by the Vicar who, notwithstanding the Commissioner's advice to the contrary, objected to the Memorialists having the use of the plan, even to taking a tracing from it; but after further undignified objection on the part of Mr. Watson, it was agreed that a tracing of the plan should be forwarded to the Memorialists.

Mr. Watson warmly urged the continuance of the churchyard as a burying ground. So much so, that at length Mr. Franks expressed his deep regret that Mr. Watson should meet this matter in the manner in which he was acting, and if the loss of burial fees were any object he for one would subscribe £10 towards Mr. Watson's loss.

The Commissioner, rather surprisingly in view of the evidence, said he would recommend to the Home Secretary that after the expiration of three years the interments should be limited to family graves and brick vaults. Mr. Welch immediately countered that the Memorialists would not be satisfied with that recommendation, and if it were acted upon they would again trouble the Home Secretary, or him failing, seek the intervention of the Archbishop of Canterbury.

The outcome of this strange wrangle is reflected in the existing gravestones in the churchyard. After the year 1869 there are no new graves. All subsequent burials were in family graves established before that date.

Dr. Frederic Hetley, one of the prime movers in seeking to close the churchyard, was himself buried in 1902 in the grave near the West Door, in which his first wife, Lady Charlotte Sarah Hetley was buried in 1867. The last interment in the Hetley grave was in 1917.

The organ, which had been originally situated in the west gallery, was replaced by a 500 guinea organ sited in the chancel in 1898. Sims Reeves sang at the service of inauguration of the new instrument. For a time Mr. Walter Hedgecock, Organist and Musical Director at the Crystal Palace, became the All Saints organist. During that period the musical services were outstanding.

In its original form, the Parish of All Saints occupied about one-third of the old Parish of Croydon, with the church conveniently centred in its own parish. Today it is somewhat incongruously at one end of a parish two miles long, while the nearby vicarage on Church Road is actually outside the parish perimeter.

All this can be accounted for by the dissections that have taken place from time to time. In 1872 the Parish of St. Paul's, Thornton Heath, was consecrated, detaching a large slice of All Saints parish in the process. Then another large area was assigned to St. Mark's, South Norwood. In 1876 the Parish of St. John the Evangelist was formed, taking its own large bite, and lapping almost up to All Saints church door.

The parish boundary between All Saints and St. John's follows the centre line of Church Road. All Saints Vicarage is on the wrong side of the line, but was especially excluded from the change, the house and very large garden being still part of the parish, but separated from it by half the width of the roadway.

Since that time part of the land belonging to All Saints Vicarage was sold for building, the first sale being of part of the garden down Sylvan Hill. The second part was alongside the Vicarage on the Church Road frontage. Though it has not always been realised, these new houses are within the Parish of All Saints, and not St. John's, as they would appear to be.

The Parish of All Saints together with the other Croydon parishes form part of the Archdeanery of Maidstone, that being at the extreme northern end of the Diocese of Canterbury, and the part nearest to Croydon.

In 1905 the Diocese of Southwark was formed out of part of the Diocese of Rochester. Christ Church, Gipsy Hill, in the See of Rochester, passed into the new See of Southwark. The total area of land surrendered by Rochester to form the Southwark Diocese had belonged to the Diocese of Winchester until the year 1877. Christ Church, Gipsy Hill was completed and dedicated in 1867, and was then, of course, in the Diocese of Winchester. This fine stone fabric, of the late Early English type, was dedicated by the Lord Bishop of Winchester, the Rt. Revd. Charles Richard Sumner, D.D.

That part of Upper Norwood in Penge has always been in the Diocese of Rochester, and remains unaffected by such changes. All Saints parish, together with the other Croydon parishes, which were styled a Peculiar to the Archbishop of Canterbury within the Diocese of Winchester, are today redesignated as being in the Diocese of Canterbury, Detached.

Chapter Seven

Days of Change

There is an air of faded bravery about the Crystal Palace Parade, like the tattered banners of another age. Neglected and shabby, it is nevertheless a thoroughbred. Its proportions are spacious and impressive. Once the Parade was a place of distinction, a high point in Norwood, where one could stroll and rendezvous when the weather was fine, a civilised place, a place suited for military spectacle and royal comings and goings. Indeed, the Parade knew such occasions well. Now, with present trends, it is no more than a traffic artery between the Upper Norwood shops and Sydenham Hill. It also serves as a down-at-heel bus terminal for a dozen or so routes. Even as a bus terminal amenities are minimal.

It is the colourful and lively past of the Crystal Palace Parade that gives it a certain ghostly quality, such as one may find in a forgotten mausoleum. It is indeed a mausoleum of vanished days and vanished glory – and this on the finest site in South London! Those desolate empty spaces on either side of the fine roadway are as accusing as a deserted concentration camp. In the mind's eye one can still see the shadowy forms of the two lost buildings which once graced them and gave the Parade meaning. On the Dulwich side was the Railway Station. How elegant it was, and imposing, a model of functional as well as architectural beauty, with its enclosing glass roof, its arches, its long echoing platforms of heavy timber, and its four lines of gleaming railway track that, beyond the platforms, met at an enchanting engine turntable.

The Crystal Palace High Level Station was built to the design of Edward Barry. The Parade lost much, both architecturally and in sheer usefulness, when the railway was closed and sent into the oblivion of so many of the better things of Norwood.

On the Penge side of the Parade was, of course, Paxton's great Khubla Khan-like pleasuredome, a dramatic cliff of glass which had the quality of changing its colour with the change of weather or time of day. Henry Williamson in his novel "The Dark Lantern" remarked on this colour change that took place on the northern elevation of the Crystal Palace when a red sunset was in the sky – "A grey mullet becoming a red mullet". That was a very noticeable feature.

The Crystal Palace has gone with the rest, but with those lost things recalled in memory, one can almost hear the staccato notes of the horses' hooves on the gritted and water-sprinkled roadway as the carriages came jingling to the main entrance, and the spanking dash of those on horseback.

Those were the great days, when the Crystal Palace Parade would take on a touch of Rotten Row. Norwood was self-assured and confident, the Parade the focal point of the Cockney crowds on their way to the delights of the Crystal Palace. It was a stimulating experience to stroll along the Parade on a fine day and just watch the people, or, from its commanding position of 360 feet above the level of the sea, pick out the features of London five or six miles away. Or to ponder on the London, Chatham and Dover Railway trains gliding below on the sleek pattern of rails as they emerged dramatically, with a flurry of white steam, from the Sydenham tunnel, and then slipped through the handsome entrance arches into the station. Then there was life and movement and promise and enthusiasm; but there is no promise or enthusiasm on the Parade today.

Camille Pissaro, the French impressionist, fled to England when the Germans invaded France in 1870. His studio was overrun by enemy soldiers and his canvases destroyed. Pissaro came to live for a while in Upper Norwood, and during his exile here he painted half a dozen or so pictures of the neighbourhood in which he had sought refuge. All are windows of those days on which to ponder, for times have indeed changed, and they have captured those lost days. Among them was Pissaro's painting of the northern aspect of the Crystal Palace from the Sydenham end of the Parade, in which he has recorded with good effect the peculiar sense of light on the glass walls, and the impressive quality of the unique building in its setting on the Parade. The scene Pissaro painted was indeed the focal point of the whole district which had been built up around it. That was Norwood's presiding genius.

Hidden from the eye, like some Pharaoh's tomb, where it lies secretly beneath the Parade roadway, is a vaulted chamber of impressive proportions. It is a place of warm colour, of red and cream brickwork, each brick fitted with geometrical precision and interlaced with ribs of stone. Octagonal pillars support a vaulted roof of remarkable strength that sustains the roadway above it and the heaviest loads that present-day transport puts on the roads.

This vaulted chamber is Byzantine in style, a truly magnificent example of the skill of the workmen who placed and cemented those red and cream bricks in their subtle arches. They were Cathedral bricklayers from Italy, specialists in the craft of building crypts of great beauty and strength, and were brought over to build this chamber. It was said that there were no bricklayers in England equal to the task.

It was constructed in 1865, to be a subway connecting the station on the one side of the Parade to the Palace on the other. Arriving rail passengers thus crossed beneath the roadway to the Palace, the architectural extravagance designed to titillate the eye and hint of the art treasures that were to be found beyond the turnstiles.

Despite the passing of more than 100 years, and the wear and tear of time and war – the place was converted into an air-raid shelter during the last war – this unique vault still glows with its immaculate brickwork. It is interesting to reflect that this subway, built in a different age, is still equal to the stresses of modern traffic.

Today this architectural treasure is in a vacuum. It begins and ends in a void, crossing as it does from one empty side of the Parade to the other. The entrance, which was from the station, is now bricked up to preserve it from the attention of vandals. Perhaps in time it will be brought back into use, by being profitably included in some new Crystal Palace development, when the present horrid desolation will be replaced by something worthy of its history.

Before the advent of the Crystal Palace, at the part where the Crystal Palace Parade now is, was a beaten track through the woods. Dulwich Wood and the Penge woods met on that high crest. From there could be followed the line of the Thames as marked by the White Tower of London and the forest of masts of the shipping as far as Greenwich Hospital, and thence over large stretches of water, on which the ships formed an ever-moving panorama. On the other side was an immense and very rich prospect over the valleys of Kent and Surrey.

Today the Crystal Palace Parade is suspended in limbo between nostalgic past and unknown, unplanned future – unplanned, that is, except for some vague future road-network involvement, in which it has been designated a Metropolitan Highway. *Sic transit!* The Parade, forlorn and shorn of its old glory, is now little more than the proverbial X that marks the murder spot!

On November 30th, 1936, when fire utterly consumed the Crystal Palace, the event was witnessed by the greatest crowds the Parade had ever known. Few could believe, as they watched the flames and felt the heat of them on that cold night, that this was the end of a legend, and nothing would ever be quite the same again. Winston Churchill was there in that huge crowd, and he was in tears as he watched the symbol of a great age melt away in moulten glass and fused metal.

After that came the Second World War, and those who mourned the Palace consoled themselves by saying that if the Palace had not been burnt down it still could not have escaped the war. The two great towers, which had survived the conflagration and stood like lonely sentinels at the extremities of the Parade, were felled because they were said to be a pointer to London for raiding German bombers, and also because the metal they contained would be useful in the war effort. The north tower was brought down by explosives at its base; the south tower was taken down piece by piece so as not to endanger surrounding houses.

The High Level Railway from Nunhead survived the war, as did the High Level Station itself. But this survival did not save the rail link between Norwood and London via the wooded scenery of Sydenham and Lordship Lane. With an utter lack of foresight, or sense of responsibility towards a whole district, but because it was expedient at the moment, the railway connection was uprooted, and the bridges and the fine High Level Station erased. With indecent speed, which forestalled any second thoughts for restoring the line in some form, blocks of dwellings were built over the empty track.

One cannot but ask oneself why a London suburb, which had so many times multiplied its population, should no longer need the High Level line, and increasingly so in the future. This was lunatic thinking by authorities who should have known better, and have thought wisely and constructively. Whatever the diminished volume of traffic in those special years shortly after the war – the last train ran on September 19th, 1954 – the massive future potential was there to make maximum use of that trackway through a populous area. As it is, the potential has been forced on to overcrowded roads which the authorities themselves insist are inadequate for their purpose.

It is little wonder that residents' societies and local amenity societies have come into being in the last ten or twelve years to protect local interests and to make protest against such high-handed encroachment by local governments and ministerial bureaucracy.

It could well be argued that the destruction of the High Level line has contributed to the non-redevelopment of the Crystal

Palace as an exhibition centre. Such a redevelopment was finally ruled out on grounds of inadequate communications!

There was no inadequacy of communications when the Crystal Palace came to Norwood a hundred years before the High Level line was closed. Railways and roads in the 1850's were adequate, or, if not, they were extended. The Crystal Palace came to Norwood in 1852 for precisely two reasons. One was that the site was the finest in London for the purpose. The other was that the railway was already there. The London, Brighton and South Coast Railway, that part which was formerly the London and Croydon Railway, passed very conveniently through Sydenham and Penge and Anerley. The swift and easy route from London was virtually on their very doorstep. It needed but a short spur from the Sydenham station through the Penge Woods to bring trains right into the Crystal Palace grounds. Such a line would bring the visitors in their thousands to the very gates of wonderland.

In October 1852 it was reported that "the rails for the new Crystal Palace Railway are now in a forward state. The railway traveller on this line may notice on his left between Sydenham and Anerley stations navvies hard at work preparing the ground. The space through the wood for the line of rails that is to run into the Palace is now cleared of trees, and presents a picturesque woodland scene, the timber lying across the way in happy confusion."

One must confess that in these days of trees so sadly diminished in numbers, where was once the Great North Wood, one winces at the term "happy confusion" in reporting those fallen woodland giants. But at least that stretch of suburban railway is still operating 120 years later. No one has as yet seen fit to close that length of line, though there have been whispers.

Such was the confidence in 1852 of the Crystal Palace project that the London and Brighton Railway went to the lengths of laying a separate line of rails from London to the Crystal Palace. This new double track was to be devoted exclusively to "Crystal Traffic", and lay each side of the main line. Specially designed locomotives were built to cope easily with the considerable gradients that existed between London in the valley and Norwood on the heights.

The local down line was on the east side of the main track. To reach the Palace it had to cross the main line between Sydenham Station and Penge Station. To avoid any danger inherent in crossings on the level, the local line ascended by an embankment and crossed the main tracks by a bridge. This method is now common practice, but in 1852 it was a novelty in railway engineering.

There was a second line from the Crystal Palace Station to the Jolly Sailor, later renamed Norwood Junction. This spur had been laid to bring materials to the Palace site during the building operations. Now, with the opening of the Crystal Palace, the Crystal Palace Company went into the railway business to the extent of buying a small locomotive and some carriages from the London and Brighton Railway, and worked a shuttle service for passengers visiting the Palace. This enabled them to pick up main line passengers for whom it was impossible to make the connection with the Crystal Palace line at Sydenham.

Ultimately the Brighton line took over this private stretch, and it became an important link in the general network. The London & North Western Railway obtained running powers to Croydon via Clapham Junction and, of course, the Crystal Palace, which was the main attraction, and used this important spur.

Two years after the opening of the Palace the Crystal Palace tunnel had been completed, which opened up a route to the West End. By December 1st, 1856, the line was opened from the Crystal Palace Station to Gipsy Hill and West Norwood and on to Wandsworth Common, where it linked up with the main line. On October 1st, 1860 Victoria Station was opened, and there were then through trains from there to the Crystal Palace.

On August 1st, 1865, the London, Chatham and Dover Railway had opened their branch line from Peckham Rye to the High Level Station alongside the Crystal Palace Parade. Thus Upper Norwood of more than 100 years ago was effectively linked up with the expanding railway system. Previous to the arrival of the Crystal Palace, the nearest station to the Upper Norwood Triangle had been Anerley. Next on the line was the Jolly Sailor, named after the local public house. It was not until 1859, when the station was resited, that the Jolly Sailor Station took the name Norwood Junction.

Equally important were the road connections between London and Norwood. As the time approached for the official opening of the Crystal Palace, road routes were widely published. That was necessary, as, for many people, travelling out to Norwood by road was like going to the back of beyond. In 1852, when Queen Victoria and Prince Albert were driving out to see how the Palace project was shaping, accompanied by outriders, a leading horseman stopped on Central Hill to ask the way to the site!

Norwood and Sydenham were still rural districts. There were farm houses with meadows and cornfields, and great tracts of woodland. There were thatched cottages, flower and herb gardens, and even windmills.

Punch published a most colourful description of a ride from London to Norwood by road, and from it one sees the violent contrasts that marked the relatively short journey, and so emphasised the fascination and beauty of the southern heights.

"The purlieus of London are not to be described", said the *Punch* correspondent. "The mind sickens in recalling the odious particulars of the immediate neighbourhood of the bridges. The hucksters and Jew furniture-shops, the enormous tawdry gin palaces, and those awful little by-lanes, of two-storied tenements, where patent mangles are to let – where Miss Miffin, milliner, lives on the first floor (her trade being symbolised by a staring pasteboard dummy in a cap of flyblown silver paper) – where the street is encumbered by oyster shells and black puddings, and little children playing in them. . . .

"You emerge from the horrid road at length on a greenish spot, which I am led to believe is called Kennington Common; and henceforth the route becomes far more agreeable. Placid villas of cockneys adorn each side of the road – stockbrokers, sugar-brokers – that sort of people. We saw cruelty vans (I mean those odious double-barrelled gigs, so injurious to horse-flesh) lined with stout females with ringlets, bustles, and variegated parasols. The leading stout female of the party drove the carriage (jerking and bumping the reins most ludicrously and giving the fat horse the queerest little cuts with the whip): a fat boy, resplendent in buttons, commonly occupied the rumble, with many children. . . .

"The villas gave each other the hand all the way up Camden Hill, Denmark Hill, etc; one acacia leans over to another in his neighbour's wall . . . one villa is just like another; and there is no intermission in the comfortable chain. But by the time you reach Norwood, an actual country to be viewed by glimpses – a country so beautiful that I have seen nothing more charming – no, not in France, nor in Spain, nor in Italy, nor in the novels of Mr. James."

In May of the year 1827 a Mr. William Hone walked across the country from Dulwich to Penge. When he reached the crest of the hill he chose a track that led him through Penge Common. The place was thickly wooded and, in his own words, "a cathedral of singing birds". But even then the common was enclosed, and was soon to be built upon. There were still remains of the hanging woods of Penge on the hillside, as beautiful, it was said, as the hanging woods of Cliveden. But they too were doomed, along with the rest of the Great North Wood.

"It is difficult", wrote Walter Besant at the close of the nineteenth century in his *South London*, "now that the whole country south of London has been covered with villas, roads, streets, and shops, to understand how wonderful for loveliness it was until the builder seized upon it. When the ground rose out of the great Lambeth and Bermonsey Marsh – the cliff or incline is marked still by the names of Battersea Rise, Clapham Rise, and Brixton Rise – it opened out into one wild heath after another – Clapham, Richmond, Putney, Wimbledon, Barnes, Tooting, Streatham, Thornton, and so south as far as Banstead Downs. The country was not flat: it rose at Wimbledon to a high plateau; it rose at Norwood to a chain of hills; between the

Heaths stretched gardens and orchards; between the orchards were pasture lands; on the hill sides were hanging woods; villages were scattered about, each with its venerable church and its peaceful churchyard. . . . If the village lay off the main road it was as quiet and secure as the town of Laish.

"All this beauty is gone; we have destroyed it; all this beauty has gone for ever; it cannot be replaced. And on the south there was so much more beauty than on the north."

The tranquil beauty of Norwood was to be changed radically with the arrival of the Crystal Palace, and it is perhaps interesting to speculate what would have been the nature of Norwood's development if the Crystal Palace had gone elsewhere. Certain it is that however mediocre the development might have been, Norwood would not have suffered the nagging emptiness of 200 acres of park land which is neither one thing nor the other. On the other hand, it might have become a wilderness of small suburban streets – which it might have done when the Crystal Palace went bankrupt in 1911 – that mars so much of south London's once fair face. On balance, Norwood is better off with the wide open spaces of the Crystal Palace Park, though it appears to be the home of lost hopes.

When Mr. Leo Schuster was a Director of the Brighton Railway he was also the owner of Penge Place, a massive and delightful property. It and some adjoining property were where the Crystal Palace Park is today. The railway ran at the bottom of Mr. Schuster's garden.

This became big business. In addition to securing for his railway the benefits of vastly augmented passenger traffic, Mr. Schuster was able to sell his estate for something like £50,000 to the Crystal Palace Company, who were in the market to buy. It must also be said that Penge Place as a site was unquestionably the most magnificent on the outskirts of London, and ideal for the purpose.

The Illustrated London News gave it a good write-up. "For beauty of scenery and perfect retirement, combined with an easy access from London, it is impossible to imagine a more fortunate situation. The park, pleasure-grounds, garden and

pasture-fields contain 280 acres, lying on a gentle slope . . .
adorned with clumps of ornamental timber, and surrounded by
a thick belt of plantations which completely separate it from
the road and from adjoining properties. . . . The situation,
sloping down into a valley and hedged in by thick plantations
affords the most perfect solitude; not a sound, not an object
within view, betrays the close vicinity of a great city. The black-
birds and thrushes sing away in harmonious rivalry, and the
rabbits dashing through the brushwood and wobbling along the
fields completes the idea of a remote rural district only disturbed
by the occasional thunder of a train dashing along the valley
below unseen but marked by a following trail of vapour. The
village in the valley is hidden, all but the tapering white spire of
the church [Penge Parish Church], by the roll of the ground and
intervening clumps of trees, but, rising beyond, the Surrey hills,
almost covered with wood, spread out in a vast panorama. . . .

"With the exception of the belt of plantations which surround
the future park of the million, very little has been done by art to
improve and develop the beauties of what Sir Joseph Paxton
has called 'the most beautiful spot in the world for the Crystal
Palace'. . . .

"It is indeed delightful to contemplate that this park, from its
position, never can be intruded upon by building speculation,
but can command solitude for centuries to come."

The same periodical, ever a staunch supporter of Paxton and
all his works, proceeded to eulogise the whole concept of a
Crystal Palace setting up shop at Norwood, and with good
reason.

"When the Crystal Palace, revived with all the triumphs of
taste and skill that are in contemplation, is removed to this
park; when four termini of railways are close adjoining the
silent highway of the Thames, and are ready to convey all
classes to the garden wilderness for the cost of an omnibus
fare – into the midst of flowers and rare shrubs in full bloom
in winter, and fountains and shady walks in summer, away from
the smoke and din of London, where all will be framed with the
view of purging and instructing by the eye and the ear, and

every debasing habit and association will be excluded – a new era in the public amusements will have commenced. The day of pot-house gardens, and the pot-and-pipe selfishness of husbands will soon pass away.

"Every year the increase in the size of London and the dearness of rent render it more essential that the masses should have the means of healthful recreation, fresh air, and amusement, without the temptation of intoxicating liquors, to refresh them after their toils. Already the improvements in our parks and public gardens have done much to improve the character of the working people in London. But the winter is no time for walks in the park, or excursions to Kew or Hampton Court. The Crystal Palace gets over this difficulty; and it is satisfactory to find that for the inhabitants of the east end of London – of Greenwich and Deptford, of Vauxhall, Bermondsey, and the suburbs on the river – the Crystal Palace at Sydenham, with the railway running into it will be nearer and cheaper than if it had been planted in Hyde Park; while a park fitted for every healthful game will be added to its other attractions."

The only real flaw in the argument was that the working classes in 1852 worked a full six days a week, while Sunday was virtually a compulsory day of rest, in which such institutions as the Crystal Palace would in no circumstances be opened. It was not opened on Sundays in Hyde Park; its chances in Norwood were nonexistent. The Sunday Observance organisations were unyielding in their demands that Sunday be kept literally as a day of rest. They opposed even the opening of the Crystal Palace Park on a Sunday, because that meant trains would run to bring people there, and the Park would have to be staffed.

Those who opposed any form of Sunday opening of the Crystal Palace were fully aware that such a closure would deprive the labouring classes of any opportunity of enjoying the Palace. Their reply to this was:

"We know that when objections are made to railway trains and museums on the Lord's Day, we are told we have no sympathy with the labouring classes, and wish to debar them from wholesome recreation. On the contrary, we rejoice in any step that can be taken to promote their health and comfort. . . . But when we hear of excursion trains and museums opened on the Lord's Day, we turn round and ask those gentlemen – 'If you have so generous, so philanthropic, so disinterested a desire for the comfort and well-being of the million – then let it be shown by one great, grand combination to release the million one half-day in the week, without diminution of the six days' pay'."

There was great argument on the matter of Sunday opening of the Crystal Palace while the new home of the glass edifice was being installed at Norwood. From this the Crystal Palace Company wisely held aloof. The outcome was a foregone conclusion, both the building and grounds remained firmly closed on Sundays, to the great cost of lost revenue to the Crystal Palace, and to the public lost recreation. But that was the way thinking ran in those days.

On Thursday, August 5th, 1852, the first pillar of the new Crystal Palace was planted on the Norwood heights. A special train brought the Directors of the Crystal Palace Company from London Bridge to Sydenham Station. From there they drove to the site, gay with surrounding marquees, flags flying, a military band playing and a large gathering of invited guests, the women in gay summer crinolines. It was a lovely day for so auspicious an occasion – perfect Queen's weather, as they said.

The Crystal Palace Directors were received in an elegantly decorated marquee. They were then conducted to a second tent in which were displayed the plans and drawings of the new building and its park and gardens. Sir Joseph Paxton, the architect of it all, explained details of his brain child. It was confidently announced that the new edifice would surpass in beauty and splendour the original Crystal Palace in Hyde Park, as that surpassed in novelty of design, material, and concept every other building before erected.

One journalist, so carried away with the promise and splendour of the whole scheme, wrote lyrically: "No attempt has ever been made until now to bring the domestic and industrious from their homes, and the idle from their ale-houses and gin-palaces by the attractions of the beautiful in art and science. The pipe, the pot, and the paper have been too often their only resources."

The ladies in their bright crinolines provided the animation and colour to the scene on the high hilltop. They were shepherded into lines around the ground, which had already been marked out to define the position of the central transept. This pleasing fancy set the stage for the ceremonial planting of the first column.

The Directors and Officers of the Crystal Palace Company were formed up into a procession, headed by six workmen dressed in their Sunday best blue jackets, blue caps, red ties and white trousers. The six carried a banner bearing the words "Success to the Palace of the People". The procession proceeded with slow dignity to the point designated for the erection of the ceremonial first column.

The actual column itself was one brought from Hyde Park, and had been part of the fabric of the original building. It had already been hoisted and suspended over the prepared socket which would receive it. Mr. Samuel Laing, M.P., Chairman of the Crystal Palace Company, performed the act of planting. First of all, a tightly stoppered and sealed bottle was lowered into the socket where it rested at a point below which the foot of the column could descend. It contained coins of the realm, a newspaper of that day, and the signatures of the principal people concerned with the translation of the Crystal Palace to Norwood. It is interesting to reflect that the bottle has never been recovered. It lies under ten feet or more of rubble dumped there during the wartime bombing of London. Nor is its precise position known.

Mr. Laing then lowered the column into place. The Royal Standard was broken from the top of the column, and a twenty-one gun salute was fired by the Royal Artillery. To present-day custom this flying of the Royal Standard was very surprising, for the Queen was not present, and the Royal Standard, the symbol of the Monarch, is exclusively flown at the royal residence or in the presence of the monarch. Nevertheless, the

Royal Standard was flown, and the Grenadier Guards band played the National Anthem. Three cheers were then called for "the People's Queen", which was given with heart-warming enthusiasm that lovely summer's day on the Norwood heights.

On the column itself was inscribed: "This Column, the first support of the Crystal Palace, a building of purely English architecture, destined to the recreation and instruction of the million, was erected on the 5th day of August, 1852, in the sixteenth year of the reign of her Majesty, Queen Victoria, by Samuel Laing, Esq., M.P., Chairman of the Crystal Palace Company. The original structure of which this column forms a part was built after the design of Sir Joseph Paxton, by Messrs. Fox, Henderson & Co., and stood in Hyde Park, where it received the contributions of all nations at the world's Exhibition, in the year of our Lord, 1851."

Mr. Laing said with great feeling: "Former ages have raised palaces enough, and many of them of surprising magnificence. We have all read of the Hanging Gardens of Babylon, the colossal palace temples of Egypt and the gorgeous structures of Ninevah and Persepolis. Many of us have seen the scattered fragments of Nero's golden palace on the Palatine hill, and the vast ruins which speak so magnificently of the grandeur of Imperial Rome. But they were raised by the spoils of captive nations, and the forced labour of myriads of slaves, to gratify the caprice or vanity of some solitary despot. To our own age has been reserved the privilege of raising a palace for the people [loud cheers]. Yet, the structure of which the first column has just raised its head into the air, is emphatically and distinctly the possession of the British people, as it is the production of their own unaided and independent enterprise."

Respectful reference was made to the Almighty. "I assure you we all feel very deeply the responsibility of our position; and although we have judged it premature and unseemly to make any formal religious ceremonial out of the present occasion, we feel not the less profoundly that in carrying out this undertaking we are but acting as the instruments of that benificent and overruling Providence which is guiding our great

British race along the paths of peaceful progress [hear, hear].
I trust that the assurance that we are all deeply and intimately
impressed with what I may almost venture to call a religious
feeling of our duties and responsibilities, will be accepted as a
guarantee that, to the best of our judgment and ability, this great
undertaking shall be constructed in the proper spirit and with a
view to noble and elevating subjects."

Mr. Laing, with a gallant reference to the ladies that surrounded and outlined the central plan with their bright silk and
muslin, said: "Figure to yourselves the surrounding area which
is now defined by a circle of beauty [cheers], converted into a
crystal dome, and raised aloft under the blue canopy of heaven,
and you will form some indistinct image of the new central
transept as it exists in the genius of Paxton, and will shortly
exist as a tangible reality for the wonder and admiration of
millions."

The surrounding ground was plentifully and gaily decorated
with flags. In the bright August sunlight, with magnificent views
in all directions, this high, empty space, now clothed with the
animation of flags and bunting, marquees and elegant strolling
guests in top hats and fashionable bonnets, had the atmosphere
and style of Royal Ascot about it. Crowds of local people from
surrounding villages climbed the green hills and, at a respectful
distance, watched the brilliant scene and enjoyed the military
music.

About 500 ladies and gentlemen sat down to a lavish lunch
as guests of Messrs. Fox and Henderson, who had the contract
to erect the building. They were the same contractors who had
built the Crystal Palace in Hyde Park, the outcome of which
was that Mr. Fox had received a knighthood, as had Joseph
Paxton. Mr. Laing presided at the lunch, and was supported by
some very distinguished people. These included Lord Ernest
Bruce, Lord F. Hallyburton, Mr. Peto, M.P., Sir John Lubbock,
Sir Charles Barry, R.A., Sir Charles Lyel, Professors Ansted,
Forbes, Solly and Wheatstone (inventor of the Wheatstone
Bridge), Doctors Faraday, Latham, Lindley and Marshall Hall,
as well as a large number of gentlemen famous in literature,

science and the arts. It was, indeed, a very distinguished gathering.

Speeches were made and healths were drunk in champagne. Mr. Laing described the site chosen as an irregular parallelogram of 300 acres, extending from the Brighton Railway where it would have a frontage of 1,300 feet, between the Sydenham and Anerley stations, to the road which bordered the top of Dulwich Wood (today the Crystal Palace Parade), where it would have a frontage towards the road of 3,000 feet. The fall from this point to the Brighton Railway was 200 feet.

The high moral tone of the Crystal Palace to be was stressed by Mr. Laing, and supported by strong murmurs of approval.

"If for the mass of our population we could provide some more refined amusements than those of Greenwich or Windmill-hill or, worse than all, the gin-palace or the saloon, we would go a great way towards advancing the character of the English nation. What was wanting for the elevation of our working classes was that very description of refinement which it might be hoped would be afforded by contemplating the marvels of nature and art in a palace like that about to be erected. . . . If the palace be made worthy of the people of England, the people of England would flock in millions to it."

That, of course, was the nub of the whole matter. The Crystal Palace Company and the London, Brighton & South Coast Railway were planning a venture which, if it came off, it was believed would provide an attraction for a million people a month, and for the railway company unending profitable daily excursions.

The Fox and Henderson party to celebrate the planting of the first column was a huge success. Speeches were plentiful, but so was the champagne, for the Victorians fully understood the art of dining at leisure. Because it was such a beautiful day, after the official entertainment was over, guests wandered the enchanting park with its perfect surroundings and distant views, fully agreeing with Paxton that it was the most beautiful place in the world for the Crystal Palace. The last of the guests did not leave until after 8 o'clock, when the August shadows were lengthening.

A prospectus issued by the Crystal Palace Company depicted in radiant terms the charm of a Winter Garden covering 18 acres; magnificent fountains worked by machinery and steam power; a gallery of sculpture, and a museum of science, arts, and manufacture. The splendours of Vauxhall, Cremorne, and Rosherville were to be thrown entirely into the shade, the Coliseum and the Society of Arts surpassed, the British Museum and Museum of Economic Geology outdone, and all the public parks, urban and suburban, made superfluous! The glamour and excitement of the year 1851 was now to become normal and unintermittent at the new Palace of Glass that was to erupt on Norwood's highest point.

The prospectus boldly claimed that the Crystal Palace should suffer no deterioration in consequence of its removal from its previous aristocratic site in Hyde Park to the more outlying Norwood, and that it would lose no part of its claim upon the gratitude and applause of the public because of its transmission from the hands of Her Majesty's Commissioners to those of the people.

One *Times* correspondent remarked dryly: "Such is the characteristic tendency of British speculation to run a winning horse to death."

The public were informed that the new Crystal Palace would not be a re-erection in replica of the Hyde Park version. Alterations were so many and so material as to leave the new building in possession of hardly any of its original features. "To the old characteristic lightness and airiness will now be added a majesty and grandeur of outline that bid fair to be surprising. The means under which the direction of the Company's advisers – Sir Joseph Paxton, Mr. Wild, Mr. Owen Jones and Mr. Digby Wyatt – have taken to effect this, are mainly the substitution for the old central transept one of greatly increased diameter and height, accompanied by two of the size of the original one near the ends of the building, and, finally, the adoption for the whole length of the nave of a circular or wagon-headed roof of the same height as those of the smaller transepts, into which it will merge."

The old central transept of the Hyde Park version became the south transept at the Norwood end of the building. The replica north transept at the Sydenham end was destroyed in the fire of 1866, and never restored.

As to whether the "majesty and grandeur" of the new building was an improvement on the appearance of the original Hyde Park version is somewhat a matter of taste. To the Victorians the Norwood Crystal Palace was an immense artistic achievement. It was more imposing with its curvilinear roof along the whole length of the nave; so much less monotonous than the flat roof of the original with its single transept. *De gustibus!* Taste alters. Today the simplicity of line of the 1851 building, its lightness and airiness, is generally considered the more pleasing, so far as pictorial records can show.

The Crystal Palace Company's statement went on to tell a receptive public that "the building will form a vast conservatory, in which differing climates will be obtained in various parts, and the characteristic vegetation of the different quarters of the world be fully represented. Among the foliage will be interspersed casts of the most famous groups and statues of the world, both those of antiquity and those of the great home and continental sculptors of the present day. Mr. Owen Jones and Mr. Digby Wyatt are travelling on an artistic tour through France, Italy, and Germany, for the purpose of collecting illustrations of Architecture and Sculpture, to be represented in the new Crystal Palace."

The visions of magnificence conjured up in Paxton's mind were almost limitless. Grandeur of presentation was now second nature to him. Almost from boyhood he had been reared and nurtured as a privileged head gardener in the lush surroundings of Chatsworth, the Derbyshire seat of the Dukes of Devonshire. Paxton had become the Duke's adviser, confidant and friend, and he had greatly beautified Chatsworth. He designed and built magnificent greenhouses and conservatories in which he reared such exotic plants as the tremendous Victoria Regia water-lily, with its five-feet diameter leaves. The limitless supply of Derbyshire moorland water had been readily available for his imaginative genius for fountains and cascades and water effects generally, and he had made full use of it. His masterpiece in water effects had been the Emperor fountain. This he had designed and built in honour of Czar Nicholas of Russia, who was to visit Chatsworth and stay there as the guest of the Duke, who was his distant kinsman.

Paxton had been on the Grand Tour with the Duke. He saw the masterpieces of European water displays, and his own thoughts took wings. The Emperor fountain at Chatsworth threw its plume of water 267 feet into the air. Now, with Penge Place under his command, he saw almost unlimited scope for his art.

The Directors of the Crystal Palace Company, encouraged by Paxton's enthusiasm, resolved that they would have a complex of fountains in the grounds, the likes of which the world had not seen. In extravagance and magnificence the Crystal Palace fountains would outrival those of Versailles. They would throw their jets of water 250 feet in the air, turning the grounds into a garden of rainbow dreams.

The one drawback was that, unlike Chatsworth with its endless water on tap, there was no such supply at Penge. *The Illustrated London News*, which at all times gave Paxton such generous publicity in his Crystal Palace venture, said: "At present there is no water to complete the picture as the eye travels down the green slopes before rising to take in the delicate prospects afforded by the opposite wooded vales, dotted here and there with villas. But from the fall of the ground it will be easy to construct a small lake, or series of basins for waterfalls. If possible, we should like to have a series of trout preserves, like those at Wolf's Den, near Heidelberg."

Sir Joseph Paxton's ambition and determination were quite equal to the challenge, though the expense was enormous. He caused a well to be sunk at the lowest part of the grounds to reach the water table under London. The well consisted of a brick shaft 247 feet deep and 8½ feet in diameter. At the bottom of the shaft an artesian boring was carried down to a further depth of 328 feet, making an impressive total of 575 feet.

Water was drawn up in quantity by a powerful steam engine and stored in a specially prepared reservoir, which of course is the present boating lake where the models of prehistoric animals are to be found. Once the lake was filled to capacity it would only require topping up from time to time to make good the wastage by evaporation and wind-blown spray from the fountains. In fact quite a lot of water was lost that way.

From this main reservoir water would be transferred to a second or intermediate reservoir on the north side of the grounds. From there water was pumped up to the top reservoir at the northern end of the Crystal Palace, close by the Crystal Palace Parade.

Those lakes or reservoirs were designed to serve the dual purpose of providing water for the fountains and cascades, and in themselves to be part of the Crystal Palace pleasureland. The lowest was termed the tidal lake, because the level of the water varied considerably. There would be a low tide when thousands of tons of water were drawn off to provide the fountains, and there would be a high tide as the expended water returned to the lake.

The intermediate lake is well stocked with fish and is conducted by an angling club, with the privilege of restricted membership. The top lake has now suffered the indignity of being turned into a car park, a sacreligeous gap having been cut in the massive brickwork that once held the water. It is now as squalidly reduced as the rest of the Parade. In its heyday it was the ornament of the North Tower Gardens, an elegant funfair with a waterchute, electric gondolas, water grottoes, firework illuminations, gas-burning fairy lights in prodigal numbers, and remarkable aquatic displays.

In the early days of the fountains, water from the top reservoir was pumped into two large square tanks, each of which held 1,500 tons of water, and were supported on cast-iron columns 50 feet from the ground. These tanks supplied the fountains inside the glass building, the nine basins on the two garden terraces, and a large circular basin on the centre walk.

A second series of fountains on a lower level, designed to throw their jets 250 feet in the air, demanded the erection of two water towers to provide the required pressure. Those twin towers, which were such a characteristic feature of the Crystal Palace, were remarkable. Some idea of their strength and magnitude may be formed from the fact that they each had to support a body of water of not less than 2,000 tons in weight, and at a height of nearly 300 feet from the ground. The constructional problems were complicated by the fact that the great mass of water was constantly in motion, caused by the water being pumped up into the tank, and its subsequent rushing down on the return journey.

The first attempt to construct the water towers turned out a failure and involved great loss to the Company, for, when nearly completed, it was found that they were insecure, and would never carry the weight intended for them, nor would they sustain the vibratory shock of the ascending and descending water.

They were pulled down. This explains the apparent discrepancy in early prints of the Crystal Palace at Norwood. Some show the building with the characteristic towers at either end, while others show the Palace towerless.

After the failure of the original towers an attempt was made to obtain the necessary head of water by placing large tanks on the top of each wing of the building. The tanks were built, and the water was in the course of being supplied. But scarcely had 500 tons been put in when the glass below began to crack, and ominous sounds of cracking rafters and bending girders warned the bystanders to make a precipitous retreat.

The outcome of this was that the celebrated railway engineer, Isambard Kingdom Brunel, was called in. He designed towers polygonal in construction, 46 feet in diameter. The tanks had to be placed at a height of more than 200 feet, and the towers which, with their load, weighed more than 3,000 tons each, had to rest on the sloping side of a clay hill.

There was always the possibility that by the bursting of a pipe a large quantity of water might suddenly be discharged. The danger was that this might produce a slip in the ground supporting the tower. Brunel therefore carried the foundations down to a great depth, creating a massive base of concrete, and on that a cone of brickwork, strongly cemented, rising above ground level. Brunel's bases for the Crystal Palace towers are still there, the one by Anerley Hill being readily visible to the passer-by.

At the beginning of November, 1853, the Queen and Prince Albert, accompanied by the King of the Belgians, his son the Duke of Brabant and an Archduchess of Austria, paid a private visit to the Palace and park. After some appalling weather, which had plagued the whole programme, the day of the royal visit was perfect, and visitors could move about without the wearing of navigators' boots. Pathways had been laid out of faggots covered with gravel, and these led as far as the shed where Mr. Waterhouse Hawkins was preparing his life-size models of antediluvian animals, which were then to be seen in their clay originals.

These and other works were explained by Sir Joseph Paxton to the royal visitors. They were shown the excavations for the great tidal lake where the antediluvian animals were to be immersed, and the network of pipes being laid to feed the fountains which, as Sir Joseph said proudly, would consume six times the amount of water thrown up by the Grands Eaux of Versailles.

It would be on great fête days that the vast streams of water would be unloosed, a volume of water one-sixth that of the cataracts of Niagara.

On the last day of the year 1853 Mr. Waterhouse Hawkins held a celebration party in his Model Room or Studio at the Crystal Palace. He also planned this party in a novel form by inviting a number of his scientific friends to dine with him in the body of one of the largest models, that of the iguanodon. They were to be seated at a table inside the actual cast. His purpose was to bring together those great names whose high position in the science of palaeontology and geology would form the best guarantee of the severe truthfulness of his works.

The restoration of lifesize models of animals extinct for 80 million years was a work of absolute veracity. The fact that subsequent discoveries and deductions have modified the concept of some of the creatures is beside the point. They remain a perfect reflection of the state of knowledge on that subject in 1853. Mr. Waterhouse Hawkins, with a distinguished scientific background, had been appointed director of the fossil department of the Crystal Palace, and in this restoration he was aided by the ideas suggested by Professor Owen.

Drawings had first been made of the skeletons of the prehistoric animals on the most scientific principles. Then the outline of the entire form had been added "according to the proportions and relations of the skin, and adjacent soft parts to the superficial parts of the skeleton, as yielded by those parts in the nearest allied living animals."

It was from such outlines that Mr. Hawkins prepared a miniature model, and after the correctness of this had been well tested, a copy in clay of the natural size was made, from which a mould was prepared, and a cast was then taken from the mould.

Details were given by Waterhouse Hawkins of the materials employed in the actual construction of one of the iguanodons that stand to this day by the Crystal Palace lake:

"Four iron columns 9 feet long by 7 inches in diameter: 600 bricks, 650 five-inch half-round drain tiles, 900 plain tiles, 38 casks of cement, 90 casks of broken stone (making a total of 640 bushels of artificial stone). These with 100 feet of iron hooping and 20 feet of cubic-inch iron ore, constitutes the bones, sinews and muscles of this large animal, the largest of which there is any record of a casting being made."

Cards were issued to the invited guests. "Mr. B. Waterhouse Hawkins solicits the honour of Professor ———'s company at dinner *in the Iguanodon*, on the 31st of December, 1853, at four p.m." The invitation was written on a lifelike drawing of the wing of a pterodactyl, spread behind a most graphic etching of the iguanodon.

It is said that 21 guests sat around Mr. Hawkins in the cast of the lower half of the iguanodon, but an illustration of the occasion shows about half that number within the cast, and the rest of the guests at a sprig at right angles to the monster.

At the head of the table, and most appropriately in the head of the gigantic animal, sat Professor Owen, supported by Professor Forbes, Mr. Prestwick, the geologist, Mr. Gould, the celebrated ornithologist, and, of course, the Directors and Officers of the Company.

Professor Owen, in proposing the health of their host, briefly explained the line of reasoning by which Cuvier, and other comparative anatomists, were able to build up the various animals of which such small remains were presented for their study.

It is notable from the artist's illustration of the feast that these eminent professors were far from being dull dogs, if one can judge from the quantity of champagne which was apparently being served by the several waiters.

A journalist reporting the occasion, wrote: "After several appropriate toasts, this agreeable party of philosophers returned to London by rail, evidently well pleased with the modern hospitality of the iguanodon, whose ancient sides there is no reason to suppose had ever before been shaken with philosophic mirth."

Evidence of the durability of Mr. Waterhouse Hawkins' work remains in the Palace grounds. The set of antediluvians he made are still almost complete, and remain a lasting and valuable monument of scientific thinking of 120 years ago.

In April, 1854 the Crystal Palace Company were reported as pursuing their great work with undiminished enterprise, and had voted the raising of a further £250,000, making a million in all. They regretted that the water towers at each end of the building would not be ready in time to exhibit the *jets d'eau* by the end of May, when the building was positively to be opened. Up to that time the sum of £679,720 had been expended under the following heads:

Purchase of land: £50,240

Purchase and removal of the materials of the original building: £95,000

Construction of the main building of the Crystal Palace: £135,050

Tunnel, heating apparatus, etc: £24,536

Wings, water-towers, etc: £34,090

Hydraulic works: £93,670

Park terraces, gardens, etc: £98,215

Plants, garden works, fountains, etc., inside the Palace: £6,450

Natural history illustrations: £11,176

Fine Arts Courts – Pompeian, Alhambra, Assyrian, Greek, Roman, Egyptian, Mediaeval, Renaissance, Italian and Byzantine: £52,500

Collection of Sculpture: £32,060

Sundry fittings throughout the building: £7,000

General expenses, including engineering staff, superintendence, officers' salaries, law and Parliamentary expenses, surveying, rent and taxes, and miscellaneous disbursements: £35,384.

No less than £1,350,000 had been spent before the opening on June 10th, 1854. This meant that the Crystal Palace was saddled with an enormous capital expenditure before it opened, and this was seriously to jeopardise its future financial stability. As far back as September, 1852, when it was proposed to raise the original capital from £500,000 to £1,000,000, *The Times* published a chilly warning about the danger of overspending, but Paxton, normally so hard-headed, .was surely suffering from delusions of grandeur. The vastly increased size of the Crystal Palace building at Norwood added enormously to the cost. His fountains and cascade in the grounds demanded that the water had to be conveyed in 10 miles of pipe, varying in diameter from 3 feet to 1 inch. The engine power to work it was 320 horse power.

Behind the façade a cold wind was blowing.

Chapter Eight

Palace of the People

During the month of May, 1854 it was announced that the Crystal Palace at Norwood would be opened with fitting ceremony on June 10th, and that Her Majesty the Queen would assist in the inauguration. Already the building was being hailed as the Eighth Wonder of the World, and in view of the Queen's deep interest in the project, her presence was a foregone conclusion. There was none of the fears that had preceded the opening of the 1851 Exhibition – fears that the reverberations of cannon firing a Royal Salute, or that great volumes of music, or even a hail storm, would shatter the glass and cut everybody to ribbons. The glass building had proved its durability, and the coming event was looked forward to with the greatest enthusiasm.

The Directors of the Company sent cards of invitation to the presidents and vice-presidents of all the learned societies, to the dignitaries of the universities, to the mayors of all municipal towns, and to many others. The Governments of France, Belgium, and Prussia, and other principal foreign powers, intimated their intention of sending commissioners. To assist in the musical arrangements, 1,000 performers of the Sacred Harmonic and New Philharmonic Societies volunteered their services free. Everybody wanted to be at the Crystal Palace on that day of days.

Enormous crowds were expected to descend on the Palace on that day, and directions were published in all the papers on how best to get there. The Brighton railway would start running special trains at 10 o'clock in the morning from London Bridge to the south wing of the Crystal Palace.

Coachmen, and others travelling by road from London, were recommended "to drive to Vauxhall Bridge, thence by the Kennington Turnpike or the Wandsworth Road to Brixton Church. Leave the Church on the right hand, and when you reach the George Canning Tavern, with its compo statue of that statesman, turn sharp to the left, and then on, crossing a narrow bridge over the dirty Effra; go on past the Half Moon through the village of Dulwich, taking care, as there are several cross-roads, to leave the church on the left hand, and the Greyhound Inn and Dulwich College on the right; keep straight on through a turnpike; and thus far you can travel without a single hill, with galloping ground from the moment you leave the stones. On passing the turnpike, the hill on which the Palace stands rises visibly. A few minutes brings you, if you are a season ticket holder or an exhibitor, to the North Transept. If you are an invited guest to the Central Transept, there, after descending, your coachman will find attendants in the Crystal Palace livery stables to take charge of your carriage and horses.

"It is understood that the route just described will be that adopted by the Royal Carriages, and will be stopped up beyond Dulwich after one o'clock. In that case a deviation may be made, to the right or left, by the more hilly roads, all leading to the North or South entrances of the Crystal Palace."

Full evening dress was the rule for all guests, so it was thought unlikely that many of them would turn up on horseback. Nevertheless, *The Illustrated London News* observed: "It may, however, be as well to mention that for cavaliers and *amazones,* there is a very delightful ride (of which nearly half is over grass) by Vauxhall Bridge, up the Wandsworth Road, over Clapham Common, to Balham Hill, and then turning into Clapham Park, keeping to the right, across by a bridle road into the upper part of Tooting Common, and so on, through the trees to Streatham Church, at Streatham keeping to the right for quarter of a mile along the Croydon Road, you reach

Streatham Common; turning sharp to the left across the common, you proceed on to Crown Hill, and then through Norwood past the Nunnery, and up the steep hill covered with public houses which have 'cropped out' under the patronage of the Crystal Palace workmen and visitors."

The description of Central Hill at this point covered with public houses gives food for thought, for today there is not a public house, nor a trace of one, along the whole length of Central Hill, from the foot of the Convent and Elder Road to the junction with Westow Hill. They must have been swept away soon after the Palace was completed and the concentration of labour was broken up.

On the south side of Central Hill, between Oxford Road and Rockmount Road, was the New Town industrial housing estate, built to house a proportion of the workmen engaged on building the Crystal Palace and grounds. New Town had the distinction of being the first of its kind in the world, and consisted of rows of terraced cottages with minute gardens. They were purely and simply labourers' cottages.

New Town also possessed three public houses. They were The Oxford, The Fox Under The Hill, and The Eagle. None exists today. The Fox was the first to go, then The Eagle, and with the complete rebuilding of the area in recent years, The Oxford finally vanished.

The New Town housing estate had the distinction of being surrounded by a high wall. There was a road entrance from Central Hill, and one small pedestrian gap in the wall at the lower end, past which the open stream of the Effra flowed. There was a narrow plank bridge crossing the stream, which gave on to fields, part of which is now the Norwood Recreation Ground.

The purpose of the high surrounding wall was obvious. New Town, by its nature, was a very rough neighbourhood, and in those days the police only dared venture into New Town in couples. On Saturday, when the men were paid, the police were content to stand by the main gate. What went on inside New Town while the week's earnings were being spent in the pubs was considered to be strictly the business of the occupants of New Town. The police were only concerned that inebriated navvies did not get out of New Town to visit other public houses. Anybody, drunk or sober, could go into New Town, but nobody who was the worse for drink was allowed out. It was a means for keeping the peace in Upper Norwood, though no doubt the public houses then on Central Hill provided their own quota of Saturday night high spirits.

Admission to the Crystal Palace on June 10th was restricted to season ticket holders, and to those with invitations. At 11 o'clock in the morning exhibitors armed with cards would be admitted to the Palace, but their assistants were not allowed in until 2 o'clock. Normal season ticket holders would be admitted between the hours of 11 a.m. and 2 p.m. They would be allowed to find seats in any part of the building, subject to police regulations, except in reserved seats or in the parts railed off in the Central Transept and Nave for purposes of the ceremony.

Seats were reserved for the Diplomatic Corps, the Queen's suite, members of the House of Lords and House of Commons, and their families, and for the families of persons assisting at the ceremonial.

A dais had been raised on an elevated platform in the Central Transept, on which a Chair of State had been placed for the Queen.

Every detail was most meticulously worked out in advance. All those connected with the inaugural ceremony were to be in their places by 2.30 p.m., half an hour before the Queen's arrival. The Directors of the Crystal Palace Company, with principal officers and others connected with the undertaking, were to assemble opposite the dais, in levée dress or full evening dress. The Archbishop of Canterbury, Her Majesty's Ministers and Officers of State, and the Foreign Ambassadors and Ministers, were to take their places on the platform to the right and left of the Chair of State. They, too, were to be in levée dress.

The Lord Mayor of London and the Sheriffs of London, with the Lord Mayors of Dublin and York on either side, and the Mayors, Provosts and other representatives of the municipal bodies of the kingdom, were to take their places in their robes of office. Places immediately adjoining were reserved for their families.

The Foreign Commissioners, the Royal Commissioners of the 1851 Exhibition in Hyde Park, and the New York Exhibition, the Representatives of the Dublin Exhibition, and of the Paris Exhibition, and the Presidents of the principal learned societies were to take their places in a space reserved for them in the Central Transept, facing the dais. Immediately adjoining places were reserved for their families.

Reserved seats for members of the House of Lords, and their families, were in the Front Gallery on the right of the dais; and for members of the House of Commons and their families in the Front Gallery on the left of the dais.

The Queen with the Royal Family and her suite were to leave Buckingham Palace so as to arrive at the Central Transept precisely at 3 o'clock, when she would ascend the dais and take her place in the Chair of State under an ornamental canopy.

On the eve of the opening excited exhibitors were distractedly arranging their stalls; carpenters were hammering away on all sides at seats and steps; women were stitching together the crimson draperies of the Queen's dais; and everywhere there was rubbish to be cleared away. It seemed quite impossible that the place could be got ready in time.

But when the Press entered the Central Transept on the following day, an hour before the ordinary visitors, they found the galleries and avenues, which the night before had been unsightly with rough deal boards and covered with dust, spotless and glowing in crimson cloth.

It was a lovely day. A bright sun and a refreshing breeze cast a charming effect of light and shade on the wooded slopes that rolled up on both sides almost to meet on the roadway that later was to be called Crystal Palace Parade.

Already the woods surrounding the Palace were crowded with gaily-dressed sight-seers, who were treating the whole occasion like a splendid bank holiday. An hour before the time of opening the doors, carriages were slowly toiling up the steep roads from Dulwich and Norwood. Trains every three minutes were depositing their passengers at the foot of the unfinished avenue which led to the south wing.

One press report said that police had scarcely taken up their positions when impatient knockings warned them that a crush was gathering outside the entrances. No sooner was the word given to unbolt than in flowed an animated crowd, armed with cards of all the colours of the rainbow.

Some cards were recognised by the police, some were not. Some people grabbed the wrong seats; the agility displayed by languid forms in flounces, feathers and lace was remarkable. Only by degrees was some sort of order restored. Police learned the comparative value of the different colours, while Sir Joseph Paxton rapidly decided on new arrangements rendered necessary by the exigencies of the moment. Thus, the best laid plans . . . !

"By one o'clock," reported *The Illustrated London News,* "almost every available part of the Nave and First Gallery were full, and the whole length of the Nave lined with fair faces and pretty bonnets – except the dais, where the Chair of State, under a canopy suspended from the roof of the Central Transept, gorgeously emblazoned with heraldic symbols, awaited the arrival of the Queen, the Prince, and her illustrious family and Royal guests.

"On the west side of the Central Transept, behind the dais, rose up an amphitheatre covered with crimson cloth, on which were seated three bands, and a volunteer chorus of 1,800 singers including some eminent vocalists, each holding in his or her hand a sheet of music. On one of the lower benches the fine white head of Lablache was to be seen, amid the celebrities of Italian and German song; lower still the solo singer of the day, Clara Novello, while from a purple velvet chair Costa took the command."

As a spectacle and pageant, the opening ceremony was more imposing than that of the Great Exhibition of 1851. There were Indian princes in white jewelled turbans and robes of gold and silver. There were the uniforms of Field Marshals, Generals and Admirals, while Coldstream Guards and the Honourable Artillery Company surrounded the dais.

Because of the cloudless sky of Italian blue, with the heat of the sun tempered by a pleasant breeze, the whole event outside took on something of a Derby Day. All the previous night people had streamed out of London to be as near the Crystal Palace as possible. There were picnic parties in the surrounding woods and fields.

Exactly on time, the Royal carriages arrived, the scarlet-coated outriders prancing in front. The standard-bearer saluted, the troops drawn up presented arms. The roadway in front of the Palace was a kaleidoscope of movement and colour. The young Queen, radiant and at the height of her popularity, together with Prince Albert, the Royal children, the King of Portugal and his brother, the Duke of Oporto, descended from their carriages a minute or two before three o'clock.

Only the Queen was not in evening dress. She wore a blue glacé silk dress, trimmed with real silver lace, and a white lace bonnet decorated with roses. The roar of cannon in a 21-gun Royal salute greeted the Queen as she set foot to ground and proceeded through a line of Coldstream Guards and Honourable Artillery Company to the Chair of State.

At the same time there was the outburst of the National Anthem from the choir and bands. It was said afterwards that this rendering of the National Anthem was so emotionally impressive that strong men were seen with the tears running down their faces. Clara Novello sang the solo parts and attained a high B flat with such power that it was heard from one end of the Palace to the other, and so profoundly impressed the policemen on duty that, against all regulations, they removed their helmets!

This was pomp and circumstance in the highest Victorian tradition. At the conclusion of the National Anthem the Queen took her seat. Mr. Laing, the Chairman of the Company, then read a short address, describing the origin and objects of the undertaking, after which he presented the Queen with a series of medals struck to commemorate the occasion. Sir Joseph Paxton then presented her with a handbook on the Palace and Park. During the ceremony a positive library of expensively bound handbooks were presented to the Queen, who replied: "It is my earnest wish and hope that the bright anticipations which have been formed as to its future destiny may, under the blessing of Divine Providence, be completely realised; and that this wonderful structure, and the treasures of art and knowledge which it contains, may long continue to elevate and instruct, as well as to delight and amuse, the minds of all classes of my people."

Then a procession was formed with Sir Joseph Paxton and Mr. Laing walking immediately in front of the Queen, and a perambulation of the building was conducted. On the Queen's return to the dais the choir and orchestra rendered the Hundredth Psalm, at the conclusion of which the Archbishop of Canterbury offered up a prayer composed for the occasion. The choir and orchestra then performed Handel's Hallelujah Chorus.

The Marquis of Breadalbane, the Lord Chamberlain, then stepped forward, and said in a loud voice: "I am commanded by her Majesty to declare that this Palace is now opened."

Immediately afterwards the orchestra once more sang the National Anthem, and the Queen departed.

Outside, the carriages dashed up and the Queen took her seat. The standard-bearer saluted, the troops presented arms, the carriages dashed away, and the greatest and most colourful piece of pageantry Norwood has ever known was ended.

Remarkably, it was a ceremony without one accident. When one recalls what a highly inflammable object the Crystal Palace proved to be on at least two occasions, it was almost tempting providence to have put so many eggs in one basket on that bright June day. The entire government of the country was contained in that fragile glass, iron and wood building on the top of Norwood's highest hill.

Chapter Nine

Two Notable Women

The interval of nearly 120 years that stretches between the Royal opening of the Crystal Palace and the present day has the effect of diminishing that glittering and somewhat ponderous ceremonial to the unreality of a puppet stage. It is difficult to feel the once living vitality and human warmth that surrounded it.

There is, however, a written record touching on the occasion, which has a tenderness and warmth that is very appealing, and is like a living voice speaking, clothing the grand occasion with the vitality of human emotions. Perhaps that is so because that verbal record is also the beginning of a love story, one that was to last for nearly 40 years.

On that historic June day in 1854, among the season ticket holders seated in solid rows at the south end of the Crystal Palace, was a young man, not yet 21 years old, who had already made his mark. He was Charles Haddon Spurgeon, a Baptist preacher with strongly Calvanistic views, who during the preceding months had been electrifying Londoners with his inspired sermons. Now he was witnessing the great occasion with a party of friends. This fact alone might well suggest his good organising ability, when one considers the hectic scramble for seats that took place when the doors were opened.

Seated next to the young preacher was an attractive girl, becomingly dressed, her hair done in the fashionable long ringlets of the day. She was Miss Susannah Thompson, a member of Mr. Spurgeon's congregation, and they had known each other for a few months. Her account of the Crystal Palace occasion, so fresh it is, reads as though that long ago event happened only yesterday. It gives the event the perspective of living people.

"As we sat talking, laughing, and amusing ourselves as best we could, while waiting for the procession to pass by, Mr. Spurgeon handed me a book into which he had been occasionally dipping, and, pointing to some particular lines, said, 'What do you think of the poet's suggestion in these verses?' The pointing finger guided my eyes to the chapter of Marriage in Martin Tupper's recently published *Proverbial Philosophy*.

" 'Seek a good wife of thy God, for she is the best gift of his providence . . . . If thou art to have a wife of thy youth. she is now living on the earth; therefore think of her, and pray for her weal!'

"A soft low voice said in my ear – so soft that no one else heard the whisper: 'Do you pray for him who is to be your husband?'

"I do not remember that the question received any verbal answer, but my fast-beating heart, which sent a tell-tale flush to my cheeks, and my downcast eyes, which feared to reveal the light which at once dawned in them, may have spoken a language which love understood. From that moment, a very quiet and subdued little maiden sat by the young Pastor's side, and while the brilliant procession passed round the Palace, I do not think she took so much more of the glittering pageant defiling before her, as of the crowd of newly-awakened emotions which were palpitating within her heart. Neither the book nor its theories were again alluded to, but when the formalities of the opening were over, and the visitors were allowed to leave their seats, the same low voice whispered again, 'Will you come and walk round the Palace with me?'

"How we obtained leave of absence from the rest of the party, I know not; but we wandered together for a long time, not only in the wonderful building itself, but in the gardens, and even down to the lake, besides which the colossal forms of extinct monsters were being cunningly modelled. During that walk, on that memorable day in June . . . and from that time, our friendship grew apace, and quickly ripened into deepest love – a love which lives in my heart today . . . ."

The courtship of Susannah Thompson, which began at the Crystal Palace on that Inaugural Day, later was to find the Palace the ideal place in which to rendezvous. Spurgeon was living in the neighbourhood of Newington Butts; Susannah's home was 7, St. Ann's Terrace, Brixton Road.

"The Crystal Palace was a favourite resort with us", she wrote. "It possessed great attractions of its own, and perhaps the associations of the opening day gave it an added grace in our eyes. In common with many of our friends, we had season tickets; and we used them to good purpose, as my beloved found that an hour of two of rest and relaxation in those lovely gardens and that pure air, braced him for the constant toil of preaching to crowded congregations, relieved him somewhat from the ill effects of London's smoky atmosphere. It was so easy for him to run down to Sydenham from London Bridge that, as often as once a week, if possible, we arranged to meet there for a quiet walk and talk. After the close of the Thursday evening service, there would be a whispered word to me in the aisle, 'Three o'clock tomorrow', which meant that if I would be at the Palace by that hour 'somebody' would meet me at the Crystal Palace Fountain."

The fountain referred to was the famous Osler's Crystal Fountain, which had been the magnificent centre-piece of the Great Exhibition of 1851. Along with Monti's beautiful bronze fountain, it had been transferred to its new home at Norwood. Monti's fountain suffered the fire of 1866, which destroyed the North Transept, but the Crystal Fountain survived in all its fairylike beauty until the final fire of November 30th, 1936. Pathetic fragments of its matchless crystal are today collector's items.

"The long walk from Brixton Road to Sydenham" wrote Susannah, "was a pleasant task to me, with such a meeting in view, and such delightful companionship as a reward. We

wandered amid the many courts which were then chiefly instruc-
tive and educational in character; we gazed with almost solemn
awe at the reproductions of Egypt, Assyria, and Pompeii, and
I think we learned many things beside the tenderness of our own
hearts towards each other, as the bright and blissful hours sped
by."

They were married on January 8th, 1856 at the New Park
Street Chapel, Southwark, where Spurgeon was the Pastor. A
London newspaper reported that "In point of numbers and
enthusiasm it far outstripped any display which the West End is
in the habit of witnessing. Shortly after eight o'clock, although
the morning was dark, damp, and cold, as many as five hundred
ladies, in light and gay attire, besieged the doors of the chapel,
accompanied by many gentlemen, members of the congregation
and personal friends. From that hour, the crowd increased so
rapidly, that the thoroughfare was blocked up by vehicles and
pedestrians and a body of the M Division of police had to be
sent for to prevent accidents. When the chapel doors were
opened, there was a terrific rush, and in less than half-an-hour
the doors were closed upon many eager visitors . . . ."

In 1857 the Indian Mutiny erupted. A Proclamation by the
Queen appointed October 7th "For a Solemn Fast, Humiliation,
and Prayer before Almighty God; in order to Obtain Pardon
for our Sins, and for Imploring His Blessing and Assistance in
our Arms for the Restoration of Tranquillity in India."

The Directors of the Crystal Palace invited Spurgeon, then
23 years of age, to conduct a service in the Central Transept on
that appointed day, and to make a collection of behalf of the
National Fund for the sufferers through the Mutiny.

Spurgeon accepted, and it turned out to be the largest congregation to which he ever preached; 23,654 persons assembled
in the Crystal Palace to join in the Observance. The collection
amounted to nearly £500, to which the Crystal Palace Company
added £200, besides contributing £50 to the Metropolitan
Tabernacle Building Fund. Spurgeon, for his part, declined to
accept any fee for preaching.

Susannah Spurgeon reported that when her husband returned home on Wednesday night after the service, he went to bed and did not wake up until Friday morning, such was his degree of exhaustion.

In 1861 Spurgeon gave a lecture in the Tabernacle at the Elephant and Castle, which was destined to attract more public attention than any which he had previously delivered. It was entitled "The Gorilla and the Land he Inhabits", and the lecturer claimed that, despite Mr. Darwin, despite the humiliaing likeness, there was a great gulf fixed between man and the gorilla. To add piquancy to the lecture, a stuffed gorilla was displayed on the platform.

At the time of the "Gorilla" lecture, the most celebrated tight-rope walker the world had ever seen was displaying his breath-taking artistry at the Crystal Palace. With bated breath, Crystal Palace audiences watched Blondin performing on a cable that was stretched the length of the Central Transept, 180 feet above the floor. The cable had been tightenend by double purchase to such an extent that its diameter had been reduced from 2 inches to $1\frac{1}{2}$ inches.

Blondin was performing such feats on the tight-rope as back somersaults, lying flat on his back, walking and somersaulting while blindfolded, walking with his feet in baskets, walking on stilts, and actually cooking and serving omelettes from a stove balanced by him on the middle point of the cable.

About the only thing Blondin never did, despite the popular legend to the contrary, was to walk on a tight-rope stretched between the Crystal Palace towers. The reason for this was that the purchase that would have been needed to make the cable taut enough would have been so enormous that the towers could never have stood the strain!

Immediately following the success of the "Gorilla" lecture, a wag wrote to Blondin a letter purporting to come from Spurgeon. It read:

"Sir, In consequence of the overflowing attendance at my Tabernacle, on Tuesday last, when I gave a lecture on the gorilla, it has occurred to myself and to my brethren the Managers of the Tabernacle, that to engage your services for an evening (say, next Wednesday) for the following programme, would result in mutual benefit. You must meet me at the Tabernacle on Tuesday next, at 12 o'clock to confirm or alter the proposed order of entertainment, which I flatter myself will be highly gratifying to all concerned.

PROGRAMME

At 6 o'clock on Wednesday evening, October 9th, M. Blondin to ascend from the platform in the Tabernacle, by an easy spiral ascent; five times round the interior, to one of the upper windows opposite to 'The Elephant and Castle', thence by an easy incline in at the first-floor window of that Inn, and return the same way to the platform. The admission to be, as at the 'Gorilla' lecture, 6d, 1s, and 2s 6d.

Yours sincerely,
C. H. Spurgeon."

The Crystal Palace was undoubtedly a factor in the lives of the Spurgeons; it exerted a nostalgic influence from the start of their courting days, and in time brought them to Westwood, on Beulah Hill.

One day, on a business visit to Norwood, Spurgeon had the sentimental desire to see the Crystal Palace at close quarters. This was in the year 1880. While driving along Beulah Hill towards the Palace, his eye was caught by a House for Sale Board at an entrance gate. For some time he and Susannah had felt the need to move to higher ground, so on returning from the Palace, he stopped at the gateway of Westwood, and walked down the drive. As soon as he saw the size and extent of Westwood, he exclaimed, "Oh, this place is far too grand for me!" and put it out of his mind.

Some days later he received a note from the estate agents telling him that the reserve price had not been obtained at the sale, and would he care to make an offer for the nine-acre estate?

By a strange coincidence, on the same day he was asked if he wanted to sell his Clapham house. As it turned out, the selling price of the one and the purchase price of the other so nearly agreed that the Spurgeons became the owners of Westwood. They moved in in August.

Apart from its private uses, Westwood became the focus point of tutors and students of Spurgeon's College, and they would spend long days there with their President and his wife.

The tower of Westwood was a popular vantage point for visitors, from which a wide extent of country could be seen. The Grand Stand at Epsom was plainly discernible, as was the tower on Leith Hill, and, when the air was clear, Windsor Castle could be seen.

There was a fine oak tree in the grounds, which came to be known as the Question Oak, because beneath its widely-spreading boughs Spurgeon invited the theological students to put any questions they pleased. It has been said that whatever question was put, Spurgeon would answer it fully and without a moment's hesitation.

On one occasion under the Question Oak, Spurgeon was asked: "Do you believe in supernatural visitations?" For reply, Spurgeon related to the students a story told him by John Ruskin, the factual truth of which Ruskin could vouch.

A widower, with several young children, was in the final stages of buying an old farm house. He had taken them with him to see their new home before finally moving into it. While he was engaged with the agent, the children set off on a tour of inspection. Presently, they found the head of a flight of steps leading to the cellars, and were rushing down them at great speed when, midway, they suddenly stopped in startled amazement, for, standing at the bottom of the flight of steps, they saw *their mother,* with outstretched arms and loving gesture, waving them back, and silently forbidding their further passage. With cries of mingled fear and joy, they turned and rushed back to their father, telling him that they had seen mother, that she had smiled lovingly at them, but had eagerly motioned them back. The father at once perceived that something unusual had happened. A search was made, and close at the foot of those narrow steps they found a deep and open well, entirely unguarded, into which, in their mad rush, every child must inevitably have fallen and perished.

The students asked Spurgeon to give his theory of the nature of the appearance. His reply was that he could not explain it, but he thought that the Almighty had impressed on the retina of the children's eyes an object which would naturally cause them to return at once to their father, thus ensuring their safety.

Many and distinguished were the visitors who came to Westwood. The Spurgeons were on friendly terms with the Archbishop of Canterbury, Dr. Benson, who visited them at Beulah Hill, and Spurgeon would be invited to Addington Palace. They were on equally friendly terms with Bishop Thorold, the Bishop of Rochester, whose palace was at Selsdon Park. The Earl of Shaftesbury, the great philanthropist, would call unexpectedly. Canon Harford, one of the Canons Residentiary at Westminster Abbey, was a close friend and constant visitor.

There was one visitor who did not prove so welcome. He professed to have come from the United States, and announced himself as Captain Beecher, the son of Henry Ward Beecher. He made himself very amiable; on leaving, he said: "Oh, Mr. Spurgeon, excuse me for making such a request, but could you change a cheque for me? Unfortunately I missed the bank, and I need some money very particularly tonight."

Spurgeon's suspicions were aroused, and he said with some severity: "I do not think you ought to make such a request to me. If you are really Mr. Beecher's son, you must be able, through the American consul, or some friend, to get your cheque cashed, without coming to a complete stranger." The man departed without his cheque being cashed.

Some few days afterwards, a man was murdered in a railway carriage on the Brighton line, not far away. When the picture of criminal Lefroy was published in the papers in connection with the murder, Spurgeon immediately recognised the features of his recent visitor.

In the grounds of Westwood was a well from which the famous Beulah Spa water could be drawn. A prospectus issued at the time of the sale of Westwood contained an analysis and an account of the virtues of the water, which were identical with those of the water obtained from the original Beulah Spa well. It compared their properties and hydropathic value with those of other medicinal springs in England and on the Continent. Spurgeon permitted a pipe to be laid from the well to take water to the nearby Beulah Spa Hotel and Hydro.

The well has long been filled in, and Westwood, the scene of so many of Susannah's charitable activities, has been razed. The drive that once led down from Beulah Hill to the house is now replaced by a public road, named Spurgeon Road. The grounds, with the lake, the bowling green, the rosary, the winding paths, the summer-houses and Victorian retreats, have been levelled and grassed over. They are now the playing fields and site of Westwood School, a large secondary school for girls. The name of Susannah Spurgeon has recently been enshrined as the name of one of the four school houses.

Half a mile away, near the top of South Norwood Hill, in a handsome Georgian mansion which was once the home of Admiral the Hon. Plantagenet Pierrepoint Carey, eleventh Viscount Falkland, is housed Spurgeon's College. This fine house was presented by Mr. C. Hay Walker in 1923, the College having outgrown its old premises at Newington.

It seems very fitting that Spurgeon's College should be in Norwood, so near where Spurgeon lived, and so near to the Crystal Palace, from which, one might say, it all began. Its modest beginnings were in 1856, when the young bride and bridegroom returned from their short honeymoon.

"We began housekeeping on a very modest scale," Susannah wrote afterwards, "and even then had to practise rigid economy in all things, for my dear husband earnestly longed to help young men to preach the gospel, and from our slender resources we had to contribute somewhat largely to the support and education of Mr. T. W. Medhurst, who was the first to receive training for the work. From so small a beginning sprang the present Pastor's College.... I rejoice to remember how I shared my beloved's joy when he founded the Institution and that, together, we planned and pinched in order to carry out the purpose of his loving heart; it gave me quite a motherly interest in the College and 'our own men'. The chief difficulty, with regard to money matters in those days, was to make both ends meet. We never had enough left over to tie a bow!"

The names of the other three houses at Westwood School equally touch on Norwood history. One is named after Vice-Admiral Robert Fitzroy, R.N., who lived on Church Road during the last years of his life. He was celebrated as a hydrographer and meteorologist, and the whole system of modern weather forecasting is based on his methods, originally devised for the use of ships at sea. He was also in command of H.M.S. *Beagle* during her famous voyage in 1831–36, with Charles Darwin on board as official naturalist to the Government.[*]

The name of Decimus Burton figures as a third house name at Westwood School. Decimus Burton was a well-known architect of the early nineteenth century. He became a Fellow of the Royal Society, and one of the earliest members of the Royal Institute of British Architects. His association with Norwood is in connection with the Beulah Spa, which was opened in 1831. It was Decimus Burton who designed the buildings and laid out the grounds. For many years his name was commemorated in Decimus Burton Road, at the Thornton Heath end of Grange Road. Now the name is lost in that respect, the entire length of the road today being called Grange Road.

The fourth school house name at Westwood is that of Catherine Marsh. Catherine Marsh became an outstanding personality for the untiring work she did for the welfare of the navvies who came to Norwood to build the Crystal Palace in 1853–54.

The Revd. Frederick Chalmers, Rector of Beckenham, Kent at that time, wrote a preface to *English Hearts and English*

---

[*] See Chapter 6, page 83.

Hands, which was a compilation from the diary of Catherine Marsh, published in 1858. He was also Catherine Marsh's brother-in-law, having married her sister.

"It is but few summers since the sun shone upon the woody heights of the Sydenham and Norwood hills, and now his rays may be seen gleaming from the crystal roof of that vast temple to the arts of peace, which has suddenly displaced the oaks and elms of the green woodland.

"Whose are the hands that reared that colossal building? Its massive iron pillars, its huge girders, the ponderous supports of its complicated roofing? . . Give a passing thought to the strength of frame and mechanical skill of the workmen who so speedily accomplished the setting up of such a fabric."

The answer to that rhetorical question is, of course, the navvies who came in their thousands early in 1853, engaged by Sir Joseph Paxton and the Crystal Palace Company, to build the vast edifice. There were 3,000 of them, their numbers increasing to 5,000. These men were the railway excavators, who, in answer to advertisements, had gravitated to the Norwood heights from all parts of the country. They were the men who with shovel and wheelbarrow were building the spreading network of railways. They were the men who had previously dug the canals of England, and were called navigators – navvies for short. The transition from digging canals to digging railway cuttings and raising embankments offered no barrier; the work, like the name, remained the same. Both called for men of brawn and muscle, capable of shifting vast masses of earth in the minimum time. Paxton knew the class of men he needed.

Catherine Marsh, with her strong humanities, her dedicated sense of duty to her fellow human beings, soon got to know these men well. She wrote in her diary: "They were the most peculiar body of men whom I have ever met. Advertised for, in this first instance, for strength alone – men, whose muscle and sinew constituted their character, and whose working powers, therefore, stood for their morale, were thus gathered together on that ground from all parts of the country. The North of England had sent most – from Lancashire, Durham and

Northumberland. But we had our Cornishmen, too, and our Kentish, and a sprinkling from nearly all the coast; a knot of kindly Scots and some warm-hearted Irish Roman Catholics.

"Wild they might be, and absolutely undisciplined, doubtless, they were; but it was difficult to judge hardly of those who received every friendly advance with a cordial but ever-respectful confidence; who combined their manly courtesy with the trust of childhood .... And here I may mention, that in all my acquaintance with working men, never have they let me hear a single oath, nor one expression which could in the remotest degree shock or pain me."

Such were the men, or a good proportion of them, who came to Norwood to build the Crystal Palace. As a breed they had become nomadic, wanderers over the countryside, settling for a while wherever work was, and then, when that job was finished, moving on to the next. Mostly these men formed themselves into little self-contained groups, who always stuck together, one acting as their leader and negotiating their joint employment.

It was their form of insurance against illness, which would mean no work and therefore no pay, and against starvation. If one of their number fell ill, the others supported him and looked after him until he was able to work again.

When the first 3,000 concentrated on Norwood, they found lodgings as far afield as Beckenham, Lower Norwood and Forest Hill, walking in each day for their labours at the Palace. Nearly 200 of them lodged in the village of Beckenham, but they were seldom seen, so late in the evening would they get back from work, to leave again early in the morning. Nevertheless, on the last day of 1853, the Sergeant of Police stationed at Beckenham said that his duty had never been so easy before in Beckenham, for their example had restrained the wilder young men.

After Christmas Eve heavy snow had fallen, preventing the navvies from carrying on with their work. Catherine Marsh soon discovered that some of the men had had no food for two days, and though a change in the weather had enabled them to resume work, their distress had increased rather than diminished. Wages were not due until Saturday afternoon, and these men were working without having had any food. Credit at shops was practically unobtainable.

Catherine Marsh's response to this emergency was to organise grand soup-making arrangements for the whole set of unfed Crystal Palace workmen during the remainder of that week, with additional meals supplied for those who had been prevented by illness or other accidents from laying by anything for a time of need. Her distress at the half-starved look of men working in the Crystal Palace grounds, caused her to organise cups of coffee and bread and butter for the men who had had no meal. This was served out in the Crystal Palace grounds.

At the end of March, 1854, England and France were in alliance to defend Turkey against Russia, and war was declared. Soon there was the common sight of the scarlet line of a regiment crossing Waterloo Bridge, with a crowd of women and children running beside it, the band playing "The Girl I Left Behind Me", and the troop train waiting in the station.

Catherine Marsh had an interview with Florence Nightingale just before she left England, but she knew there was no hope of her being sent to the Crimea, because she had not had any training as a nurse. However, there was other important work for that indefatigable woman, and it centred around the navvies at the Crystal Palace.

In October, 1854, Paxton insisted on the urgent need to send navvies to the Crimea to assist the army in building roads, earthworks, and all essential services.

Lord Panmure, Secretary of War, wrote to Sir Joseph Paxton at his Crystal Palace home, Rockhills, on April 24th, 1855: "Her Majesty's Government has decided upon forming a Corps of Navigators to be employed in the Crimea upon the duty of forming entrenchments and other earthworks. Your great experience in the employment of these workpeople marks you out as the person probably the best qualified to afford aid to Her Majesty's Government in the selection of persons to take charge of the superintendence and management of the Corps. I have accordingly the honour to request that you will favour me with any suggestions you may have to offer with respect to the formation and organisation of this Corps."

Paxton accepted, on condition that he should receive neither remuneration nor reward for his services. Certainly the navvies he had employed would be available for service in the Crimea. The concept of the Army Works Corps, as it became known, developed rapidly. The men were not to be armed; they were not to be put into uniform; they were to be paid wages; their officers were to have a distinguishing dress, but no badges of military rank.

The first 1,000 men were recruited at the Crystal Palace. They were fully equipped for the job, and while waiting at the Crystal Palace before being transported to the seat of war, slept in bell tents in the Palace grounds. However, this first detachment of the Army Works Corps met with considerable delay in its embarkation for the Crimea, and the men were in consequence remanded to the neighbourhood of the Crystal Palace. Catherine Marsh kept in closest touch with the men and their officers; then a report reached her that the men would leave the Crystal Palace to go on board the following morning, June 18th.

Catherine Marsh and her sister drove to the Crystal Palace grounds, to be there at eight o'clock in the morning to take leave of the men, who had come to regard her as their fairy god-mother. Here is her account of the occasion.

"The men were gathered in groups in front of their tents. An officer of the Corps kindly arranged them in companies of fifty – comprising two 'gangs' in each, with the 'gangers' at their head – to be addressed separately . . . .

"Previously I had offered to take charge of any portion of their large wages which they chose to empower me to receive from them during their engagement in the Crimea, to deposit them in the Savings' Bank, in the form of a Friendly Club, and to keep a private account for each man.

"A large number of men gladly accepted this proposition. Many of them requested us to forward to needy relatives a portion of the money thus saved, which varied from ten to twenty shillings weekly. Not only wives and children were thus provided for, but amongst the majority, who had no such ties, an aged mother, an infirm father, a widowed sister, a sickly brother, or orphan nieces, were remembered, with a generous care for their comfort in 'this time of their wealth' by those who toiled for it night and day in the service of their country, and in many cases paid for it by laying down their strong, young lives on that unhealthy shore.

"Strangers, as the majority of those who ˜daily arrived to swell the ranks necessarily were to us, and the rest only friends of a few weeks standing, I thought it but right to give a stamped receipt to each man for the money-order which had been drawn out in my name, and carried these receipts to the Crystal Palace grounds on the afternoon of the 18th."

There was a surprising response. The men of the Army Works Corp flung the receipts back into Catherine Marsh's carriage with something approaching shouts of disdain at the supposition that they could possibly require such a pledge of honesty from such a friend and lady. Catherine Marsh, in her turn, wrote on the back of the money-orders their "Wills" – the disposition of the property so entrusted, should they not be spared to return to claim it.

Before the first detachment left the Crystal Palace, Lord Panmure paid a visit to the Corps Headquarters in the grounds. He inspected officers and men, and complimented them on their appearance and turnout. The effect on some of the men was unfortunate. About fifty of them sallied forth to Penge, got themselves intoxicated, formed a ring, and indulged in friendly fisticuffs.

Two women onlookers became alarmed and insisted on a policeman nearby to enter the ring of men and stop the fight. The policeman argued reasonably enough that if they were left alone they would soon be tired of fighting under a burning June sun and would sleep it off in the shade. But if he were to use his staff on them they would be roused into tigers.

But the women were insistent, and to begin with the navvies were prepared to move their ring to some distance. But when the policeman followed up with a second attack, using his truncheon, what has since been described as the Battle of Penge began. The sparring men turned on the armed policeman. A second policeman came up, and together they fought desperately against massive odds, but by sheer force of numbers were compelled to retreat to the house of the first policeman.

The crowd of navvies followed and broke in. It was little short of a miracle that the two policemen escaped with their lives. The rioting navvies, for good measure, terrified a local butcher, and wrecked his shop.

A fresh force of police arrived, and the navvies principally concerned in the fight gave themselves up. The rest dispersed.

About an hour later the men of the Corps turned up at the Crystal Palace Office for their afternoon roll-call. Hearing rumours of the recent fight, they stopped to find out particulars. As luck would have it, at that moment a fresh detachment of police arrived. Having been informed that two of their comrades had been murdered, they were in an ugly mood, and supposing that the men around them were the guilty ones, began laying about with their truncheons and making arrests. A highly dangerous situation had arisen, and this was made worse by a great crowd of navvies pouring down from the top of the hill and from the Penge gates to the Palace grounds. They immediately went in to attack the police and rescue the arrested men.

The police stood up to defend themselves against overwhelming numbers, and it seemed as though something like slaughter was imminent. And then a remarkable thing happened, which undoubtedly saved lives. An open carriage with two ladies in it, driven by a coachman, drove between the navvies and the small body of police, and came to a halt in the middle of the seething mass. One of the ladies stood up in the carriage, and vehemently addressed the crowd of some five hundred men with already upraised missiles. The men recognised her at once; she was Catherine Marsh, and she was white with anger. "The first man who throws a stone is my enemy! We will have no more fighting today, by God's help! Haven't we had enough of it already – two policemen nearly killed, and seven of our poor fellows perhaps to be transported for life, or hanged, if the wounded men die. Go back and give over, for my sake . . . ."

A brief silence followed Catherine Marsh's outburst, then one of the men said: "Do you go away, ma'am. We wouldn't hurt you for anything, but it's not fair to hinder us paying off the police."

"We don't want to vex you," said another navvy, "but we will set our mates free."

"They shall be set free," replied Catherine Marsh, "those innocent men whom we have seen taken prisoners before our eyes. If there be justice in England, they shall be free to go with you to the Crimea. I pledge myself not to rest till it is done. Will you trust me?"

There was a momentary silence among the men, followed by a short conference among the leaders, who then cried out: "Trust you to the world's end!"

"Then prove it by going back within the Crystal Palace gates."

In five minutes Catherine Marsh was left alone with the police and their prisoners. The police gratefully admitted that Miss Marsh had saved a deal of bloodshed, and immediately released one prisoner for whose good character Catherine Marsh could vouch, and promised to deal gently with the remaining prisoners.

By the time the first ship sailed from the Thames to the Crimea Catherine Marsh had been able to prove to the magistrates that the men taken prisoner in the second phase, when she arrived in her carriage, were innocent of the previous fight. They were set free and resumed their position in the Army Works Corps.

The immediate outcome of the Battle of Penge was that the men were at once embarked at Blackwall, to keep them under control and out of temptation's way. A message was thereupon sent from the Corps Commander to Catherine Marsh that the men were embarking that day. By 7 o'clock in the morning Catherine Marsh and her sister had entered the Crystal Palace grounds, and remained until nine, taking leave of the men, and thanking them for their forebearance over the matter of the police.

"After shaking hands with each man, I took my leave, but was requested by an official to return, to hear the subject of a communication which had been passing from the men to the foreman of the Corps. It was to express the united wish of these warm and grateful hearts that I should go out with them to the Crimea, to keep them straight, and to be with any of them who should die out there, in their last hours. And they humbly begged to know if they might take the best place on board for me, and pay for it amongst themselves."

This Florence Nightingale of the Crystal Palace was not able to accept the invitation, but before the first battalion of the Army Works Corps sailed for the Crimea, she visited the men on board ship. When she was rowed out to the *Barrakpore,* off Blackwall, the navvies manned the rigging like sailors, and welcomed her with cheers.

Early in August the second battalion was formed, and as before, Catherine Marsh and her sister visited the new candidates for the Corps. Sir Joseph Paxton's office invariably notified Catherine Marsh of any movement of men or ships, such was the tradition and respect built up around this remarkable young woman.

The last detachment of the Third Battalion was selected during the month of November at the Crystal Palace. Volunteers were at the rate of 1,000 per day. For the most part these men had very little means for their support during the time of waiting on the chance of being chosen. Catherine Marsh reported that numbers were unable to afford lodgings, and therefore slept without a roof over their heads in the damp cold November nights. Many were almost starving. A pieman, who came down from London, brought about two hundred "hot penny pies" – a marvellous supply of nourishment for those who had had no meal in the course of the day. These Catherine Marsh dispensed.

"It was a fine thing to see several hundred men fall back, leaving a ring around us of only the absolutely famished men, not to trespass on the little kindness, although many of those who retired had had but one meal in the course of the day."

Characters were required of the men before the appointments for selection could be made. Catherine and her sister turned Beckenham Rectory into an office, in which they wrote for, and received characters of, artizans of all descriptions, and of railway labourers. There was a scarcity of work at that time and crowds of men endeavoured to gain admission at the Crystal Palace gates. At Beckenham Rectory men queued daily from 9.30 to 3.30.

The Third Battalion was the last of the Army Works Corps to be sent to the Crimea. On May 8th, 1856, the *Cleopatra* anchored off Portsmouth, and the first 600 men of the Army Works Corps returned home. On May 18th Catherine Marsh and her sister went to meet the whole body of the men then returned, in the Crystal Palace grounds. They were told afterwards that all that day, until they arrived, 300 men lingered at the Crystal Palace gates watching each carriage that arrived, waiting for Catherine Marsh to appear.

With each successive returning ship from the Crimea, notice would be sent to Catherine so that she might rendezvous with the returned Works Corps men at the old spot in the Crystal Palace grounds. This enabled her to see almost all the men who returned from the Crimea.

Of Catherine Marsh herself, she was a woman with unflagging interest in people and public affairs. She had a unique capacity for gentle sympathy and for being able to enter into the feelings of others. She had great power of enjoyment; she was completely unselfconscious, with a perfectly natural manner, and a keen sense of humour. She lived to the great age of 94, being born the year before Queen Victoria, and was two years older than Florence Nightingale whom, in some respects, she resembled. She died on December 12th, 1912.

In a letter to her, when she was between 80 and 90 years old, a stranger wrote: "Well do I remember that story being told to us by my father, of how he stood with his mates facing those angry navvies, outnumbered by them many times over, in the most dangerous position it had ever been his misfortune to find himself in, and how you, a young lady, came upon the scene and did what few, if any, men would have dared to do single-handed, and by your courage and presence of mind undoubtedly saved the constables from serious injury, if not from death."

Catherine Marsh was indefatigable. To the last, such was the enduring impact of those Crystal Palace days, her thoughts and energies turned to the navvies and their needs. In her ninety-third year she wrote to the Press firmly pointing out the spiritual needs of the men who were building the Canadian Pacific Railway, and her appeal met with a warm response.

Chapter Ten

Fountains for Pleasure

Wednesday, 18th June, 1856 was the day fixed for the Royal Inauguration of the Crystal Palace fountains, reputed to be more elegant and more imaginative than those of Versailles. This long awaited occasion came two years after the opening of the Crystal Palace. The delay had been a great disappointment to everybody, and had been brought about by the discovery that the original water towers, built at the same time as the Palace, were unsafe. As was explained in Chapter 7, new towers, designed by Isambard Kingdom Brunel, were erected in their stead. It had been a costly business. But now all systems were working, and Paxton's fountains would be revealed in all their glory.

The water temples, classical Greek in style, the cascades, the two large waterfalls, and the fountains of the grand lower basins were now to be displayed to their full perfection, together with the fountains already in operation. These latter consisted of the fountains within the Palace, the nine basins on the two terraces, and the large circular basin on the centre walk, which did not derive their supply of water from the two great towers. In the grand display there would be *jets d'eau* thrown to a height of not less than 250 feet. It would be an occasion almost rivalling that of the original opening in 1854.

The day itself was an occasion of elaborate toilettes and fashionable attire and, as it turned out, proved to be an event as elegant as Royal Ascot. Hours before the timing of the water display, London Bridge station was almost completely blocked by the crowds bound for the Crystal Palace. By 2 o'clock, thousands of visitors had already arrived, and the lawns were dotted with animated groups of people. On the terrace and in the open corridors facing the centre transept there was a long, slowly moving line of bright dresses sauntering in the sunlight, holding aloft thousands of little parasols. The day was another perfect example of Queen's weather, with only one or two little white clouds floating like feathers against the deep blue sky.

Numbers of visitors had ascended the mound where the rosary was situated, and were watching the weather-vane on top of the flagstaff. This interest in the weather-vane was to try to discover which way the spray from the fountains would be blown.

The basins from which the new jets of water were to be hurled into the air were situated on either side of the broad centre walk, near to the grand central fountain. Below that were the water temples and cascades which emptied into the grand north and south basins. These twin basins were huge lakes of water, bordered by stone coping, and were as big as football pitches. In fact, in later years that was to be their fate – to be filled in to become a football pitch, a sports ground, a running track, and a dirt track. Today the International Sports Centre occupies that area, with its Stadium on one side and the Sports Hall on the other.

Together with the six fountains on the Italianate terrace, this huge assembly of waterworks comprised 11,788 jets. On the day of the Royal Inauguration long trails of smoke were curling skywards from Brunel's twin towers, indicating that the steam engines were at work pumping water up to the 1,576 ton capacity tanks at the top. All round could be heard the murmurous sound of invisible rushing water.

The twin water temples were gilded and gleaming. A poised and shining Mercury stood on one foot on each domed roof. Around the cornices were the heads of cupids, seemingly sucking little bits of lead pipe, from which, later on, water would spurt.

The broad sheets of water of the grand lower basins were dotted in all directions by little black stick-like objects poking above the surface. Closer inspection showed them to be the metal mouths of water jets.

It was said by one spectator on that inaugural day that "the surface of the tranquil water served as a mirror to reflect the brightly moving pattern of different coloured dresses of the forms walking along the path at the edge of the lakes. It struck one that this vast expanse of water with nothing but the black sticks shining on its surface, had a naked, deserted look, and that a few statues would have broken up its monotony. As the fountains themselves never play longer than one hour at a time, the water during the other hours of the day, remains without any ornament to interest the visitor."

The same spectator, impressed with the colour and animation of the occasion, and not without an appreciative eye for a pretty girl, has left this graphic description of a Victorian summer's day.

"It seemed like the beauty show of all England. There was one Venus in a silken dress, delicately green as an opening bud, and from her temples hung long flaxen ringlets that, as she nodded her head to the music of a band, vibrated with elastic grace about her lace-covered bust. There was another, in a transparent muslin that allowed a waist, slender as a wrist, to be discovered, whilst a foot, encased in a white kid boot that would have pinched a Cinderella, peeped out from under the worked border of the petticoat.

"A third held in her hand, almost small enough for a letter-clip, a parasol of fluttering lace, which cast a transparent shade upon a countenance which must be accustomed to, at least, its ten matrimonial offers per diem. Some of the fair audience were listening as intently to the music as if a secret were being whispered in their ears, with their large sentimental eyes opened, until the long lashes bent like springs against the lids; others were unconcernedly chatting together with a lively indifference, asking whether 'so-and-so was in the gardens'."

It was reported that at least a hundred policemen were lolling about in the Palace. In honour of the Queen's visit, their Berlin gloves were white as turbots, and their uniforms brushed as free of dust as the cloth of a billiard table. They passed their time in examining the model manure carts, and highly varnished ploughs, or in trying to establish intimacy with the damsels managing the cotton spinning machines. The attendants were watering the plants, and a beautiful odour of freshness filled the air. The atmosphere seemed blue with the reflection of the bright sky above the glittering glass roof, and made the white statues appear as cool as snow; and gave a mystic grace to the baskets of flowers suspended half way in the air, with their shoots and drooping branches hanging downwards, as if making for the parent earth again.

"On our way to the Alhambra Court, we passed by the ornamental water in the centre of the nave. The lilies have grown out of all knowledge. The leaves of the Victoria Regia, which last year were scarcely bigger than dinner plates, have grown into the dimensions of the paper hoops employed at a circus. The Hall of the Abencerrages was filled with ladies. They were seated upon the red cushions at the side and were gazing up at the wonderful roof, with its small round windows of stained glass, flooding the gilt mouldings with purple, crimson and yellow rays, until the dome seemed one crumpled mass of jewels. One of these young ladies, wearing a dress of Indian muslin and a dainty bonnet with jessamine sprays meandering over the white sides of dotted lace, whispered in a luxurious mellow voice that she could stop a week in this beautiful abode."

It is recorded in the journals of the day that as the time of the Queen's arrival drew near, the crowd arranged themselves on each side of the gravel walk up which the pony carriage was to pass. Ladies, we are told in one account, stood on chairs, while the gentlemen took their chance to see as best they could. Some of the more obstreperous girls were restrained from pushing forward with such appeals from uniformed policemen as, "For heaven's sake, ladies." One girl in white muslin with cherry-coloured trimmings, broke the ranks twice, and drew from a worried constable, "Why don't you gentlemen keep her back?"

To quote again the observer with a sensitive eye for the ladies: "In a short time all the apple-green, the pink, the lemon-yellow dresses, the pert satin jackets, the tantalising rose-tinted cloaks, the aerial white, blue, and lilac bonnets, were ranged into a thick hedge on each side of the path. The National Anthem suddenly was heard above the hum of voices to strike up at the other end of the park. The Royal Artillery band took up the air, and the Coldstream musicians followed their example. Then arose the shout of 'The Queen has come!' Then a sound of hissing and spitting and spirting, followed by the loud roar of rushing waters filled the air, and the fountains sent foaming columns high up towards the sky. Between the temptation of the fountains and the expected arrival of the Queen, the elegant crowd scarcely knew which way to look or what sight to sacrifice. The uncertainty was soon put an end to by a heavy shower of spray, which, carried by the wind, came down on the devoted bonnets with stormy drenching violence. In an instant the crowd was in agitation, scampering off to drier spots. The roses and lilies and jessamine twigs in the bonnets drooped their wet heads and hung in damp disorder. Everybody laughed, and delicate parasols, scarcely larger than mushrooms, were in vain opposed to the torrent. Those who had umbrellas used them, but those who were less fortunate took to their legs."

During all this spray-swept confusion, the scarlet-coated outriders in front of the Royal carriage made their appearance. In the first carriage rode the Queen with the Prince Consort, the Regent of Baden, and the Prince of Prussia. Next followed a phaeton, in which was riding the fifteen year-old Prince of Wales, the Princess Royal, and Princess Alice. The youthful Prince of Wales was obviously thoroughly enjoying the general drenching, of which he had had his fair share.

"As soon as the Royal party had gone by," the record has it, "a rush was made towards some other spot where the carriage would again have to pass. Away went the crowd, scampering over wet grass, the most delicate of kid boots plunging heedlessly into ankle-deep puddles, bounding over paths, scrambling up slopes, until the desired locality had been reached. In these enthusiastic flights how many toilettes were deranged was proved by the spoils left on the grass.

"The fountains were certainly wonderful, and went as high as steam engines and tall towers could send them. The two monster jets sent up their streams of opaque crystal so high into the air, that the neck ached with keeping the head thrown back, as you watched the topmost spray jerk and jerk towards the clouds. Around the base of some of the fountains, jets had been so arranged that the lines crossed and recrossed one another, making a kind of lace-work border, something similar to the wire-work bordering that encircles a flower bed. The waterfalls at the base of the cascades fell in a smooth sheet, that roared and splashed as it tumbled into the basins below, and above them the water came gurgling and foaming down the stone steps of the cascade itself, marking with lines of white spray the edge of each descent. On either side, the bronze figures spirted out their silvery streams, and above all the temples poured forth from their gilt domes a heavy stream of glittering water. On every side were seen the foaming mounds spirting out from countless jets. The air was filled with a roaring sound, and was as cool as in a grotto. At some of the fountains, the spray falling in the sunlight became dyed with bright rainbow tints, or else it formed a thin silvery cloud, which the wind carried away until it melted into the distance."

This dazzling occasion almost certainly represented the highest fulfilment of the Crystal Palace, and of the energy and talent of Joseph Paxton. This was the high-point. The palace of glass, already the Eighth Wonder of the World, was Paxton's creation, the fountains were his magic, an ephemeral dream world, and the Queen was there to see it and signify her approval. This was a moment to remain fixed in time.

The inevitable anti-climax came when the Palace turncocks made their appearance, and with their big iron keys began their circular walk of turning off the water. The magic hour was over. Slowly the different jets decreased in height, until at last the silvery streams ceased altogethcr, and the nozzles of the pipes again appeared like black stumps above the quiet surface of the basin.

A journalist who was present at this first water display wrote: "To compare the fountains of the Crystal Palace with those of Versailles is about as absurd as to compare English with French cookery. They are two entirely different things. The one is substantial, the feast gigantic and soon satisfying; the other is light and elegant, so that even when the entertainment is over, the appetite still remains. At Sydenham, the display of water partakes something of the baron-of-beef style of banquet; it is the intensest feast of fountains to be obtained. But the display once over, what remains? A blank sheet of water. Now, at Versailles, whether the water is playing or not, the fountains are still interesting from the sculptures about them, which certainly help to destroy the monotony of a vast watery expanse, and please the eye and excite the imagination. Both styles are essentially distinct, and both of them come as near perfection as they in their various characters can approach."

While such a comparison as that puts the now legendary Crystal Palace fountains into perspective, the day of the inauguration of those fountains must be rated as a golden one in the pre-Disneyland magic of the Palace of the People. To close, in retrospect, that golden day, one should again quote the words of one who was present at the time: "Soon the crowds set in for the railway terminus. As the hour grew late, the gentlemen boldly lighted their cigars, and openly smoked in hitherto forbidden places. The ladies who valued their dresses avoided the crush at the door of those impatient to get away, and many who prized an uncrumpled skirt above a speedy return home, had to wait patiently until past nine o'clock for an opportunity of making their escape from the gardens."

Edward Whymper, the celebrated mountaineer, and the first man to climb the Matterhorn, wrote in his diary: "June 18. My mother was presented today with a season ticket for the Crystal Palace at Sydenham, and went today to witness the opening of the grand fountains and waterworks there. It was said that they were thrown to a height of 250 feet and many say they surpassed the boasted one at Versailles. I shall try to see them. The Queen went today and got drenched by them, the spray being blown right over her."

Whymper did not visit the Crystal Palace until September of the following year. He clearly believed in looking after the pennies. He wrote in his diary, dated September 7, 1857: "At the Crystal Palace, Sydenham, being the first shilling day on which the great fountains and the whole system of waterworks have played, I had determined that I would wait until such a day arrived, as I did not see the use of paying more for this. There were a great many people there, although not altogether of the choicest sort, but I was much pleased with what I saw, although it was so far windy that the fountains at no part of the time could be seen to much advantage."

It may be noticed that Whymper did not enthuse to the extent of one writer who expressed the opinion that "the richest visions of the Arabian Nights and Persian Tales seemed more than realised as one gazed on the gorgeous scene."

The setting for the fountains was one of considerable magnificence. The length of the upper terrace with its handsome stone balustrade was 1,576 feet, and its width 48 feet. The granite pedestals on either side of the steps leading from the centre transept were 16 feet by 24 feet. The width of the central flight of steps was 96 feet, and this was also the width of the grand central walk.

The lower, or Italianate terrace, along which were ranged the first and top six fountains, was 1,664 feet long between the projecting wings of the building, and 512 feet wide. The total length of the garden front of the wall of this terrace, which was formed with alcoves, was 1,896 feet. The total length of the broad central gravel walk from the building to the end of the garden in a direct line was 2,660 feet.

There is considerable significance in those measurement figures, for it will be observed that they are all multiples or sub-multiples of 8. That exact multiple was strictly adhered to throughout, both in the measurements of the building, much of which was in 24 feet square units, and in the grounds. There, the width and length of the walks, the width and length of the basins of the fountains, the length of terraces and breadth of steps were multiples of 8. This factor of 8, adopted by Paxton, undoubtedly produced a harmony of layout, satisfying in its sense of tranquillity, that is largely lost in the present Crystal Palace park.

There was enchantment in the formal Italian garden, with its basins and fountains and brilliant flowers, the flower-beds cut in the lawns. These flower-beds were truly a Victorian feature which in their day delighted the eye of the beholder, and, indeed, continued to delight the majority until the final loss of the Crystal Palace. Critics, on the other hand, have described Paxton's Italianate garden as *Gardenesque,* a combination of advanced gardening blended with vulgarised aesthetic values. Whether that be the truth or not the Italianate garden reflected accurately the taste of the time.

Below and beyond the lower terrace was the English garden with its winding paths and wealth of shrubs, and the white forms of marble statues. There were the groves and lawns, the green slopes of the park, and still further off, beyond the Palace grounds, an extensive view of rural scenery, cornfields and long hedgerows, the spire of Penge Church, villages half hidden in the trees, and the long line of blue hills to mark the distant horizon.

When on April 20th, 1855, the Emperor of France, Napoleon III, and the Empress Eugénie stepped out upon the balcony in the company of Queen Victoria and the Prince Consort to look at the gardens, they were, it is reported, struck with the splendid panorama of field and woodland. They were also deeply impressed with the acclamation of 20,000 people on the terrace, who cheered with fervour, according to *The Times* report. "What a place for a fête!" exclaimed the Emperor, who was not enjoying the same popularity in France. "It is superb!"

Below the great central fountain were the water temples and cascades, on either side the central walk. The cascades extended for a distance of 600 feet from the water temples, and were 120 feet broad. At the foot of the twin cataracts the water fell 30 feet in a smooth stream into the two great ornamental basins. Each of these basins was 784 feet in length, with a diameter in the semi-circular centre portion of 468 feet.

The water temples were 60 feet in height, and octagonal in shape. The water was forced up the hollow columns to the domed roof whence it spread over the whole surface in a glittering film, and fell over the sides to form a transparent curtain.

A guide book of the day informed the visitor that there were swans, ducks, Muscovy geese and Mandarin ducks swimming on the waters of the great basins and added that "velocipedes for hire are kept in the caverns beneath the waterfall, and they are much favoured by boys out for a holiday."

Chapter Eleven

A Progress of Music

Until the late 1960s, when so many old houses in Norwood were biting the dust, there stood on the north side of Beulah Hill, west of Hermitage Road, a semi-detached villa named Roselawn, not greatly altered in appearance since the early years of the nineteenth century. There lived, from 1821 to 1834 Thomas Attwood, the musical composer, pupil of Mozart and organist of St. Paul's Cathedral, where he is now buried. To that house in Norwood came the composer Felix Mendelssohn-Bartholdy as Attwood's guest in 1829 and again in 1832.

Attwood had been one of the first to recognise Mendelssohn's musical genius when the young composer came to London in the spring of 1829. On his return to London from his tour of Scotland and Wales, Mendelssohn had met with an accident, being "thrown out of a cabriolet and very severely wounded in the leg". The injury kept him two months in London. It was while tied to his lodgings that he received a generous hamper from Thomas Attwood, whom at that time he had never met.

"On top were splendid flowers which are now smelling deliciously round my fireside; under the flowers lay a large pheasant; under the pheasant a quantity of apples and pies."

As soon as he was sufficiently convalescent, Mendelssohn was invited to come out to Norwood to be Attwood's guest at his house.

"I must above all things describe the place", wrote Mendelssohn with studious thoroughness. "This is Norwood, famous for its good air, for it lies on a hill as high as the cross of St. Paul's – so say the Londoners – and I am writing late at night in my little room with the wind howling wildly outside my window, whilst the chimney fire burns very quietly.

"I have had a walk of two miles today, and the air has really had a very salutary effect on me; in the three days that I have been here I can feel how much stronger and healthier I have become."

At the time of this visit, Mendelssohn was 21 and Attwood 64. Attwood lived there with his wife and daughter. A stable attached to the villa housed a white donkey, an essential member of the Attwood menage. The animal was thus described:

"In Norwood lives one of the most distinguished donkeys that ever ate thistles – but he lives entirely on corn! A plump, milk-white animal, full of vivacity and talent, appointed to draw a very diminutive four-wheeled vehicle. In the said vehicle sat Felix, who by and by got out of his carriage and walked with us; and a caravan, consisting of one lady, four young men, the vehicle with the milk-white donkey and three dogs, moved placidly up the hill and into the village."

There is a musical composition by Mendelssohn entitled *The Evening Bell*. It bears the date "Norwood, Surrey, November 1829", and is a little piece for harp and pianoforte. The circumstances surrounding the composition are that a large party of friends had been to Roselawn to meet Mendelssohn, who had to return to London that night. He was in high spirits, and had been extemporising on the piano in his best manner, accompanied on the harp by Attwood's daughter. While the music was in progress a ring was heard on the gate bell. It was the coachman announcing the arrival of the carriage that was to carry him back to London. The summons was unheeded. It was repeated again and again, till at last Mendelssohn reluctantly dragged himself away from his friends.

Back in his lodgings in London, and before going to bed, he sat down and composed the piece, and next day sent it to

Attwood and his daughter with a dedication in his own hand-writing. The melody of *The Evening Bell* is frequently interrupted by the gate bell note (A) – an affectionate echo of that musical evening on Beulah Hill.

Mendelssohn's *E Minor Cappricio* (*op. 16*) is likewise dated Norwood, Surrey, November 18, 1829, though the music was actually composed in Wales.

In the spring of 1832 Mendelssohn was once more under Attwood's roof. He had gone there for a few days' rest and to collect his thoughts after hearing of the death of his old master, Zelter, the intimate friend and correspondent of Goethe. All was the same as before at Norwood, except that he could now smell the lilac, enjoy the apple blossom, and perform his gymnastics in the garden.

It was on this second visit that he composed part of *Son and a Stranger,* while a lasting memorial of Mendelssohn's friendship for Attwood is furnished in the dedication of *Three Preludes and Fugues for the Organ* (*op. 37*) to his Norwood friend.

While Mendelssohn was staying on Beulah Hill, a note was sent by Attwood to Vincent Novello at 67 Frith Street, Soho.

"Sunday, May 27, 8 o'clock

Dear Novello, Mendelssohn has just received some MSS of Sebastian Bach, which he proposes trying this morning. Hope you will meet him at 11 o'clock, Yrs Truly, Thos. Attwood."

When in the late 1960s Roselawn fell to the picks of the harbingers of suburban progress, the "A" bell, which to the end rang with a true "A" note, was duly salvaged to be retained as a wistful echo of those distant days.

In 1855, Mr. Willert Beale, a partner in the firm of Cramer & Co., had the object in view of organising the New Philharmonic Society to establish concerts which should be heard at moderate prices. To find a hall big enough, in which performances with band and chorus on a large scale could be given with due effect to a large audience, was a first essential.

The new Crystal Palace building at Norwood seemed to Beale a likely place, and he went to inspect it. The centre transept was a vast, empty expanse, the corners occupied by palm trees and other gigantic tropical plants. There was no organ then; that was yet to come. The temporary orchestra, which had been erected for the Royal Inauguration on 10th June of the previous year, had been dismantled after the opening ceremony.

Beale at once saw the possibilities for music being presented at the Crystal Palace on a large scale. He was given a letter of introduction to Sir Joseph Paxton, who was living at Rockhills, which was contiguous with the Palace grounds at the junction of Crystal Palace Parade and West Hill (now Westwood Hill).

He was received cordially by Paxton. Beale spoke flatteringly of the beauties and attractions to be found in the Palace. He then expressed the opinion that for continued public support other amusements would have to be offered.

Paxton disagreed, and said that in his view the gardens and fountains, the various Fine Arts Courts and wealth of statuary, the objects of art and the department of tropical horticulture were sufficient to keep the Crystal Palace permanently attractive to a paying public.

"It would be ignoring the experience of the past", he said, "were we to arrive at any other conclusion."

"There is one art", Beale replied, "which I venture to think has been strangely neglected in your arrangements hitherto."

"And what may that be?", Paxton asked with a touch of impatience.

"Music."

"Music!", exclaimed Sir Joseph. "Have we not Mr. Schallehen's band in the Music Court?"

That was so. Herr Schallehen was the first Musical Director of the Crystal Palace. He had been a Prussian army bandmaster, but otherwise without distinction. It was said that he was now at the Crystal Palace because a member of the Royal Family had suggested him. He had put together an extraordinary band, consisting of 62 brass, 1 piccolo, and 2 E-flat clarinets.

Beale explained his idea of making the central transept available for the performance of orchestral music on a large scale.

"Never with my consent", said Paxton curtly. "Never shall this place be turned into a bear-garden such as it would become were we to have more music in it than there is at present."

On that unsatisfactory note the interview ended. However, Beale was not to be put off so lightly. He called on Mr. Farquhar, Chairman of the Crystal Palace Company, at his city office. Mr. Farquhar liked the idea and promised to put the matter before the board. Beale himself then immediately circulated all the Directors of the Company with details of his plan for popular music on a large scale. Scott Russell, the engineer, and one of the Directors, immediately invited Beale to meet him in the central transept to discuss the idea. At the end of the meeting Scott Russell said enthusiastically, "If I pay for it myself, the experiment shall be made."

It was indeed owing to Scott Russell's determined support that the first concert was given on June 4th, 1855. A distinguished cast of singers and instrumentalists were engaged, which included Madame Alboni, the then leading contralto, Herr Ernst (violin), and Mr. Charles Hallé (pianoforte).

Alboni, however, became so alarmed when she inspected the great emptiness of the transept the day before the concert that she went home and took to her bed. A medical certificate was sent to explain why she could not sing. She was, fortunately, replaced by Madame Amadei, a contralto in voice and appearance remarkably like Alboni, and the public received her with applause. The occasion was a pianoforte concert, and not a performance with band and chorus such as Beale had proposed. Nevertheless, the receipts were very good and the Directors were well satisfied with the experiment.

A second concert was given, and this time Alboni was quite ready to sing. Other concerts followed, held in the north, or tropical, end of the Palace.

The musical fame that was to come to the Crystal Palace, and to establish it as the leading musical centre in England, owed much to two men. They were George Grove, the Crystal Palace's first Secretary, and August Manns, who became the Musical Director. They were men of remarkable character and integrity, and they developed a partnership and understanding in the quality of musical programmes that was second to none.

George Grove, an engineer by profession, had become Secretary to the Society of Arts in 1850, in succession to Scott Russell. He then became Secretary to the Crystal Palace at Norwood in 1852, and he and his wife came to live in their new house, Church Meadow, Sydenham. For the rest of his days, Grove lived at Sydenham, becoming the centre of an artistic coterie, and remained devoted to the musical progress of the Crystal Palace.

August Manns, like Schallehen, had been a Prussian army bandmaster. For eight years he had been in Herr von Roon's Regiment, having previously conducted at Kroll's Winter Gardens in Berlin. In the spring of 1854 Manns resigned from the regiment. Schallehen then engaged him on 1st May, 1854, at a salary of £3 a week, as sub-conductor to his Crystal Palace band. This was in addition to his playing E-flat clarinet in the band, conducting for Schallehen at rehearsals and performances as often as it pleased him and composing music for the band.

Such an arrangement was not to last long. A grand fête was arranged for September to celebrate the Anglo-Franco-Turkish alliance, and Schallehen instructed Manns to compose a quadrille on the national airs of the three countries for the pianoforte and band parts.

Proof sheets of the printed music for the piano announced "The Royal Alliance Quadrille: Composed by Henry Schallehen". August Manns realised that, because of his contract, he could not object to Schallehen's name appearing as author, but when he learned that Schallehen had received £50 for the copyright of the arrangement, Manns was indignant. He felt himself entitled to the £50, seeing that his salary was £3 a week, while Schallehen's was £600 per annum. He protested. Schallehen replied coolly that he was the owner of all such work that Manns did for the Crystal Palace band, and that his services were no longer required.

Manns was thus dismissed. In reply, he wrote a letter to *The Musical Times,* giving in full the details of his treatment. The letter was published; furthermore, *The Musical World* made a positive response in its editorial columns to this appeal by an unknown foreign musician. Outlining the whole situation, James W. Davidson, the eminent editor and musical critic, said: "There is but one step to take, and we trust the Directors will take that step. It is to restore Herr Manns to his place in the orchestra and to discharge the man who, without talent and character, acts the part of tyrant over the unfortunate men who are his superiors in everything but salary."

Schallehen in reply produced his contract, showing the clause in which the work of his subordinates' brains went to him. Unabashed, he held on to his pound of flesh.

This unsavoury incident did not pass unnoticed by the Directors of the Crystal Palace Company, and particularly by George Grove. He was shocked at the treatment meted out to Manns; he was aware, too, of the discredit it brought on the management.

Grove made it his business to keep in touch with Manns, who had taken up an engagement in Amsterdam, and was able to assure him that his complete reinstatement was only a matter of time.

He was as good as his word. By the middle of October 1855, Manns was back at the Crystal Palace with the appointment of conductor of the band. Schallehen had gone.

In an article he wrote for the *Dictionary of Music,* Grove said: "The music at the Crystal Palace was at that time in a very inchoate condition. The band was still a wind band, and the open centre transept was the only place for its performance. Under the efforts of the new conductor things began to mend. He conducted a Saturday Concert in the Bohemian Glass Court the week after his arrival. Through the enlightened liberality of the Directors, the band was changed to a full orchestra, a better spot was found for the music . . . and the famous Saturday Concerts began."

On August Manns' appointment, *The Musical World* offered its felicitations. "Herr Manns has a capital opportunity of distinguishing himself. His resources are sufficient to constitute one of the finest bands in the kingdom . . . . Herr Manns is too intelligent a musician not to appreciate the nature of his resources and the requirements of the public. It may be safely predicted that the music at the Crystal Palace will be one of its principal attractions within a short time after the instalment of the new director."

It was not long before Manns, with the strong backing of Grove, persuaded the Palace Directors to convert the brass band into a Symphony orchestra with 16 first violins, 14 second violins, 11 violas, 10 'cellos, 10 double-basses, and woodwind and brass instruments. Programmes were adjusted, and Manns began slowly but surely to educate his audiences to an appreciation and understanding of the great masters of music, and to bring before them the works, not before heard in England, of composers like Schumann and Schubert.

Many years afterwards, in generous recognition of August Manns, Grove said: "The great glory of the Crystal Palace music is the perfection in which it is played. There is no doubt that we play many of the greater works better than they do anywhere else in England . . . . And to what is this due? To the devotion and enthusiasm, the steady, indefatigable labour of my friend Mr. Manns. Possibly no one but myself is in the position to know really how very hard he has worked, and how much he has done behind the scenes to ensure the success of the performances that do him such infinite credit."

August Manns was almost alone in enlightened musical appreciation in those days of 1856. In April of that year a selection from Wagner's *Tannhauser* was performed at the Palace. In his memoir on Manns, H. Saxe Wyndham records that the score from which it was played by the Crystal Palace orchestra had been stealthily copied by Manns from a full-score of the opera brought by a young Polish Count to Posen in 1848, where the Prussian Infantry Regiment No. 5 (in the band of which Manns was first clarinet) had its garrison. Those excerpts from *Tannhauser* played at the Palace comprised the beginning, end, and some of the Venusberg music of the overture, Tannhauser's pilgrimage, the *Festive Tournament March,* Wolfram's

Evening Star song, and other selections. Manns conducted the first performance from the actual scores copied by him during the space of three days and three nights when the full-score was lent to him.

In those musically Philistine days, and with prejudiced music critics, it took the combined efforts of Grove and Manns to present on March 15th, 1856 the *D Minor Symphony* of Schumann. The critical world was uncompromisingly hostile to the cause of Schumann. Manns' sympathies for Wagner met with so little encouragement that works like *Die Meistersingers* overture had to be avoided. The only exception to this was the *Tannhauser* selection.

Manns was very much a voice crying in the wilderness, and he was continually urged to avoid the works of unknown and unappreciated composers, which meant almost anybody other than Handel, Haydn, Mozart, Beethoven, and Mendelssohn. Schubert and Schumann were particularly to be avoided. Then the score of Schubert's *C Major Symphony* came into his hands. Manns himself had never heard the *C Major Symphony* until he performed it in the rehearsal room. Then he eagerly sought out George Grove and urged him to come and listen to it. Grove came, though convinced in advance that the work would never receive the approval of a Crystal Palace audience. But when he heard it played, the effect on Grove was profound, and it was then that his love and enthusiasm for Schubert's genius sprang to life and led him into active research into Schubert's compositions.

Manns afterwards wrote: "I have reason to believe that my performance of the *C Major Symphony* in 1856 was the first in England, although I remember hearing one of the members of my then very small band speak of a rehearsal of it under the late Dr. Wylde, when at the close of the first movement, the principal horn called out to one of the violins, 'Tom, have you been able to discover a tune yet?' 'I have *not*', was Tom's reply. I quote these remarks made by two of the foremost artistes in Costa's band (then the only band in England) in order to show how great was the prejudice at that time against any compositions which did not come from the sanctified Haydn, Mozart, Beethoven, and Mendelssohn."

The impact of August Manns at the Crystal Palace was slowly but surely cultivating popular taste. By 1858 the Saturday Concerts were so successful that they were being imitated in London by bold attempts to provide the public with shilling classical music.

Sterndale Bennett in his *Forty Years of Music* wrote: "What a boon the Saturday Concerts were to amateurs who hungered and thirsted after better things than could be found in town . . . . This state of things sufficiently accounted for the Saturday rushes to Sydenham, not only of cultivated amateurs, but of professionals also. All that was great in the London musical world might have been seen at Victoria Station in the winter Saturdays . . . . It was not a company of many opinions, but a band of worshippers having one faith and one soul."

By 1859 the Saturday Concerts had become an institution. Oscar Beringer first appears on the programmes in 1857 as an *infant protigé,* giving daily recitals and playing with the orchestra. This lasted for the best part of nine years.

Queen Marie Amelie, the widow of Louis-Philippe, used frequently to come to the Crystal Palace concerts, when Oscar Beringer was the solo pianist. He said that one day the old Queen sent him by her equerry a purse and a bag of sweets. His personal problem was whether to keep the sweets as a royal souvenir, or eat them. He ate them.

George Grove in his pursuit of music was sitting one evening in the gallery during a Schumann concert at St. James's Hall when he noticed a young man peering through the glass panel of the gallery door.

"Who is that engaging-looking young man?" he enquired of his companion.

"Oh, that's Sullivan", was the reply. "He's just come back from Leipzig." Leipzig was then the most important centre of music in Germany.

Arthur Sullivan was introduced to the Secretary of the Crystal Palace, and out of that meeting a warm and enduring friendship was formed between the two.

While at Leipzig, as the first holder of the Mendelssohn scholarship, Sullivan had composed his *Tempest* music. This he now sent to George Grove. So far, only the work of the greatest composers was being performed at the Crystal Palace. Grove immediately discussed Sullivan's *Tempest* with Manns.

On Saturday April 5th, 1862, the *Tempest* music, composed by a young man of nineteen years of age, was performed at the Crystal Palace. At the end he received an ovation. This first work of an unknown created a great sensation in musical circles; all the critics were at the Palace, and on the Monday Sullivan woke up to find himself famous. The *Tempest* was repeated at the Palace on the following Saturday. The music charmed all those who heard it, including Charles Dickens, who was present at that memorable event. Afterwards he went round to see Sullivan, accompanied by Chorley, *The Times* music critic. Dickens grasped Sullivan's hand and said "I don't pretend to know much about music, but I do know I have been listening to a very great work."

In this way, at the Crystal Palace, was laid the foundation of Arthur Sullivan's musical career, in which George Grove constantly encouraged and helped him. The musical success of the *Tempest* put Sullivan into the best musical circles, which at that time included such great names as Jenny Lind and her husband, Otto Goldschmidt. There was Frederic Clay, who later composed *I'll Sing Thee Songs of Araby, She Wandered Down the Mountain Side* and *The Sands of Dee*, whom Sullivan first met at Grove's house at Sydenham. It was Fred Clay who was to introduce Sullivan to W. S. Gilbert, who together created the world-famous Gilbert and Sullivan operas.

Sullivan took up residence in Sydenham, renting a room over a shop. It was while he was living in Sydenham that he composed his *Sapphire Necklace* music. To help him eke out a livelihood, Grove appointed him Professor of Pianoforte and Ballad Singing at the Crystal Palace School of Art.

He became a constant visitor to the Grove household, and was equally welcomed at the homes of the Scott Russells and the von Glehns. The three families formed the inner coterie of Sydenham society, and all were highly musical. Scott Russell was on the Board of Directors of the Crystal Palace. An engineer by profession, he had been engaged in the building of the ill-starred steamship *Great Eastern*, which had been designed by Isambard Kingdom Brunel. That had been an unhappy association between the two men.

There was something enigmatical about Scott Russell. At times he had secret thoughts of his own; at others he was eager and fulsome, as, for example, when he so whole-heartedly helped Willert Beale introduce concerts into the Palace. Yet he proved to be no friend to Arthur Sullivan. Sullivan was to fall deeply in love with one of Scott Russell's daughters. This was reciprocated; later, there was an unofficial engagement. It never got beyond that because Scott Russell did not approve of his daughter being affianced to a musician. They were forbidden to be more than friends, in the traditional Victorian manner. Nor was there a Victorian elopement in reply. Scott Russell's daughter remained obedient to her father, and the engagement was broken off. Sullivan never married.

Sullivan's *Tempest* music had put the young composer on a pinnacle, but many queried his lasting qualities. Then his *Symphony in E Flat* was produced at the Crystal Palace in 1866. The quality of the work fully converted those who had doubted his durability. The concert, under August Manns' conductorship, consisted mainly of excerpts from Sullivan's works, with his *Symphony in E Flat* as the *pièce de résistance*. Jenny Lind, popularly styled the Swedish Nightingale because of her exquisite soprano voice, was on the platform, and drew all London to the Palace, so that more than 3,000 people listened to this first concert of any importance by Sullivan.

Sullivan's old music master, John Goss, wrote to him. "I rejoice that I was at your concert, and that I can heartily congratulate you on all points. It was a great triumph, and that Madame Goldschmidt [Jenny Lind] should have given her help crowned it to perfection."

Jenny Lind possessed what Sullivan declared was the most beautiful voice that he had ever heard. She enslaved London, and between Sullivan and Jenny Lind was formed a friendship broken only by death.

On the afternoon of Sunday December 30th, 1866, a fire broke out at the north end of the Crystal Palace. It occurred at a time when the Palace was empty, except for a watchman, a policeman and an attendant in charge of the aviary and monkey house. At 1.20 in the afternoon all was apparently safe and sound. Before 2 o'clock it was a furnace.

People tried to get into the building, but were unable to do so for nearly an hour. The three men inside had been making ineffectual attempts to put out the fire themselves. When those outside got in they acted vigorously, and with the aid of some loitering navvies, whom they called in to join them, tore up flooring to try to check the advance of the flames, and sent for more massive help.

Captain Shaw, who commanded the London Fire Brigade, sent most of his men on in advance by train. The engines, horse-drawn, came up as quickly as they could, arriving on the Crystal Palace Parade by half past four, and the progress of the fire was halted. The wind, fortunately, was blowing away from the Palace; had it been the other way, nothing could have saved the building. The whole of the Natural History collection, the Alhambra, Byzantine and Assyrian Courts, the Royal apartments, the Library and Printing Offices, and a great deal else were destroyed. Nearly all the monkeys and livestock perished, though one eagle was saved by a man who, risking its beak and talons, carried it to safety under his arm.

The loss was estimated at between two and three hundred thousand pounds. The Palace was grossly under-insured, and all that was recovered on insurance was £20,000. The North End and Transept were never rebuilt, because the money was not there.

Perhaps one of the most dramatic events in the musical history of the Crystal Palace was when George Grove and

Arthur Sullivan, almost on the spur of the moment, went to Vienna in an attempt to locate the lost portions of music of Schubert's *Rosamunde*. Grove's ambition was to complete the *Rosamunde* score, the beauty of which was so impaired by the absence of large portions of it.

Grove, as has been said, first came under the spell of Schubert when Manns rehearsed for the first time the wonderful *C Major Symphony* in April 1856. From then on Grove had set himself to find out all he could about the lost and unknown compositions of Schubert. He had put himself in correspondence with Herr Spina, the great Viennese music publisher, and out of that correspondence were forthcoming further portions of the *Rosamunde* music, and also the *Unfinished Symphony*, which Manns then presented for the first time in Britain at the Crystal Palace.

Grove and Sullivan arrived in Vienna in October 1867. Extracts from Grove's letters to Olga von Glehn at Sydenham convey all the romantic thrill of the quest.

"I must tell you of our extraordinary good fortune since we came to Vienna. It has been quite wonderful; everything has happened to our wish and advantage. Spina the magnificent has behaved like a prince. . . . We have got from him three more pieces of *Rosamunde* music and overture, a *Stabat Mater*, a *Trio for Violin,* etc, all most interesting and some of them first rate (all by Franz Schubert), and he has given me many pieces of printed music, a bust of Schubert, an original letter of Beethoven's, and has behaved in the most charming and kind way. . . .

"Today we went to Spina's house. Spina produces a pile of MS music as big as a portmanteau and says 'Here is all that I have that you wish to see. . . .' First we spend an hour in incoherent raptures, then we . . . begin to go through it thoroughly. Then we take the things we like into the other room, and Arthur plays, and we decide to have, or not to have . . . . Some of them turn out charming, equal to anything of Schubert's or anyone else's, so they have to be played over and over again.

"At last all is examined . . . then Spina comes in for a final talk and we play him about 10 of the best of the things, and he has raptures and pats Arthur on the shoulder, and says how much gratified he would be to hear something of *his*, on which Arthur plays some *Day Dreams*, and Spina embraces him."

But they had as yet failed to locate the chief object of their journey – the principal lost portions of *Rosamunde*. Neither Spina, nor Dr. Schneider, a relative of Schubert's, had been able to complete their quest for them. On a previous visit to Dr. Schneider they had succeeded in getting two Symphonies and an Overture, but no *Rosamunde*.

Grove and Sullivan paid a last visit to Dr. Schneider to bid him farewell before leaving Vienna. "The doctor was civility itself, he again had recourse to the cupboard and showed us some treasures which had escaped us before. I again turned the conversation to the *Rosamunde* music. . . . Might I go into the cupboard and look for myself? Certainly, if I had no objection to being smothered with dust. In I went, and after some search, during which my companion kept the doctor engaged in conversation, I found at the bottom of the cupboard, and in its furthest corner, a bundle of music books two feet high, carefully tied round, and black with the undisturbed dust of nearly half a century. . . . When we had dragged out the bundle into the light, [we] found that was actually neither more nor less than what we were in search of."

They had found the part-books of the whole of the music of *Rosamunde*, tied up after the second performance in Vienna in December 1823. They sat up till 2 o'clock in the morning copying the missing parts.

On March 28th, 1868, the long-missing folios of the *Rosamunde* were performed for the first time before an English audience at the Crystal Palace.

Professor Ebenezer Prout, at that time one of the professors in the Crystal Palace School of Art, wrote afterwards: "I well remember the excitement at Sydenham when Grove returned from Vienna bringing back with him the newly discovered music to *Rosamunde* which had been lost for nearly fifty years.

. . . Few who were present at the first performance of the music will have forgotten the immense effect made by the two *Entr'actes* and the lovely *Ballet-air in G Minor*. Schubert's great *Symphony in C* was a *cheval de bataille* with Manns. I have never heard such splendid performance of that work as under him. Hardly less fine was his reading of the *Unfinished Symphony in B Minor,* which he was the first to bring to a hearing in England."

Prout's regard for Manns was of the highest. "Manns devoted his energies to the Saturday Concerts which obtained a reputation second to that of no concerts in Europe for the performance of the highest-class orchestral music. . . . I do not believe that during the many years over which the concerts extended any piece was ever presented with insufficient rehearsal. The Crystal Palace Orchestra thus gained a reputation for highly finished performances."

Those were the golden years of the Crystal Palace as a centre of music, and Grove and Manns worked together as an inspired team. *The Times* music critic wrote that the 1866-67 season had been the most brilliant ever known at the Crystal Palace – "a succession of orchestral performances without parallel in this country, and unsurpassed in any other. Never in England . . . have the symphonies of Beethoven been performed as under the direction of Herr Manns at the Crystal Palace."

Sterndale Bennett in his *Forty Years of Music* wrote of "the vogue of Schubert in 1867-68, when work after work unheard of before in this country was produced at the Crystal Palace with loving care, and received with fervent admiration. . . . It seemed to us that the shining glass-house at Sydenham had become the temple of a new and gracious gospel. . . . At this time, and for many years after, the Crystal Palace Concerts flourished as though nothing could extinguish or even dim the 'vital spark' which burned within them. They stood firm as the Pyramids, and we never dreamed for them an evil time."

An outstanding feature of the musical history of the Crystal Palace was the series of Handel Festivals. Those massive orchestral and choral occasions represented the supreme fulfilment of the Victorian love of the biblical theme expressed in oratorio. In that field Handel was supreme.

As the time approached for the centenary of Handel's death, attention was turned to the Central Transept of the Crystal Palace as being the only area of sufficient magnitude to contain the choir and orchestra. It was determined to hold a preliminary festival in 1857, in order to test the building for musical purposes. The arrangements were entirely under the supervision of the Sacred Harmonic Society, and this preliminary performance was styled *The Great Handel Festival.*

The principal vocalists were Madame Clara Novello, Madame Rudersdorff, Miss Dolby, Sims Reeves, Montein Smith, Weiss and Formes. The chorus consisted of 2,000 voices and the band of 386 instrumentalists. A large organ was erected expressly for the occasion. This was the famous Handel organ, said to be one of the finest in the world, and was built by Messrs. Gray and Davidson. With various additions and alterations over the course of years, the organ ultimately consisted of 4,568 speaking tubes.

Michael Costa conducted *The Great Handel Festival,* and the selected pieces were the *Messiah, Judas Maccabaeus* and *Israel in Egypt.* It was a great success, despite certain acoustical defects, and the Centenary Festival was given the go-ahead.

The Gentleman's Magazine for July 1857 reported on the event as follows:

"The 'Handel Festival' at the Crystal Palace has drawn great numbers to Sydenham this week. Fortunately, the weather, though sharpened by the east wind, has been very fine and sunny. The first performance on the 15th drew an audience of 11,129 persons, and afforded a brilliant spectacle. On the 17th, when the Queen and her distinguished guests attended the celebration, the numbers of persons within the Palace, 11,649, did not much exceed that of the first day, but the number outside was much greater. The lanes and woods between Dulwich and the Palace were at an early hour lined and occupied by ranks of well-dressed persons four or five deep, the ladies predominating. Within the Palace, the effect of such a large assemblage of the gentle sex was very striking. Viewed upon the level they looked like a flower-covered prairie; but when seen from a high gallery, they took the form and regularity of a garden, the blocks being all separated by well-marked divisions, allowing free ingress and egress, but each block closely packed with fashionable occupants. The Queen arrived at the Palace a little before one o'clock. With her was the Archduke Maximilian of Austria, Prince Albert, the Princess Royal, and Prince Frederick William of Prussia, the Princess Alice and the Prince of Wales. The reception of her Majesty by the people, followed by the National Anthem, was very stirring. As soon as the audience had settled themselves for the concert, a photograph of the whole scene, with the royal box as a centre, was rapidly taken, and before the first part of the oratorio was over, well-finished copies, framed and glazed, were laid before her Majesty and her guests. It was observed that the Queen beat time with her fan, and Prince Albert with a roll of music. An obstinate demand was made for a repetition of 'See the Conquering Hero Comes.' Mr. Costa hesitated, and looked towards the Queen, who, bending forward, sided with her people against the dictator of the day. Before the Royal Party left Sydenham, Prince Albert conducted the Archduke through the grounds. They were dogged by mobs of visitors. A body of police, acting in military fashion as a corps of observation, moved from place to place, and occupied positions that would have enabled them to interpose between the Princes and the crowd had it been expedient. The Queen did not reach Buckingham Palace on her return until 6 o'clock. On the last day nearly 18,000 persons were present."

The *Commemoration Festival* accordingly took place in the Crystal Palace on 20th, 22nd, and 24th June 1859. It was a greater occasion than the previous festival, the chorus numbering upwards of 2,700 and the band augmented to 460. Costa once more directed. To avoid dispersion of sound, and direct it towards the audience, the sides and back of the orchestra were enclosed with wooden screens and the whole covered with an enormous awning of oiled and hardened canvas. The three performances and a public rehearsal drew 81,319 visitors.

Michael Costa conducted the series of festivals up to and including the *Seventh Triennial Festival* in 1880. Sims Reeves, the great English tenor of those days, was one of the pillars of the Handel Festivals, but in the course of time he was to become a casualty. It was over what became known as "the Battle of the Pitch". Costa had introduced into the Sacred Harmonic Society what was called the Philharmonic Pitch, which was a good half-tone higher than the so-called *diapason normal,* the pitch followed in Germany and France. The Philharmonic Pitch produced an instrumentally brilliant effect, but it proved a severe strain on many trained voices, including Sims Reeves, Charles Santley, and Adelina Patti. Patti, when singing with an Italian orchestra, had the tone lowered to suit her voice.

August Manns, too, supported the demand for the *diapason normal,* though he recognised the enormous expense of lowering the tone of all such instruments as could be lowered, and the replacement of those that could not. Military bands were obviously not interested in changing their instruments, and Costa flatly refused to listen to the demands of singers to accept any reduction of tone to the Sacred Harmonic Society. It was not until 1895 that the leading orchestral society in England, the Philharmonic, set the example by officially lowering its pitch to the *diapason normal,* and others were thereby forced to follow suit. To this day a number of North Country brass bands keep to the brilliant Philharmonic Pitch.

But until 1895 the battle raged. Chorley, the music critic of *The Times,* made a vigorous attack upon the abnormally high pitch in England in comparison with that on the Continent. This drew an approving letter from Sims Reeves, written from his home, Grange Mount, Beulah Spa, Upper Norwood, which stood at the junction of Beulah Hill and Grange Road, his garden backing on to the Spa grounds.

Dated November 10th, 1868, Reeves' letter said: "I read with great interest your comment . . . that it is high time the pitch of our orchestras should be adapted to the normal diapason used in France and Germany. Your complaint is one which I have strenuously, although in vain up to the present, insisted upon. . . .

"So strong is my conviction upon this subject that some time back I intimated to the Committee of the Sacred Harmonic Society my final decision, notwithstanding grave reasons for my coming to a contrary determination, not to sing for that Society so long as the pitch of the orchestra was maintained at its present height and until it was, as you suggest, 'assimilated to the normal diapason of France'."

Sims Reeves took part in the Handel Festival of 1874 at the Palace, but that was to be his last appearance in the great choral gatherings. He declined to sing in the 1877 festival. This was quite a break with tradition. Reeves had sung in the preliminary Handel Festival in 1857 and all subsequent festivals, and his greatest triumphs in sacred music were achieved at the Crystal Palace. His departure was a serious loss.

Another tradition was soon to be broken. The festival of 1880 was to be Costa's last. Two years later the Sacred Harmonic Society was dissolved, with the result that the *Eighth Triennial Festival,* to be held in 1883, devolved on the Crystal Palace, which took the sole management of the great undertaking. Then, on the eve of the festival, Costa suffered a severe stroke, from which he died the following year. He had dominated the Handel Festivals, and with this major emergency it seemed that the festival would collapse.

It was said that no one could replace Costa. Then August Manns stepped into the breach and took over the control of the gigantic event. He met with resistance. Some of the older members of the chorus showed definite signs of mutiny at any departure by Manns from the Costa tradition, but Manns with his unruffled, urbane manner was able to show that he knew as much about the Handel Festival as Costa. Manns had been present at every rehearsal since 1857, and in some respects he could have given Costa some useful pointers.

In terms of financial receipts, the 1883 festival broke all records. It was unanimously agreed that the performance surpassed all previous efforts, and attained an artistic finish never before approached. The 4,000 singers picked from all parts of the kingdom, and the 440 instrumentalists formed, as one critic put it, "the greatest musical machine of all time". The attendance was a record, totalling 87,784 persons.

Manns conducted the festivals up to and including that held in 1900. Then he handed the baton over to Frederic Cowen for the *Seventeenth Handel Festival,* at which Edward VII and Queen Alexandra gave their patronage for the first time.

During those strenuous years, Manns conducted the Saturday Concerts with unabated zeal. The Crystal Palace shone in South London like a bright star. Dr. Campbell, the blind Founder and Principal of the Royal Normal College for the Blind, chose Norwood for its setting because of the close proximity of the Crystal Palace and its musical reputation. The College was founded in 1872. Blind himself, Francis Joseph Campbell's aim was to give his pupils the highest possible education, not only in music – which came first – but in every field of scholastic work, so that they might meet their sighted fellow-beings on equal terms.

Dr. Campbell was given letters of introduction to George Grove and August Manns. When he met Manns, Campbell said that he had chosen Norwood so as to be close to the best musical centre. That to him was of essential importance. He now asked if his blind pupils could be allowed free entrance to the concerts.

"Not only all concerts," replied Manns, "but to all rehearsals as well."

Manns in his turn visited the Royal Normal College, situated on the west side of Westow Street. It had begun with a few pupils in two small houses in Paxton Terrace. The Mount on Westow Street was the first real property purchased. Manns became a valued friend of the blind students. He also became one of the examiners of the College.

The Saturday Concerts at the Palace proved themselves an important feature in the musical education of the students at the Normal College. Alfred Hollins, the blind musician, who became outstanding as a master of the organ, and also had considerable ability as a composer, was a distinguished pupil at the College on Westow Street at the time of Dr. Campbell.

"What an unspeakable boon those concerts were to us blind music students no sighted musician can imagine. It was through them that I learned to know and appreciate practically all the classics; they were my opportunity of hearing for the first time compositions which are now firmly established, and come to me over the wireless as familiar works, first heard at the Palace half a century ago, although often new to my friends."

When Alfred Hollins first went to the College in 1878 it consisted of three buildings; a house called The Mount, the house in which Dr. Campbell lived, and the main college building. The extensive grounds were laid out in terraces, so constructed that the blind students could walk freely in them, and a large meadow. The Normal College lay behind a belt of trees and a handsome brick wall that flanked Westow Street on the west side, the extent of which is now occupied by a car park. The grounds at the back occupied the area now called College Green. The main building was a four storey structure, specially designed for college purposes, with a great hall large enough to hold 500 people comfortably. In the hall was an organ, a large platform at one end and a gallery at the other. In his autobiography, *A Blind Musician Looks Back,* Alfred Hollins recalls that "annually, for many years in succession, a Christmas tree was given by the Archbishop of Canterbury – to be unveiled by a lady of high rank, such as the Princess Frederica of Hanover." Her father, the late King of Hanover, had been blind, and had found great solace in music.

Soon after Hollins came to the Normal College, Mr. A. J. Eyre, who composed *Service in E Flat,* was appointed organist at the Crystal Palace. There were two organs in the Palace, the great Handel organ in the centre transept, and a small three-manual organ, built by Walker, in the concert room. Hollins made himself acquainted with Eyre, and asked to be allowed to examine the great organ.

Eyre was very kind, and invited Hollins to explore the organ. "I stood at the treble end of the console, and for the first time felt those huge draw-stop knobs on their slanting jambs", Hollins wrote afterwards. "There were seventy-seven altogether." Eyre made Hollins gasp with astonishment by asking him to play the Handel organ. "I chose one of Bach's fugues, which did not require any changing of stops. Eyre was very pleased. So, it would seem, were the audience.

"At a later date, when I was preparing to give one of the afternoon recitals, I used to go to the Palace at six in the morning to practise. To be in that enormous building when everything was quiet except for the squealing of the parrots was an eerie experience. I felt the same thing when I practised in the Albert Hall, and again in some of the big auditoriums in America – a kind of deafening sensation, very difficult to explain."

Over the years August Manns conducted the Saturday Concerts with continued artistic success. Many brilliant composers attended what had become a Mecca of music. On March 22nd, 1884, Dvorak visited the Palace and conducted some of his works in person. In 1886, the Abbé Liszt stayed at Westwood House, Sydenham, near the Crystal Palace. There were two concerts during the visit, and Manns arranged that they should be devoted entirely to Liszt's works. Liszt himself was present at the concerts, and at the rehearsals as well. The concerts were magnificent, and Liszt was enthusiastic. "I did not know till today", he exclaimed rapturously, "that I had written such beautiful music."

It was reported in *The Musical Times* that from his place in the front row of seats immediately beneath the conductor's desk, Liszt more than once rose to shake Manns cordially by the hand and to bow to the audience, whose applause and cheers reverberated throughout the enclosed area.

Before returning home, Liszt was in the concert room to hear his *St. Elizabeth* produced under the conductorship of Dr. Mackenzie. The composer fell asleep while listening to his own music!

The anecdotes are endless, and they come back like whispers from another age, of the aura that surrounded the Crystal

Palace in those vanished days. The curate of that time at St. Bartholomew's Sydenham, the Revd. A. T. Davidson, has left behind a lively description of the visitors who called on George Grove in his lovely timbered house at Sydenham: "There were distinguished people of all kinds, travellers connected with the Palestine Exploration, a musician or two, and friends who had come to dine after the afternoon's Concert at the Crystal Palace. There were endless stories and endless jokes . . . till at length came eleven o'clock – what might be described as 'closing time' on Saturday evenings at Lower Sydenham – when Londoners had to leave in order to catch the 11.22 train to Victoria.

"Many were the distinguished people I met – Arthur Sullivan, John Hullah, Henry Leslie, Joachim, L. Straus, Stockhauser, Gounod, Ferdinand Hiller, W. H. Lecky, F. W. Myers, Holman Hunt."

In April 1895 there was printed and published at the Crystal Palace a catalogue of the principal instrumental and choral works performed by the Saturday Concerts from October 1855 to May 1895 – a period of 40 years. The total number of compositions performed was 1,550, of which 195 were symphonies, suites, etc. The total number of overtures, marches, entr'actes and detailed orchestral works was 585. Concertos, masses, cantatas and other choral works, 194. The works of 300 composers were produced.

On April 12th, 1895 a concert took place celebrating the 33rd anniversary of the second performance of the *Tempest* music at the Palace. Arthur Sullivan wrote to Manns from Paris. "How much do I not owe to you, my dear old friend, for the helping hand you gave me to mount the first step of the ladder! I shall always think of you with gratitude and affection – Ever yours sincerely, Arthur Sullivan."

A remarkable concert took place in October 1895. It was devoted solely to works by British composers who had made their first appearance at the Saturday concerts. They included Sullivan, Parry, Mackenzie and Stafford.

The golden heart of Manns was never more clearly evinced than when Joseph Holbrooke composed and orchestrated *The Raven.* He was advised to send it to Manns. Manns immediately invited Holbrooke to come and see him at his house in Harold Road, Upper Norwood. Holbrooke could not accept the invitation as he was playing a piano in a provincial pantomime. Then, later, he was unexpectedly in London. He was practically penniless at the time, but was able to get to Norwood to see Manns who invited him to lunch. "It was the best meal I had eaten for weeks", said Holbrooke afterwards.

Manns told Holbrooke that he proposed presenting *The Raven* at one of the Saturday Concerts. Holbrooke had to confess that he could not accept the offer as he could not pay for the orchestral parts. Manns' reply to this was to have all the parts copied at his own expense. It was not the first time he had done that. *The Raven* was duly produced under Manns' conductorship.

"I sat in front," said Holbrooke afterwards, "in a world of amazement, listening to my own music, which I heard *for the first time,* if I exclude the attendance at rehearsals. The effect it produced on me is indescribable. I defy the most bloated genius to describe his soul in torment or ecstasy!" At the conclusion of the performance the applause was very slight, but persistent, and did not stop until Holbrooke went on to bow, making, as one of the critics remarked, "a raven-like spectacle in very *outré* clothes." "If that writer had only known the reason for this", said Holbrooke later. "I had no money to buy white collars, or pay for the washing of them, so I had to wear a muffler round my neck, and my shoes were very bad."

Arthur Sullivan died in 1900, at the age of 58. He and George Grove had both been knighted in 1883 for the services they had rendered to the Art of Music in England. Sullivan's close link with the Crystal Palace was honoured by an In Memoriam concert on December 8th, 1900. It was conducted by August Manns. The programme included the *In Memoriam Overture,* selections from the *Festival Te Deum,* the *Martyr of*

Antioch, the *Golden Legend,* the *Tempest* music, the *Merchant of Venice* music, and *Oh hush thee, my babe.*

George Grove had died the previous May. With the exception of August Manns, he had outlived his contemporaries who had been at the opening of the Crystal Palace on that memorable June 10th, 1854.

There appeared in the *Oxford Magazine* of May 13th, 1903, the following:

"The Honorary Doctorate of Music was yesterday conferred on Mr. August Manns. . . . In his tenure, lasting over forty years, of the Directorship of Music at the Crystal Palace, Mr. Manns carried on with unceasing enthusiasm a nobly artistic work, the influence of which on music in England is beyond all calculation. All these years daily concerts were given at which the entire literature of great orchestral music was played over and over again; and during the bulk of this time there was literally hardly any orchestral music worth mentioning to be heard in England outside Sydenham. The full band of the Saturday Concerts was famous throughout Europe. Mr. Manns first taught us to know Schubert and Schumann and many others, and, though a foreigner himself, had always the warmest welcome for British music. The star of the Crystal Palace began to wane when London concert-givers entered into the results of Mr. Manns' single-handed labours, and a new management with no love of art in its soul maimed, and finally dismissed, the superb band. Mr. Manns has never sought official distinction . . . so we rejoice, even though tardily, Oxford has done all that lay in its power to show its appreciation of a great life work, which is one of the landmarks in the history of English art."

Though he had constantly eschewed public honour, in the King's Birthday Honours List August Manns was the recipient of a Knighthood. This was made possible because he had only lately become a naturalised Englishman. That same day the pupils of the Royal Normal College for the Blind came to August Manns' house in Harold Road and there serenaded him. There were letters of congratulation from Elgar, Sir

Herbert Parry, Sir Alexander Mackensie, Joachim, William Wallace, Prout, Fritz Hartvigson, and many more.

Sir August Manns made a speech to the Whitefriars Club on January 29th, 1904. In it he said: "When I began my work in 1855 at the Crystal Palace, I could scarcely find half a dozen English composers whose works were suitable for the Crystal Palace Saturday Concerts. The catalogue of music performed at those concerts since 1855 contains the names of 343 composers, of whom no fewer than 103 were born and trained in England. First-class performances of choral and orchestral concerts are now successfully established throughout Great Britain."

That was the proud epitaph of the musical splendour of the Crystal Palace, for truly the Crystal Palace led the way, and the rest followed.

Manns' last occasion at the conductor's desk was on 11th June, 1904, at the Crystal Palace Jubilee. Mendelssohn's *Hymn of Praise* was performed.

On March 1st, 1907, August Manns died at White Lodge on Beulah Hill, the house into which he had moved the year before, and his passing marked the end of the golden age of Crystal Palace music.

26. The Beulah Spa; a fashionable resort in the 1830s.

27. The Beulah Spa. It was proposed that a Georgian crescent should overlook the Spa, but this ambitious scheme only remained a dream.

28. Claude Grahame-White in his Farman biplane, making a demonstration flight at the Crystal Palace, June 1910.

29. The Army airship, *Nulli Secundus*, made its flight from Farnborough to London and then to the Crystal Palace in 1907.

30. E. T. Willows' airship at the Crystal Palace, 1910.

31. 1868. The first aeronautical exhibition, held at the Palace. On display were aeroplanes and helicopters.

32. Grove's house at Sydenham; the rendezvous of the famous.
33. George Grove, first Secretary of the Crystal Palace.

34. The Crystal Palace from Anerley Station, 1854. The towers had yet to be built. Part of old canal is seen in the foreground.

35. The High Level Station linked the Crystal Palace with the City and West-End. The line was closed in 1954 and the station demolished.

36. The railway fly-over at South Norwood, 1845. It carried the atmospheric line over the steam line to Brighton. It was the first railway fly-over in the world.

37. Forest Hill Station, Atmospheric Railway period, 1845.

38. Margaret Finch, the Norwood Gypsy Queen. Famed as a fortune-teller; the local publicans paid for her funeral.

39. The Gypsy House, Norwood, 1808. Home of the Gypsy Queen.

40. All Saints Church and School, Upper Norwood, 1862.

41. The school-house. It was pulled down in 1972. Architect, James Savage.

42. The Jolly Sailor, 1815. It backed onto the Croydon Canal.

43. Roselawn, Beulah Hill. Felix Mendelssohn stayed there.

44. Balloon ascents by Professor Glaisher and Coxwell.

45. Poster advertising the Health Suburb, 1900.
46. Balloon posters – Beulah Spa and Crystal Palace.

47. Centre-piece of the Crystal Palace – the great Handel organ. One of the finest in England, it was destroyed in 1936.

48. The Crystal Palace was all things to all people. Skipping could be performed with an automatic skipping rope.

49. 1909. Local 'Terriers' at the Crystal Palace. Brock's fireworks and John M. East's theatrical flair simulated all the thrills of aerial attack.

50. The author's home, The Sycamores, Beulah Hill. The house today is much as it was in the 1860 photograph. Built in 1690, the house was enlarged in 1780.

51. November 30th, 1936. The 82-year-old Crystal Palace was destroyed by fire.

52. An aerial view of the desolation where the Palace had stood.

53. Architect's drawing of Little Menlo, Beulah Hill. Once the home of Colonel Gouraud, English agent for Thomas Edison. The first perfected phonograph was demonstrated there before a distinguished audience.

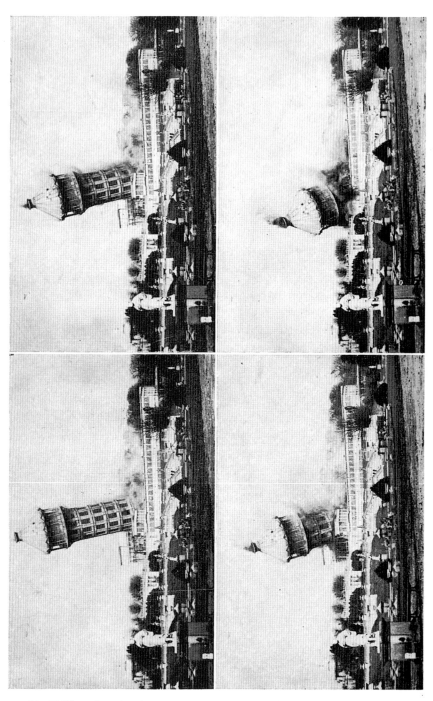

54. Felling the North Tower in 1942. The South Tower had been taken down piece by piece so as not to endanger property. The towers had been designed by Isambard Kingdom Brunel to supply water to the fountains.

Chapter Twelve

Balloons at the Palace

Ballooning displays by professional aeronauts was one of the popular entertainments from the first years of the nineteenth century. Ascents were made from all the Metropolitan gardens, such as Cremorne, Vauxhall, Pentonville, Surrey Zoological, the New Globe Pleasure Grounds, Mile End, and the Beulah Spa. Charles Green was one of the great veteran balloonists of the eighteen-thirties. He made a spectacular voyage across the Channel in his Vauxhall balloon, landing at Nassau in Germany. The result of this was a balloon fever.

The pastime could not be described as being particularly intellectual, having about it the style of a circus performance. Nor, for that matter, were the professional aeronauts particularly intellectual men. Their research into matters aeronautical was mostly limited to obtaining maximum financial reward and publicity for their outlay and skill. To the public the spectacle was one of colourful daring, visible evidence that man was reaching for the stars. One awe-struck woman cried as she watched an ascent, "They're going straight up to heaven!" Another, writing to a friend about a balloon voyage she had recently made, said, "the idea that I was daring enough to push myself, as I might say, before my time, into the presence of the Deity, inclines me to a species of terror."

A young man named Henry Coxwell became an enthusiastic balloonist. In 1849 he gave ballooning demonstrations on the continent, and had the distinction, when the wind was carrying him from Hamburg towards Keil, of being shot at by soldiers in the belief that he was a Danish spy. When he landed he found bullet holes in the envelope of the balloon.

By 1852 Charles Green was gradually relinquishing aeronautical duties. West-end gardens, as well as those in the East-end of London, were now all eager to secure the professional services of the enterprising Henry Coxwell. In due time Coxwell's services were sought by the Crystal Palace Company, to establish ballooning in the Palace grounds.

Coxwell wrote afterwards: "I had been asked for some time to do what I could in this way, and began to make inquiry as to the facilities for inflations. Fortunately a friend of mine, Mr. Magnis Ohren, Secretary of the gas works at Sydenham, took a lively interest in the proposal, and was well qualified in this respect, as he had officiated and simplified matters in Hamburg, when I took up Prince Paul Esterhazy. His assistance materially simplified this matter, in which there were certain difficulties to surmount, and also unavoidable expenses to be incurred on the part of the General Manager of the Crystal Palace."

The expenses referred to concerned the cost of laying gas pipes of adequate diameter from the Sydenham gas works to the point of inflation, and for a time the directors were reluctant to outlay so much money. Meanwhile, the refreshment caterer, who was about to have a benefit at the Crystal Palace, thought it would add to the popularity of the occasion if he were to make an ascent in a small balloon, borrowed from the Cremorne Gardens.

The Cremorne aeronaut, Mr. Lythgoe, visited the Palace to find out what could be ·done by using existing gas pipes of small diameter. He succeeded in inflating the balloon and making a successful ascent. This opened the way for the introduction of larger balloons, and the General Manager of the Crystal Palace was not slow to press home the advantage. Adequate pipes for the job were laid from the Sydenham gas works to the balloon ground, which was sited not far from the

North Tower. Henry Coxwell made his first Crystal Palace ascent in the year 1859.

Such ascents became very popular at the Crystal Palace. Passengers were usually taken up to 2,000 feet to enjoy the view and see the Palace and grounds laid out below them. High ascents were uncommon, and little was known about the speed and direction of upper air currents.

Considerable impetus was given to the subject of ballooning following a meeting of the Committee of the British Association. The committee had been experimenting with Lythgoe's Cremorne balloon, the purpose being to make meteorological observations at a great elevation, if that could be achieved. The balloon, however, proved itself incapable of attaining the desired height, the envelope being old and porous, so that the gas leaked away.

Coxwell expressed the opinion that a balloon should be specially built for the purpose, with adequate internal capacity and general construction to make possible the scientific requirements of the British Association. There would be no time to build such a stupendous envelope out of silk; that would have taken six months to manufacture, and would cost at least £2,000. Coxwell proposed using a kind of American cloth, a material possessing great strength. The envelope when inflated would be 80 feet high, with a diameter of over 50 feet, and a cubic capacity of 93,000 feet.

The enterprising aeronaut thereupon made the balloon at his own expense. He then stated through the medium of a local newspaper that he was able to provide the right balloon for the intended meteorological experiments of the British Association, which would consist of a series of observations in the upper regions, with a view to determining the laws of storms and other atmospheric variations by instruments of the most delicate and accurate construction. Coxwell was a firm believer in advertisement.

James Glaisher was an eminent scientist at the Royal Observatory, Greenwich, and was Superintendent of the Magnetical and Meteorological Department. In 1861 he became one of a group of distinguished scientists of the British Association, including Admiral Fitzroy, Sir David Brewster and Sir John Herschel.

Coxwell's balloon was inspected by Colonel Sykes, Lord Wrottesley, Professor Glaisher, and other gentlemen of the British Association. The balloon was immediately accepted for this important scientific mission, and Glaisher announced that he would himself go up in the balloon and make the scientific observations. The best possible instruments were procured, and Mr. Glaisher set to work to practise himself in manipulating and reading the instruments, so that he might do so accurately and quickly when up in the balloon.

Mr. Glaisher would sit at one end of the car, facing his instruments, which were mounted on a wooden table resting on the sides of the car. Henry Coxwell would be at the other end of the car, or, more often, be seated in the ring of the balloon where the lines from the netting containing the envelope were linked at the circular ring with the ropes supporting the car. Coxwell's preference for this airy perch was that he had more sensitive control of the valve line.

At Glaisher's feet were a pile of cushions in a basket. When descending and nearing the earth, he would thus be able quickly to remove the scientific instruments and pack them among the cushions so as to avoid them being broken by the shock of landing.

The charge for each scientific ascent in the Mammoth Balloon, as it was called, when Mr. Glaisher and Coxwell were the only occupants, was about £50. As the resources of the British Association would only permit a comparatively few solo ascents being made, Mr. Glaisher would, on other occasions, accompany Coxwell on his ascents from the Crystal Palace, when he would pay the fee of an ordinary passenger, approximately £5.

On these public trips in the Mammoth Balloon, in a car crowded with passengers, Mr. Glaisher would fix a smaller board outside the car, on which he would mount his instruments. On two noteworthy private ascents from the Crystal Palace, the balloon attained altitudes of 22,884 feet and 24,163 feet respectively. Altogether, 28 ascents were made by Mr. Glaisher in Coxwell's balloon between the years 1862 and 1866. The greatest height recorded in this series was one made on 5th September, 1862, from Wolverhampton, when the instruments showed the balloon as attaining more than 29,000 feet. It is likely to remain for all time a record achievement without the aid of oxygen or a pressurised cabin.

The balloon would be inflated with coal gas. Generally, great care was taken as to the quality of gas provided. The product of the last distillation of coal is composed of light gas of weak illuminating or heating power, but the best for ballooning. This specially light gas would be stored in a separate gasholder for that purpose; only by this means would the balloon attain the greatest heights.

Ascending from the Palace on 18th April, 1863, the balloon rose to a height of 24,163 feet. During that ascent the ground was obscured by heavy mist. After 1 hour 30 minutes the balloon was at 10,000 feet, and directly below was a sea of fog, with the twin towers of the Crystal Palace emerging out of it. The balloon then began to move south, still ascending.

Mr. Glaisher recording the flight, said: "When we were four miles high, on descending, we began to reflect that possibly we might have been moving more quickly than we expected, and it was necessary to descend till we could see the earth below. The valve was opened rather freely at 2 hours 34 minutes, and we fell a mile in 3 minutes. We descended quickly, but less rapidly, through the next mile, and reached the clouds at 12,000 feet from the earth, at 2 hours 42 minutes. On breaking through them at 2 hours 44 minutes, still 10,000 feet from the earth, I was busy with my instruments, when I heard Mr. Coxwell exclaim, 'What's that?' He had caught sight of Beachy Head. I looked over the car, and the sea seemed to be under us. Mr. Coxwell again exclaimed, 'There is not a moment to spare; we must save the land at all costs. Leave the instruments.' Mr. Coxwell almost hung to the valve-line, and told me to do the same. . . .

"When a mile high, the earth seemed to be coming up to us. There were two rents in the balloon, cut by the valve-line, these we could not heed. Up, up, the earth appeared to come, the fields momentarily enlarging; and we struck the earth at 2 hours 48 minutes at Newhaven, very near the sea– of course with a great crash, but the ballon by the very free use of the valve-line had been crippled and never rose again, or even dragged us from the spot on which we fell. Nearly all the instruments were broken. . . . The whole time of descending the four miles and a quarter was about a quarter of an hour only."

On 31st May, 1863, Glaisher and Coxwell attained 24,000 feet in one hour and 12 minutes after starting. "We left the Crystal Palace with an east wind and at about 4.48 the Palace appeared directly under us. When one mile high the deep sound of London, like the roar of the sea, was heard distinctly; its murmuring noise was heard at greater elevations. At the height of 3 or 4 miles . . . the plan-like appearance of London and its suburbs; the map-like appearance of the country generally; and the winding Thames, leading the eye to the white cliffs of Margate and on to Dover, were sharply defined. Brighton was seen, and the sea beyond, and all the coast-line up to Yarmouth. . . . Towards Windsor the Thames looked like burnished gold, and the surrounding water like bright silver. Railway trains were like creeping things, caterpillar-like, and the steam like a narrow line of serpentine mist. All the docks were mapped out, and every object of moderate size was clearly seen with the naked eye. . . . Ships, visible even beyond the Medway, looked like toys."

Glaisher gives an interesting description of the Crystal Palace aeronaut. "At the moment of departure, in Mr. Coxwell alone is vested the right to let go; Mr. Coxwell, hand upon the catch, his countenance is fixed. He looks stern, and is apparently staring at vacancy; but he is not. If the sky be partially cloudy, he watches till he is midway between the cloud that has passed and that which is coming, so that he may have a clear sky. He knows that in every wind there are periods of calms, and if he can start in one of them he avoids much rotatory motion."

By 1865 the scientific use of the balloon, notably by James Glaisher, had created an interest in aeronautics outside the showman bracket. From his own experience with such professional aeronauts as Coxwell, Glaisher felt that the field of aeronautics had so far barely been touched upon. He and several others with the scientific approach came together and conceived the idea of forming a society to foster and develop the science of aeronautics, which had stagnated for so many years, and to increase the knowledge of aerology, and so put the whole subject of aeronautics on a scientific and reputable footing.

And so, out of Professor Glaisher's balloon ascents with Coxwell at the Crystal Palace and elsewhere, was kindled the idea which became the Aeronautical Society of Great Britain. Today it is the Royal Aeronautical Society. The inaugural meeting was held in the London house of the Duke of Argyll on 12th January, 1866, with the Duke presiding. Professor Glaisher, F.R.S., delivered the opening address, in which he said that in the hands of private individuals the progress made in aeronautics had been for any useful object almost nil. The great expense attending the necessary experiments combined with the absence of scientific and mechanical attainment on the part of aeronauts generally, considered in conjunction with the fact that their balloons were often in profitable requisition for purposes of amusement, had doubtless contributed to the present uninteresting and unsatisfactory condition of the science of aeronautics. With the exception of some of the early experimenters, aeronautics had scarcely occupied the attention of scientific men, nor had the subject of aeronautics been properly recognised as a distinct branch of science. Performances had been resorted to in order to pander to the public taste for the grotesque and hazardous, which had tended to degrade the subject that had been, till very lately, looked upon with contempt by scientific classes.

In the third year of its existence, the Aeronautical Society organised an Aeronautical Exhibition, the first of its kind. The venue chosen was the Crystal Palace. It was opened on 25th June, 1868, and for eleven days it was an enormous success, both with the scientific world, and the general public, who had suddenly become airminded.

There were 77 exhibits, which included aero-engines, models, kites, and plans. Of the sixteen aero-engines entered and submitted for the £100 reward offered by the Society for the best engine, seven were powered by gas or explosive fuel. There were examples of rocket propulsion. Regarding the models, some were on the heavier-than-air principle, others were lighter-than-air.

The outstanding model flying machine was the work of John Stringfellow, the design of which was based on W. S. Henson's prophetic design in 1843. This remarkable flying machine, so essentially modern in appearance, was a triplane with a ten-foot wing span, driven by twin screws. Stringfellow's steam engine for his triplane was awarded the Society's prize of £100. It was a marvel of lightness and efficiency. Together with its boiler it weighed only 13 lbs. It took only seven minutes to develop one horse power, and was the lightest steam engine in proportion to its power to be constructed to that date.

Stringfellow's triplane was supported on a wire a hundred yards long stretched inside the Crystal Palace, the Palace authorities having forbidden any attempts at free flight within the building on account of the danger of fire.

The machine was demonstrated many times, and it was noted by observers that after a certain velocity had been achieved, the machine left the support of the wire and rose up, lifting the wire with it. Once, when the wire broke just after the start, the aerial buoyancy of the model under power achieved so light a descent that when it landed no damage was done.

At a meeting of the Aeronautical Society, held during the Crystal Palace exhibition, John Stringfellow related that his model flying machine had, in 1847, flown successfully. At that time it had been in the form of a monoplane. After the Crystal Palace exhibition closed, the Stringfellow machine was tested in the basement of the building. When launched in the air, the triplane descended through the air on a gentle incline, with apparent lightness, until it was caught in a canvas curtain held up to break its fall. The observers' impressions were that had there been sufficient fall from the launching point, the model would have recovered itself and maintained level flight.

Stringfellow's lead in the matter of heavier-than-air flight was undisputed at the exhibition. He had drawn heavily on the earlier work in the aeronautics field of Sir George Cayley and W. S. Henson, and had produced an aeroplane that was to be the forerunner of the modern concept of a heavier-than-air fixed-wing machine. He was received in the Royal Box at the Crystal Palace by the Prince and Princess of Wales, who were greatly impressed by what they had seen.

Of the model heavier-than-air machines at this historic exhibition, two were fixed-wing aeroplanes, two were helicopters, and the remainder were ornithopters, or flapping-wing machines. Stringfellow had in almost every important feature anticipated the modern wing structure, and only failed to reach outstanding success by the lack of suitable engine power, and – equally important – financial backing to enable him to continue his experiments.

His engine was ultimately sold by his son to Professor Langley, Secretary to the Smithsonian Institute in Washington, D.C., where it is one of America's most precious exhibits. There is also in the Smithsonian Institute a replica of the flying machine Stringfellow exhibited at the Crystal Palace. The whereabouts of the original model are not known.

A power-driven helicopter was exhibited by a Mr. W. H. Phillips. It was not shown in flight at the exhibition, but the inventor claimed that in June 1842, on Primrose Hill, he had flown a helicopter model weighing two pounds. Steam was delivered at high pressure from the extremities of eight arms carrying four fans. When released, the whole apparatus mounted into the air faster than any bird. The distance travelled was across two fields, where the machine was found minus the wings, which had been torn off on landing. Phillips' claim was accepted by a number of experts, and his model was regarded as the first machine which had risen into the air by steam power.

A second model helicopter displayed at the Crystal Palace was the invention of the Viscomte Ponton d'Amecourt, which was credited with having risen to a considerable height under its own steam, but was not tested at the Crystal Palace.

Another outstanding exhibit was a glider, reputed to have borne a man in mid-air. It was the invention of a Mr. Charles Spencer, by profession a teacher of gymnastics. The framework of this machine was a marvel of lightness and strength, and was composed of umbrella wires and wicker-work.

This glider on display in the Palace had been previously referred to in an article in *The Times* of April 9th, 1868, under the heading "Swimming or Flying". The writer had discussed the feasibility of man sustaining himself in the air by his own muscular exertion, and mentioned Charles Spencer's assertion that he could not only effect this feat, but that he could sustain flight for several yards. In this glider, only the year before, Mr. Spencer had succeeded in flying for a distance of 14 feet. Indeed, Mr. Spencer had made what might almost be called the first gliding experiment of modern times. He had claimed that by 1868 he would be able to fly or glide the length of the Crystal Palace.

At the meeting of the Aeronautical Society on Friday, July 3rd, 1868, marking the close of the Crystal Palace exhibition, the Hon. Secretary, Mr. Breary, reported that Mr. Spencer, whom he described as "one of the best teachers of gymnastics in the country", by running down a small incline in the open air, and jumping from the ground, had, by action of the wings, been able to sustain flight for a distance of 120 feet.

Mr. Charles Spencer then told the meeting of an experiment he had made that day at the Crystal Palace. He said that at 6 o'clock that morning, in the presence of Mr. Stringfellow, he had tried out his apparatus in the Transept of the Crystal Palace. The apparatus was suspended by a long rope from the roof, and when he had taken up his position in the machine he had moved his arms, operating the wings, and he was raised in the air. He said that he found the down-stroke had great effect. He proposed to practise every morning, and he hoped in a fortnight or three weeks to be able to improve and complete his apparatus. Through the power of the wings he had been able to jump from 15 to 20 feet; the week before last he had flown 120 to 130 feet. He found that when he made such a jump it was quite possible to fly.

The Aeronautical Exhibition had been an unqualified success, but as the Society itself admitted, it still left them ignorant of the basic principles of flying. The Jurors of the Exhibition, at the end of their report, were bluntly honest. "It remains now", said the Report, "to be considered how far the Exhibition has forwarded the science of aeronautics. With respect to the abstract question of mechanical flight, it may be stated that we are still ignorant of the rudimentary principles which should form the basis and rules of construction. No one has yet ventured to give a correct experimental definition of the primary laws and account of power concerned in the flight of birds, neither, on the other hand, has any tangible evidence been brought forward to show that mechanical flight is an impossible one for man."

Henry Coxwell, the Crystal Palace aeronaut, was curiously upset by the formation of the Aeronautical Society, and deeply offended by its exhibition at the Crystal Palace. Because this scientific body did not admit professional balloonists to its membership, but kept themselves strictly to the scientific approach, he took the whole thing as a personal insult.

"What I find fault with," he wrote in *The Aerostatic Magazine,* which he himself edited, "is that a body of scientific men should come forward to introduce a new era in aerostation when it was soon evident that they could not even manage ballooning... It is only too apparent by reference to an early prospectus, that the chief scheme of the formers of this Society was to suppress professional aeronauts, and to establish a sort of balloon company...

"It has been rumoured, too, that my professional reputation was to be extinguished on these very grounds [Crystal Palace grounds], where I had so often exerted myself for years, to amuse the public and benefit science. I was not myself alarmed at being so easily put aside, but was grieved to see aerostation thus trifled with and disgraced."

The disgruntled Mr. Coxwell said scathingly: "To argue with gentlemen who never had at their command the motive powers essential for aerial transit would be to labour in vain . . . Would, for the sake of their own credit, that they had not in a corporate capacity entered the threshold of the Crystal Palace."

Despite the offence taken at the time by Mr. Coxwell, who felt himself slighted, the fact clearly emerges in retrospect that the Crystal Palace aeronautical exhibition marked the first step forward in the long and painful progress towards a scientific understanding of the problem of mechanical flight. It was an historic event. From then on, with many pauses and failures, the Crystal Palace was to remain a focus point of aeronautical endeavour, the developing of new ideas, and displays of aviation as it is understood today.

Chapter Thirteen

Aeronauts: The Next Phase

The inspiration of the 1868 Aeronautical Exhibition at the Crystal Palace was not to find an echo in the years immediately following. Ballooning remained firmly on its popular course, with gala events and displays still largely in the hands of showmen-aeronauts. A shapely Miss Leona Dare, becomingly dressed in close-fitting tights, brought gaping crowds' hearts into their mouths by ascending from the Crystal Palace balloon ground, near to the North Tower, hanging on by her teeth to a trapeze slung below the balloon car. This enterprising young woman was carried elegantly to a dizzy height before being hauled into the car by her manager, Signor Eduardo Spelterini. This was the world of circus, and drew the crowds through the clicking turnstiles. It also provided gratis entertainment for the local inhabitants outside the grounds, who, as intimate neighbours of this gigantic fun centre, expected to enjoy such free entertainment from time to time. As with Brock's Fireworks Night, it was all part of the stimulating life of Victorian Norwood, Sydenham and Penge. But such aeronautical ascents as those made by Miss Dare hardly represented the scientific progress envisaged by Professor Glaisher, F.R.S.

In 1870 another aspect of ballooning, of a possibly more scientific, and certainly of a more sinister nature, emerged when in the summer of that year Henry Coxwell received at the Crystal Palace an urgent invitation from the Prussian Government to go to Cologne with two of his balloons, for the purpose of instructing a newly raised detachment of army aeronauts.

Under Coxwell's instruction, the technique of inflating balloons was practised and carried out by German soldiers. N.C.O.'s and men were taught the care and maintenance of balloons and balloon fabric. Coxwell also made many ascents with the German officers on the balloon course, teaching them all the finer points of ballooning.

A series of balloon ascents was instituted for training purposes, and the Prussian Commanding Officer frequently issued his orders to inflate and go up, notwithstanding fresh winds and hazardous conditions. Although the instruction side was Coxwell's province, the degree and rigours of training lay in the hands of the Commanding Officer. The conditions were sometimes far from those Coxwell would have tolerated at the Crystal Palace. But the Prussians had complete faith in his skill, and were always ready to face any dangers, satisfied that they were acquiring sound aeronautical training. It can be fairly said that the high efficiency of the subsequent German military aeronauts owed much to the sound teaching of the Crystal Palace balloonist.

In 1871 Thomas Moy, an engineer, in collaboration with a Mr. R. E. Shill, designed and built a heavier-than-air flying machine, which they called The Aerial Steamer. It had none of the classic beauty of Stringfellow's aeroplane. Two wings were set fore and aft, and twin propellers were placed between the wings. The steam engine developed about 3 horse-power and drove the six-bladed propellers, which were slatted, and had rather the appearance of windmill sails.

This somewhat ungainly contraption was tested out on a circular track laid in the Crystal Palace grounds, and steamed round it at about 12 miles per hour, propellers whirring. Moy, who will always have a place in aeronautical history for his persistent advocacy of heavier-than-air flight, read a well-reasoned paper before the Aeronautical Society, in which he had calculated that to achieve flight his machine would have to attain a speed of 35 miles per hour. As with his predecessors in the field, Moy was defeated by the inadequacy of his power unit. His Aerial Steamer steamed in the Crystal Palace grounds in vain, and his experiments were inconclusive.

The first fatal balloon accident at the Crystal Palace occurred on 29th June, 1892, in which Captain Dale, the professional balloonist, lost his life, as did one of his passengers. *The Star* headlined the event: "An Ascent for the Edification of School Children suddenly turned into a Terrible Tragedy."

Captain Dale had been aeronaut at the Crystal Palace for six years. He had succeeded Mr. Wright, who had followed Henry Coxwell. Dale was considered a skilled, experienced and courageous aeronaut.

On this particular day a great crowd of spectators were there to see the balloon go up. It was noticed that when the balloon was laid out on the grass for inflation, a rent in the fabric had been discovered near the neck, and this Mrs. Dale herself repaired. When all was ready Captain Dale gave the order to let go. With him in the car were three passengers, one of whom was his teenage son. The balloon rose quickly, and in a few minutes had reached an altitude of 600 feet. Suddenly, the spectators were horrified to see the envelope distort and collapse. A large rent appeared in the top part, and the gas rushed out almost instantaneously.

There had been other instances of balloons bursting in mid-air, and the passengers coming safely back to earth. In such an event the deflated fabric takes the form of a parachute within the netting that surrounds the balloon. Coxwell himself once had such an experience, when a passenger in a balloon. A 16 foot rent appeared, and the balloon parachuted safely into a street in Pimlico.

Captain Dale did not have that good fortune. The balloon fabric twisted into all manner of shapes, and dropped like a stone. The unhappy occupants could be seen throwing out ballast and everything which could possibly lighten the car. The balloon fell with a heavy thud on the grass between the Maze and the Lower Lake. Captain Dale died almost immediately;

the three passengers were taken to the Norwood Cottage Hospital, where one died, but Captain Dale's son and a Mr. Mackintosh made a full recovery.

The cause of the accident, as was discovered at the inquest, was due to the weakness of the envelope, the fabric of which was old and thin from years of use. This envelope had been made up by Dale and his wife from material they had selected from three earlier balloons. One can only marvel that neither Dale nor his wife appreciated the danger that lay in employing such worn out material. Furthermore, only a few days before they had been given clear warning of the danger. The fatal ascent was only the third ascent made by the balloon. The second ascent had been made from the Crystal Palace on the previous Monday week. Then the balloon had suddenly fallen at Blackheath, with a two-foot rent in the envelope. In that instance the balloon had parachuted, falling about 2,500 feet in 3½ minutes. Except for bumps and bruises, no one was hurt. But the underlying cause of the accident clearly failed to register, and was to cost Dale his life.

After that, there was no more ballooning at the Crystal Palace until April, 1893, when Percival Spencer made an ascent. Percival Spencer was one of a famous trio of ballooning brothers, Arthur, Stanley and Percival, and of the same family of professionals as the Charles Spencer whose glider had figured in the 1868 Aeronautical Exhibition. One of Percival Spencer's passengers on that April ascent was Mr. Mackintosh, survivor of the Dale tragedy, who was quite obviously a man with nerves of steel. The occasion drew great crowds.

From then on ballooning was resumed in earnest at the Crystal Palace. Balloons were regularly to be seen drifting over Norwood and Sydenham and Dulwich and Penge, and became a familiar local feature.

What can best be described as Heath Robinson ideas in the matter of flying were being constantly presented – and sometimes tried out – in the later years of the nineteenth century. A Penge grocer named F. W. Bennett was indomitable in this respect. He invented what he termed an aerial bicycle. In purpose it was an auxiliary to a balloon, and by attaching it to a balloon it would convert it into a dirigible. A framework with bicycle pedals and rotating handles mounted in a balloon car would drive vertical and horizontal propellers. This crazy affair was actually mounted in one of Spencer's balloons at the Crystal Palace, and it was duly tried out. An *Evening News* correspondent was present at the trial, and gave this description:

"A big fan, something like the screw of a steamer, projects over the front of the car, and is worked from the inside exactly like a bicycle, while between the balloon and the car are two more such fans, which are to drive the balloon up or down. These fans are worked by the driver turning a handle just on a level with the face.

"It was too foggy for a regular ascent to be made, so the balloon was held captive at a height of about 60 feet, by four men with ropes. The balloon certainly moved in the desired direction, but no amount of pedalling would make it distance those attendants, two of whom strolled calmly behind and two ahead . . . . The invention will be exhibited at the Crystal Palace during the National Cycle Show."

During this trial Mr. Bennett pedalled furiously with his feet and hands, with precisely no visible effect on the balloon. It was tried out several times at the Crystal Palace and then, as was inevitable, passed into oblivion.

On 14th September, 1898, Stanley Spencer very nearly equalled the unbroken record of Coxwell and Glaisher, who had reached an observed height of 29,000 feet. Dr. Berson, a German scientist from Berlin, ascended with Stanley Spencer from the Crystal Palace on a scientific high altitude mission. For this purpose the balloon was inflated with pure hydrogen.

When the aerostat left the Palace grounds it ascended in an almost perpendicular line at a rate of 1,000 feet per minute for 10,000 feet. After that, the air currents bore the balloon in a south-easterly direction. They attained a height of 27,500 feet, and were by that time breathing oxygen through their respirators. The reason why they did not ascend higher than 27,500 feet was that there were only four bags of ballast left out of the twelve with which they had started. Spencer warned Dr. Berson that it would be reckless to throw any more ballast away, as they would need it for making a controlled descent.

On account of the amount of gas lost at the higher levels, on the descent the balloon took on almost the form of a parachute. Then a strange manifestation happened. Sand that they had *previously* dropped over the side began pattering down on the top of the balloon. The balloon had been dropping faster than the released ballast, and the sand only overtook the balloon as it slackened its downward pace in the denser atmosphere. At one time even the released empty sand bags had seemed to float *upwards*, and only later overtook the descending balloon.

The balloon made a perfect landing, and the whole enterprise was a worthwhile scientific voyage, which was curiously marred by Stanley Spencer claiming it as a world altitude record, which it definitely was not. "I am inclined to think", he said in an interview with *The Daily Telegraph*, "that our ascent was really the record. I know that Glaisher and Coxwell reported that they had reached 29,000 feet, but after my experience yesterday I doubt it. I have been ballooning all my life, and I may reasonably be supposed to have become accustomed to rarified air, and Dr. Berson also has had much experience. Now we both found asphyxiation becoming severe at 25,000 feet, and would certainly have been unconscious before 27,000 feet but for the oxygen gas. Glaisher and Coxwell had no oxygen and I really cannot see how they could either of them have been conscious at 29,000 feet. I think that some error must have been made."

This, of course, was a foolish and quite unwarranted statement, and was quickly refuted. Stanley Spencer, in a letter to the *Belfast News,* then had the presumption to write: "With reference to the supposed high ascent of 29,000 feet by Messrs. Coxwell and Glaisher, I say, as I so often have said, that taking into consideration the old style of apparatus used, and perhaps the unreliability of the scientific instruments of those days . . . . I do not believe that such a height as they mention could possibly have been reached by them."

In this statement Spencer was once again ignominiously defeated. The published reply was cold and to the point. "The means then employed at Greenwich and Kew in testing and verifying such instruments was just the same as at the present day, so that it is certainly astonishing to find Mr. Spencer now writing of 'the unreliability of the scientific instruments of those days', as if it were two or three hundred years ago instead of only thirty-six years, the interval between the two ascents under discussion. Mr. J. Glaisher was a Fellow of the Royal Society and one time a president of the Aeronautical Society. At the time of those ascents in 1862 he was the superintendent of the Meteorological Department in Greenwich Observatory."

Dr. Berson took no part in this ill-considered claim. As it was, before making his scientific ascent from the Crystal Palace he made a point of visiting James Glaisher, who was then living in retirement in South Croydon, to seek the advice of a great scientist and elder statesman in scientific matters.

On Bank Holiday Monday, 8th August, 1899, Spencer nearly suffered the same fate as his predecessor, Captain Dale, due entirely to his own forgetfulness. In the presence of the usual Bank Holiday crowds, the balloon in which Stanley Spencer was ascending with two passengers rose splendidly, and veered over in the direction of West Norwood. As it was crossing the foot of Gipsy Hill at an altitude of 500 feet, its occupants were seen to be throwing out sand in heavy quantities. A large rent had appeared in the lower part of the envelope.

Losing shape, the balloon began to fall at speed. It landed with a crash on the roof of one of the semi-detached villas in Victoria Road (now Victoria Crescent). The car itself slid down the side of the house, grazing the brickwork. Before it reached the ground, the upper part of the balloon became entangled in the chimney-stack, and the fall of the car was checked. It overturned and the three occupants were unceremoniously shot out in a heap on the lawn, remarkably without injury.

Spencer, with extreme *sang froid,* immediately hurried back to the Palace, as it were dismissing the incident as of minor importance, and proceeded to supervise the captive balloon ascents which were in progress. Nevertheless, he must have felt a complete fool, though a lucky one. He had forgotten, on ascending from the grounds, to carry out the aeronaut's first rule – to untie the neck of the balloon. This essential procedure ensures that the internal pressure of the gas shall always be equal to that of the outside air by allowing any excess gas, due to expansion, to escape. As it was, with the neck tied, during the ascent the internal pressure exceeded that of the air, and the envelope burst. Spencer was lucky to make so safe a landing, but obviously the collapse of the balloon over Gipsy Hill was bad for his image.

Two weeks later Spencer laid on a public demonstration at the Crystal Palace to prove conclusively that no particular risk was attached to balloon ascents if ordinary precautions were taken. He also decided to show that when a mistake had been made it was still without danger. A miniature balloon was specially arranged to exhibit the faulty arrangement in which the mouth of the balloon had been kept closed. The balloon was liberated with the neck secured, and weighted with ballast. Spencer explained that at 2,000 feet the balloon would burst, and then descend safely in the form of a parachute. The balloon, however, did not burst, but continued to ascend until it was lost in the clouds.

To make up for this non-event, Spencer made an ascent himself, ostentatiously undoing the neck of the balloon as he left the ground.

The Spencers were indeed showmen. They were among the first to provide parachute drops as an attraction. To begin with, they made their own drops, but they quickly appreciated that a pretty girl in tights, rather after the style of Leona Dare with her balloon trapeze act, was more of an attraction. It was occasionally a problem, when the desired height was reached, to persuade the girl to make her first ever parachute jump, and it was sometimes found expedient to help her out of the basket with a quick push. After the first successful drop, the young lady, radiant in the glamour of her tights and the cheers of the crowd, was quite ready to repeat the performance. Viola Spencer, a cousin of Stanley, made 146 such drops in 6 years, and was said to be a fearless parachutist.

By the turn of the century a fresh and significant attitude toward ballooning was emerging. Professional ballooning had been on the decline since about 1895, while a new, well-off section of the society with leisure and money was taking up the new thrill and delight of motoring. This had boomed after the famous Emancipation Act of 1896, which made it legal for motor cars to travel at speeds up to 12 miles per hour instead of the previous 4 miles per hour with a man carrying a red flag walking in front.

In the year 1900 the Automobile Club's 1,000-mile Motor-Car Trial ended at the Crystal Palace. And there, so to speak, the motor car and the balloon confronted each other. Not incongruously, the new breed of motorists saw a complementary relationship between the balloon and the motor car, as a thrilling and intellectual sport. Men like Frank Hedges Butler, a wealthy wine merchant, the Hon. C. F. Rolls, later, in partnership with Henry Royce, to give the name to the motor car, and Charles Pollock, a fashionable solicitor, adopted amateur ballooning as a elite sport. Ballooning became the smart thing to do, and the Crystal Palace, which ever since the eclipse of the old pleasure gardens at Cremorne had been the Metropolitan centre for balloon ascents, took on a new enthusiasm.

It became the rage. The amateur balloonists would ascend from the Crystal Palace, and elsewhere, while their friends would chase after them in their motor cars. This balloon versus motor car was in itself an exciting challenge, and private bets were laid as to whether the car would arrive at the landing point at the same time as the balloon. With the macadam roads of those days, poor sign-posting, and bad minor roads, considerable skill was required to follow a balloon floating freely over the countryside. Good map-reading was essential.

The motor cars, too, with their primitive petrol and ignition systems, and non-vulcanised tyres, demanded skilful driving and nursing on their sometimes long and tortuous cross-country runs.

It is not without significance that an "Emancipation Garage", as it was termed, stood at the top of Anerley Hill, adjoining the Royal Crystal Palace Hotel. This Robin Wood garage, until long after the 1939–45 war, displayed the sign "Established 1896". Robin Wood, who started the garage, was a Gypsy, son of a ganger who had been at the building of the Crystal Palace.

In those early years the Robin Wood garage was the only place in the Crystal Palace vicinity where petrol could be obtained, and at week-ends it was a sight to behold the splendid motor cars, their owners in heavy greatcoats with motoring caps and goggles, driving up to the Robin Wood to be filled up with petrol from the great stock of two-gallon cans in the forecourt of the garage.

Robin Wood, son of the original Robin Wood, was gathered to his Gypsy forebears after the 1939–45 war, and the garage passed into new ownership. It is still there to serve petrol and perform other garage functions, but the name Robin Wood has vanished, as has – surely unnecessarily – the proud "Established 1896" sign. There are very few Emancipation Garages left in the country today, and many famous Edwardians filled up at the Robin Wood.

The Spencer brothers played their part in this new enthusiasm for ballooning, of which the Crystal Palace was a principal centre. They taught the amateurs the tricks and skills of ballooning, and built their balloons for them.

Another important development was to take place in the ballooning scene, and this too started at the Crystal Palace. It so happened that Charles Rolls, Hedges Butler, and Butler's daughter, Vera, had planned a Scottish motoring tour in September, 1901. The car developed a fault, and the tour had to be abandoned. Vera Butler suggested that they should make a balloon ascent, and they accordingly engaged Stanley Spencer's services.

The 4th September was a very calm day, and when they ascended, in the presence of a large number of friends who had come to see them off, the Crystal Palace remained directly below until they reached a height of about 5,000 feet.

The three passengers began to discuss the advantages enjoyed by French amateur balloonists in following their sport. The three-year-old Aero-Club de France had been formed to encourage all forms of aerial activity. Vera Butler said that a similar organization should be formed to combine and further the interests of ballooning in England. This was agreed, and in this manner the Aero Club of the United Kingdom was born at 5,000 feet above the Crystal Palace. Formalities were to be completed as soon as possible.

"A few days later", said Hedges Butler, "the name of the Aero Club of the United Kingdom was registered at Somerset House through the Secretary of the Automobile Club, the committee of which institution looked to our Aero Club to control the science and sport of balloons, airships and aeroplanes in Great Britain."

Before long, Aero Club ascents from the Crystal Palace were commonplace, and the Club itself had three balloons built which could be hired by members. In the year 1902 some interesting automobile versus balloon contests took place. On one occasion Charles Rolls was the "hare", while the motor car chase was undertaken jointly by members of the Aero Club and the Automobile Volunteer Corps. Rolls himself gave a good description of the chase as seen by him from his balloon.

"Nearly a dozen cars started from the Crystal Palace, and quite a good many of them kept up with us for quite a long time; one of them in fact seemed to hold us easily until we got to Guildford. We could see the cars quite well when low down, but we lost sight of them when we got above the lower level of clouds. Still, then we could hear the horns so that we knew somebody was close. Several dropped out of sight, but one of them was so near us in Guildford that we had a talk with the occupants.

"Beyond Guildford there were no roads whatever for him in our direction. It seemed to us in the balloon to be a stretch of rather barren country there. We followed the Hog's Back travelling along a line parallel with it until we went over Farnham. Beyond Farnham, as it was getting dark, we thought it time to come down, so, seeing nothing of the cars, we made a descent into a field . . . . We had to empty the balloon and pack it without assistance, which, with a large balloon of that size, is rather a difficult thing to do. Then one of us had to set out on foot to try to find some living person. Eventually we succeeded in getting a cart, which conveyed us to Herriard Station, thence we went in a light railway to Basingstoke, about six miles, when we heard one or two cars had been asking for us, so they could not have been too far away.

"They took the wrong turning. It was amusing to us to watch the cars trying to follow us. They would take a road thinking it was just the one that followed our course, but we could see long before they found it out that the road they were taking ended in nowhere."

An enthusiastic balloonist of those heroic days was the Revd. J. M. Bacon, who made many ascents from the Crystal Palace. His hobby was making scientific observations, some of which he reported in a paper he read before the Society of Arts. He recounted that he had been aloft from the Crystal Palace during the night flight, and at cock-crow he had heard the challenge from a farmyard below. It was answered from a score of others in close neighbourhood, and then further afield – further yet, much further, till almost from an infinite distance the shrill, penetrating calls fell on his ear. The open country was to the eye of the balloonist without break of continuity as far as the neighbourhoods of farmyards was concerned. From the fowls' point of view, all the land was a connected whole. When, then, at night any single cock might crow, did a wave of crowing spread throughout all England? He could see no escape from this conclusion.

Frank Hedges Butler on a similar balloon flight, which took him in the direction of Brighton, reported on the ceaseless singing of nightingales swelling into one great chorus from 2,000 feet below. All night, too, the peewits called, and the cuckoos only rested for two short hours. The moonlight was so brilliant that Butler and his companions could read the evening papers. At 2 a.m. the lark began. Once they heard a mournful moaning, like the cry of a wounded dog, and concluded that it was a fox caught in a gin.

The formation of the Aero Club was an unqualified success, and lighter-than-air flights enjoyed a dramatic renaissance. In place of the showmen, balloon meetings at the Crystal Palace and, later, Hurlingham and Ranelagh, at which fashionable Edwardian society turned up in strength, had about them the flavour of Royal Ascot. Indeed, that halcyon period before the Great War might be termed the Golden Age of aeronautics. There were hare-and-hounds races, point-to-point and long distance. In the last instance, it is interesting to note that the Aero Club made strict rules concerning members venturing out over the sea, because of the hazards and potential dangers to possible rescuers.

The greater number of these meetings were held at the Crystal Palace, and, as the Aero Club interest developed, as many as a dozen balloons were being regularly flown over England.

In Paris the famous Brazilian, M. Santos-Dumont was flying his guided airship. In October 1901 he circled the Eiffel Tower, and Frank Hedges Butler on behalf of the Aero Club invited him to visit England as the guest of the club, and asked if his airship might be exhibited at the Crystal Palace. Santos-Dumont accepted, and the airship was brought direct to the Palace and assembled there. By a coincidence, the concert room of the Crystal Palace, which had been arranged to receive the airship, was of exactly the same length, 34 metres, as Santos-Dumont's airship shed at St. Cloud.

Inflated with air, the dirigible was first put on public exhibition on Easter Monday, 1902, and it was confidently expected that the little aeronaut would be making a number of ascents from the Crystal Palace in June.

At the Crystal Palace Santos-Dumont made a slight, nervous figure, with hollow cheeks and restless unsatisfied eye, as he stood near his towering airship in the concert hall. The airship itself was described as a thing of airy lightness and grace combined with a latent sinewy strength. The cigar-shaped balloon of light yellow-coloured, varnished Japanese silk had been inflated to its fullest extent, and appeared almost transparent as it soared above the framework of pinewood attached to its swelling bulk by innumerable thin copper "piano" wires.

Santos-Dumont announced that he was willing to make a demonstration as to what could be done in flying the airship. He said that on a day between June 15th and June 30th he would make a flight from the Crystal Palace to Richmond Park, from there to Hyde Park, and after that to fly over Fleet Street before returning to the Palace.

At the end of May, in preparation for this trip over London, the airship was dismantled and transferred by Santos-Dumont's own staff to a special airship shed that had been built for him in the grounds of the ascent enclosure. Santos-Dumont himself returned from Paris, and on that same afternoon it was discovered that severe damage had occurred to the deflated envelope. The skin of the balloon had become rent and torn in some inexplicable manner after being placed in the basket in which it had been carried to the grounds. There were numerous clean cuts which could only have been made with a knife; there were also tears with rough and jagged edges. Santos-Dumont and his two French assistants affirmed that the injury could only have been the result of wilful action.

"I am quite sure it was done through malice", said Santos-Dumont. "I mention no name and I suggest nothing, but of the fact I am quite convinced."

The Crystal Palace authorities engaged detectives, who discovered nothing to account for the damage. When a rumour began to spread that the damage had been inflicted by Santos-Dumont himself, the little Brazilian became furiously angry, and when he overheard a man make a sneering reference to the mystery, Santos-Dumont tweaked his nose and demanded satisfaction. A duel in fact never took place, and the incident was smoothed over. Santos-Dumont never flew his airship at the Crystal Palace, or elsewhere in England for that matter, as he affirmed that it could only be repaired in France. As a compensation, it was patched up and once more put on display in the Crystal Palace.

The mysterious disaster to the airship was turned to advantage by the Spencers. Stimulated by the fantastic success Santos-Dumont had had in France, where his airship flights had thrilled and delighted the Parisiens as he cruised over the boulevards, the Spencers had built an airship similar in size and plan to that of the little Brazilian.

It was brought to the Crystal Palace, and on 23rd June a preliminary captive ascent was made in the grounds. It had been inflated with hydrogen, and now occupied the shed intended to house the Santos-Dumont airship. On this first ascent it was held by long ropes, the men below walking in response to the airship's movements. The ship answered its helm, and showed no signs of rolling. It was an historic occasion, being the first airship with a man aboard to make an ascent in this country. Throughout the summer it was one of the sights of the Crystal Palace, and some thirty excursions were made round the football ground. The sponsors were Mellins Food, and the airship carried the name MELLINS in large letters.

On the 19th September the airship was cast off and sailed magnificently above the glass roof of the Palace. Spencer, who was alone on the airship, successfully navigated the North Tower and headed for London, progressing over Dulwich and Herne Hill, bringing the suburbs to a standstill with the note of his engine coming from the skies. It had been Spencer's intention to circle the dome of St. Paul's, which would have been conclusive evidence that the airship was fully under control. The impression conveyed to the casual observer was that the machine was under anything but perfect control, for at times it whirled in an eccentric manner due to air turbulence, while at other times it behaved well. The ship did not make St. Paul's, but passed over the West End, with the throbbing of the engine distinctly heard above the London traffic. It left the entire population of London gazing skywards. Eventually it alighted at Harrow after a fifteen mile journey. It was a personal success for the Crystal Palace aeronaut, but the verdict was that while Mr. Spencer was able to manoeuvre his ship, in the end he landed where the wind would have carried him had he been in a balloon without any steering apparatus.

The indefatigable Mr. Bennett, the Penge grocer, was so inspired by Spencer's airship performance that he stated to the Press, which printed it: "I am confident that I can make a figure 8 between the two towers of the Crystal Palace, and I hope next spring to go from the Palace across the Channel and come back again in about 6 hours."

Mr. Bennett was described as the sanguine inventor of an airship of which he had at the time only a model. He required £600 to construct the real thing, which consisted of a gasbag with a triangular frame below which contained the car and the driving gear. There were to be 10 electric motors, 5 on each side, each driving two propellers. These would be controlled by a lever which would be so managed as to raise the ship and drive it along. At the stern would be propellers driven round by the inrush of air behind the ship as it travelled at 60 miles per hour. These propellers would drive a dynamo which would provide the power to work the motors that worked the side propellers. In front would be another propeller by which the ship would be steered.

As a master touch, above the balloon was to be a canopy which could be opened with a lever worked from the passenger car; this was to be opened in mid-air to "take the buoyancy" – in other words to help carry the weight of the affair. It was also expected to be useful in the event of the balloon collapsing, Mr. Bennett's anticipation being that in that eventuality he would "come down slowly at an inclined plane".

The Star, reporting the invention, added drily: "Mr. Bennett thinks he has satisfactorily tested all the theories on which his ship is designed. But these airship inventors are so buoyant in their hopes."

It may be added that Mr. Bennett's figure of 8 never took place between the Palace towers, nor were his theories, including that of perpetual motion, put to the test.

In September, 1903 Stanley Spencer had another crack at sailing an airship from the Crystal Palace, with the hope of circling the dome of St. Paul's. He had a new airship, larger than the previous one, with a more powerful engine, and the project was sponsored by the *Evening News*. The airship quickly became one of the attractions of the Crystal Palace. The framework, with passenger car and propeller, was exhibited in the great central hall, where it was seen by large numbers of people, who then visited the balloon ground where the huge envelope, 93 feet long by 24 feet in diameter, was receiving its first inflation of coal gas.

On 17th September the airship, now inflated with hydrogen, set off on its attempt to round St. Paul's and return to its starting point at the Crystal Palace. Huge crowds gathered at the Palace to watch the start. At about ten minutes past five Stanley Spencer ascended, and after making a few circles and manoeuvres over the grounds, headed for London, passing over the water tanks in the North Tower Gardens. On the Crystal Palace Parade, overlooking the High Level station, big crowds watched the airship making straight for the City, travelling at a good speed, and holding a fairly straight course.

The yellow gasbag could be plainly seen for a long time against a cloudless sky, but at last it disappeared into the haze hanging over the Metropolis.

Soon after 3 o'clock an enormous crowd had gathered near St. Paul's, and had to wait over two hours. People were gathering thickly on the Cathedral steps, and soon the pavements round St. Paul's and all down Cannon Street and Ludgate Hill became quite black with men and women. There were people with craning necks by London Bridge, and westward the pavements looked impassable at Holborn Viaduct. A large number of police had to be called in to keep a clear passage for the traffic.

The airship appeared at 27 minutes past 5 o'clock, and all traffic came to a standstill. The crowds cheered as the ship was seen to alter course, but it was soon evident that the breeze was too strong. Although Spencer was trying hard, he could not bring the nose of the airship westward of the face of the dome. The ship drifted farther to the north, and was finally lost to sight. It was not capable of making headway against a wind of 15 miles per hour.

"The airship", said Stanley Spencer, "descended at Barnet as gently as a butterfly." After that it was deflated of its hydrogen and transported back to the Crystal Palace for another attempt.

This second attempt was made on October 1st, again with a large and appreciative audience. The airship swept in great circles over the Palace grounds amid the cheers of the crowd – except for one man, a Merionethshire farmer paying his first visit to London.

When the airship began to move the farmer declared that it was the result of "black art magic", and added that he should now believe his black lambs were killed by sorcery. Perspiration poured from his face, and when he beheld Mrs. Spencer get into the car to be photographed with her husband, he exclaimed, "Surely the law will not allow a lady to kill herself." He was manifestly relieved when Mrs. Spencer stepped out again, but when the ship began to ascend and manoeuvre overhead the Welsh farmer ran about in terror. To his wife afterwards he said: "It made circles like a bird, skipped like a girl, and skated in the air like our young squire on the ice. You must never doubt the wonderful tales of the Old Testament about the horses drawing chariots in the clouds. I wonder what St. Paul would have said about it."

This attempt to circle the dome was less successful than the previous voyage. On this occasion Spencer lost his way in mid-air. He went in the direction of Nunhead, and before long the airship faded from the sight of the Palace spectators.

The *Evening News,* sponsor of the flight, published Spencer's own account of how things went wrong.

"After reaching an altitude of 500 feet I found the air very cold and damp, and this, by chilling the gas, caused it to contract and lose some of its buoyancy. I made a number of evolutions which proved that I had complete control of the ship, and then looked for my course to St. Paul's. I could not see it, nor could I distinguish any distant landmarks. The haze was so thick that it was impossible to pierce it more than ¼-mile. There was a mist, too, between me and the ground, making the country look quite unfamiliar. I had, of course, my compass, and I pointed the ship in a northerly direction.

"But I had over-estimated my powers of finding my way by the compass alone. I could only guess how far I was being taken out of the bee-line by the influence of the air currents . . . . and I could see no prominent objects to guide me till I got to Peckham. I was surprised to find myself there. In fact, I had been lost in mid-air. Just at this time, while I was beginning to despair of making St. Paul's, the airship began to descend through the spilling of gas. I had parted with nearly all my ballast, and had no means of making her seek a higher level. If I went on, it meant that I should come down on housetops – an unpleasant prospect.

"Then I turned, hoping to make the Palace again, though I could not see it. I steered in that direction, but the airship descended still lower, till, after covering ¾-mile, I arrived over Peckham Rye, where there were thousands and thousands of people cheering as they watched me. Having parted with all but a pound or two of ballast, I had to give up the idea of reaching the Palace. I descended in the Park. I came down about 5 o'clock."

The airship was deflated in the County Council's works yard at Peckham Rye Park, and sent back to the Crystal Palace by road. A great crowd of men, women and children flocked to the Rye, cheering and shouting with wild excitement, and greatly hampered the work of stowing the ship.

In addition to the substantial sum already guaranteed for expenses, the *Evening News* offered Spencer a handsome money prize if in the course of three attempts he succeeded in performing the great feat of starting from the Crystal Palace, steering the ship round St. Paul's, and returning to the Palace. In one of the little speeches, which he was so fond of making before any ascent, Stanley Spencer glowingly pictured the time when he would have a 100 horse-power airship.

Both that and the prize for circling the dome of St. Paul's remained out of his reach. In November 1905, Stanley Spencer accompanied the Prince of Wales's party to India. He had been appointed official aeronaut, the Prince wishing to include a series of balloon ascents during his tour. On his way home Spencer contracted typhoid fever, and died at Malta on 26th January, 1906. He was still a young man not yet having reached the age of 40.

In the year following Stanley Spencer's last attempt to fly from the Crystal Palace to St. Paul's and back, a remarkable echo of the Santos-Dumont business of the slashed airship at the Crystal Palace in 1902 took place. In June, 1904 the famous little Brazilian was invited to demonstrate his airship at the St. Louis World Fair, and to make a flight on Independence Day. This invitation Santos-Dumont accepted, and he and his crated airship duly arrived at St. Louis, but when the envelope was unpacked it was discovered that 48 cuts had been made in the envelope, through four layers of silk, varying from 20 inches to 3 feet in length.

The Exposition Police Chief, Colonel Kingsbury, after he and his detectives made a full examination, declared bluntly that the injury to M. Santos-Dumont's airship called attention to the fact that one of Dumont's assistants possessed a knife like that which must have been used to cause the rents. Santos-Dumont himself was furious at the statement made by Colonel Kingsbury that he himself had disabled – or caused to be disabled – the airship because he was afraid to fly it. He declared that both the balloon at St. Louis and the one at the Crystal Palace had been injured by some malicious or irresponsible crank. "It cannot be repaired except in Paris", declared M. Santos-Dumont, and himself returned to Paris, abandoning the proposed flight.

Rats were blamed, but acquitted of the charge. "More like frogs", said a wag who appeared to share the same view as Colonel Kingsbury.

So, the mystery of the Crystal Palace slashing was duplicated in a sinister manner at St. Louis. Colonel Kingsbury officially reported his opinion that M. Santos-Dumont himself had had his airship mutilated to avoid making the ascent.

Yet, if that was Santos-Dumont's own act, why did he do it? The mystery still remains, for no one could accuse him of fear; his flying record was one of great enterprise and daring. Following these enigmatical incidents, he was yet to become an intrepid pioneer in heavier-than-air flight, in which his bravery was unquestioned, and in which he excelled. By 1906 he had abandoned the steerable balloon for the aeroplane.

Down at West Norwood, mid-way between the Thurlow Arms tavern and Tulse Hill station, in the Norwood Road, lived Sir Hiram Maxim, American by birth, and a naturalised Englishman. A practical scientist, and author of many inventions including the formidable Maxim gun, which was the forerunner of the modern machine gun, he was an authority on heavier-than-air flight. With the previous limitations of steam as the power unit, he had constructed an enormous aeroplane at Baldwyn's Park. It had virtually become airborne, restrained only by the confining rails which held it, until one day one rail had broken and the great bird had half risen and then crashed. Now, in West Norwood, Sir Hiram was busy on another project. He was, at the same time, noting the airships that rose uncertainly from the Crystal Palace on the hill two miles away.

"The successful flying machine", insisted Sir Hiram Maxim, "will be built of a substance heavier than air. It is not possible to make a balloon strong enough to be driven through the air at any considerable speed, and at the same time be light enough to rise in the air."

At his house near Tulse Hill, once the home of Lord Thurlow, Sir Hiram Maxim was constructing his latest invention. By March, 1904 it was revealed as a "captive flying machine", as he termed it. It was rearing its gaunt head over the roof of his house, and somewhat resembled the skeleton of an inverted umbrella. The huge, upward-pointing ribs were ten in number, and depending from them on strong wires were ten wooden, fish-shaped cars eighteen feet long. The contraption was a form of suspended roundabout, and the passengers were carried in the wooden flying boats, which swung more widely outwards the faster the machine revolved. Other apparatus could be substituted for the wooden flying boats.

One of these merry-go-rounds was to be installed at the Earl's Court exhibition, and a much larger one at the Crystal Palace. A third would be going to Blackpool. Those at Earl's Court and Blackpool were for amusement only, while that at the Crystal Palace, the home of every sane or crazy idea, was intended for public entertainment and also for research into aerodynamics. Meanwhile, the prototype at West Norwood was wildly popular with children for miles around, who only had to present themselves at Maxim's door to be given free rides to their hearts' content. Large numbers of well-known and famous people also visited Sir Hiram Maxim's workshop, including General Baden-Powell, who was to found the Boy Scout movement.

At the same time as Sir Hiram Maxim's machine was being erected in the Palace grounds on the mound which had been the Rosary, Major B. S. F. Baden-Powell, younger brother of the future Chief Scout and an active member of the Aeronautical Society of Great Britain, was conducting a series of highly entertaining experiments on one of the lakes at the Crystal Palace. He had built himself a water chute, down which he would slide at increasing speed in a light boat. This he had provided with crude aeroplane wings. Sometimes the wings would be monoplane in construction, sometimes biplane.

A boat sliding down a well-greased water chute takes a high leap in the air after striking the water. With the wings added, instead of making a short jump, the boat and its passenger would make a more prolonged flight over the water. Sometimes, if the boat slewed out of centre on its descent, the tip of one wing would strike the water and everything would end in entertaining disaster. As to what the scientific value of all this added up to is doubtful, but it certainly contributed to the gaiety of the Crystal Palace of 70 or so years ago.

On the 7th August, 1904, after the installation of Maxim's flying machine at the Crystal Palace, in place of one of the gondolas that hung suspended, a huge mechanical bird-like object, 20 feet long, with outstretched wings, was propelled round and round, at the end of wires, at a calculated 130 miles per hour. There were controls attached to the wings whereby their angle could be altered slightly, so that the line of flight could be varied.

After several dummy runs, a Mr. Metcalfe Wood carried out a daring experiment on the wooden aeroplane. He took up a prone position along the fuselage, and when maximum rotation was achieved the speed of his flight was 100 m.p.h., at a height of from 70 to 90 feet in the air. When two journeys had been safely accomplished, Sir Hiram Maxim attached a steering handle, connected by cords to the kite-like rudder and to the wings. Metcalfe Wood was then able to direct his own course within limits. At the moment of greatest velocity his flight was practically independent of the leading $\frac{3}{4}$-inch iron cable, which was slack. Thus, the wooden aeroplane was at that stage airborne.

What it all proved was another matter, but Maxim's Flying Machine remained an active source of amusement at the Crystal Palace for many years. Sir Hiram himself agreed that since science had at last provided a petrol motor with the weight of a barn door fowl and the power of a horse, it only required time and money to solve the problem of heavier-than-air flight.

Among the famous figures that have passed across the colourful tapestry of the Crystal Palace, that of Samuel Franklin Cody must be included. Not to be confused with his friend and namesake, Buffalo Bill Cody, he, like Buffalo Bill, was a show-man, a roughrider and sharpshooter. Like Maxim, he was a practical man, an inventor, and an American by birth, who became a naturalised Englishman and served his adopted country faithfully.

He first made himself famous on account of his man-lifting kites, which were used by the War Office for aerial observation and photography. With his grouped kites he was lifting men 3,000 feet in the air. Some of Cody's early kite-flying experiments were performed at the Crystal Palace.

Cody built a glider in 1905, and flew in it before Sir Hiram Maxim. Cody also experimented with kites as a means for propelling boats on the sea, and for providing a means of signalling from a boat when in distress. This remarkable man nearly crossed the Channel by means of a kite in the year 1903.

With further plans of this nature in mind, Cody sailed a kite-drawn boat over the lower lake at the Crystal Palace. The kite measured 15 feet across, 4 feet deep, and 2 feet thick. It was a kite with a box-shaped body, with two wings, and four fins below. Cody had in mind a plan to cross the Atlantic from Europe to South America by kite-traction, and he tried out on the Crystal Palace lake a craft he had designed for the purpose.

Cody was a civilian officer employed at the Army Balloon factory at Farnborough, where he played a considerable part in the design and construction of the first Army dirigible. This airship was named *Nulli Secundus,* and was completed for trials in the year 1907.

On Saturday, 5th October, the *Nulli Secundus* flew from Farnborough to London. Its arrival over the Metropolis brought London to a standstill. It flew low over Whitehall and Buckingham Palace, where it manoeuvred, and circled the dome of St. Paul's.

"Our turn round St. Paul's was very sharp", said Cody afterwards. "We kept within a space no bigger than the churchyard."

At times the Army airship flew so low that the crowds in the streets could see the workings of the mechanism and the movements of the occupants, Colonel Capper, Cody, and Lieutenant Waterlow. The *Nulli Secundus* was finally turned into the wind to make the return journey to Farnborough, but the wind – as was so often the case with those early dirigible balloons – was too strong. A logging of the airship's movements after that makes interesting reading:

12.20. Steers south, crossing Thames just east of Blackfriars.

12.30. Above Kennington Oval. Ship visible from many distant parts of London.

12.45. Strong wind springs up from the west and makes progress slow.

1.00. Going westward towards Clapham. Consultation between Capper and Cody as to advisability of alighting.

1.45. Ship lowered to 200 feet at Clapham Common. Orders signalled to Engineers following to send for more gas. [This was due to the sudden drop in temperature. Colonel Capper would have landed the ship, but there were too many people on the Common to make such a manoeuvre feasible.]

2.00. Ship unable to make more than 2 m.p.h.: Decide to go to Crystal Palace, at Norwood.

2.20. Arrive at Crystal Palace. In descending, Mr. Cody blows siren, which brings thousands of spectators to the scene.

The *Nulli Secundus* made a safe descent on the cycle track, touching down so gently that the aluminium keel made scarcely an impression on the grass. A detachment of sappers of the Royal Engineers were already there awaiting them. There was an immediate rush of spectators to the landing spot, who were restrained with difficulty by the sappers and police.

To everybody's astonishment, the *Nulli Secundus* was seen to be thickly covered with cobwebs, which had been picked up in the air during the flight. This phenomenon was as unexpected and remarkable as that which occurred in July 1904, when

Spencer on a balloon flight from the Crystal Palace, accompanied by Lawson Wood, the artist, and two others, was at a height of 4,000 feet over Banstead. Darkness was setting in, and the balloon was suddenly surrounded by a flight of bats. Again, the Rev'd. J. M. Bacon on one of his flights found floating around his balloon seeds which had germinated. They had risen thousands of feet into the air.

The *Nulli Secundus* was secured and left under guard for the night. The next day, however, was unfavourable for a return flight to Farnborough, while on the following day the airship was so saturated with water from the previous heavy rain that it would not lift off. It was estimated that there were between four and five hundredweight of water in the rigging. On the next day there was more heavy rain, and another postponement. The day after started fine and calm, but about 9 a.m. a sudden south-westerly gale sprang up, and soon the *Nulli Secundus* was tugging hard at the ropes and rolling alarmingly. As the lurching continued many of the stay rods were bent or broken. All the staff in the Palace grounds were summoned to help the sappers. It then became absolutely imperative to deflate the balloon, and the 75,000 cubic feet of hydrogen was released. By the time Colonel Capper and Cody had arrived the airship was ready for removal by road to Farnborough.

A spectator suggested that the Union Jack should be placed over the remains of the airship, but Cody retorted that the Union Jack was only placed over a corpse, and the airship was by no means dead yet. Damage was very slight, and it would have been perfectly feasible to put the airship into the air again with the replacement of some of the stay rods.

As it worked out, the *Nulli Secundus* never flew again. Her voyage over London to the Crystal Palace was her greatest hour and swan song. A larger and structurally stronger vessel, Army Airship No. 2, was built in her stead.

The spectacular voyage of the *Nulli Secundus* quite overshadowed a fine balloon record that was set up from the Crystal Palace on the day of the arrival there of the military airship.

On October 12th a large balloon, named the *Mammoth,* sponsored by *The Daily Graphic,* left the Crystal Palace on a long-distance flight. Under the charge of the professional aeronaut, A. E. Gaudron, and with two passengers, J. L. Tanner and C. C. Tanner, the balloon ascended at 6.25 p.m. Nineteen hours later the balloon and its occupants descended in Sweden. Two new records were made. The balloon crossed the North Sea from Great Yarmouth to near Sonderrig in Denmark, the 360 English miles over water easily surpassing the previous achievement of Sir Claude de Crespigny in 1883. By travelling 702 miles – the distance between Norwood and Bracken, Sweden – the longest journey by balloon from England was set up. The attempt had been to make a world distance record. It failed, however, to break the distance record set up by the Comte de la Vaux for his voyage from Vincennes to Korostichell in Russia, a distance of 1,193 miles, in October 1900.

In recording this flight made by A. E. Gaudron, *The Daily Graphic* said: "Beside this natural advantage of making the ascent from the grounds of the Crystal Palace, there are strong sentimental reasons. As long ago as 1868 an exhibition of ballooning and aeronautics was held at the Crystal Palace, which has always for Englishmen been associated with the science. From it innumerable ascents were made by Wright, Coxwell, Dale and others. In September 1901, the balloon *City of York* ascended from the Crystal Palace with Mr. Frank Hedges Butler, when he founded the Aero Club. In May 1902 the Prince and Princess of Wales witnessed a balloon ascent from the Crystal Palace. Here, too, were exhibited the war balloons from Ladysmith. In 1904 there were interesting motor car and balloon races. Mr. A. E. Gaudron, the captain of the *Mammoth,* has made many ascents from the Palace, which has, indeed, earned the title of the nursery of ballooning in England. The exhibition of the double-deck car of *The Daily Graphic* balloon is appropriate, and the crowds at the Crystal Palace every day gaze at it."

For the next two years there were no outstanding flights from the Crystal Palace, though ballooning went on with enthusiasm, and the Norwood skies were constantly enlivened by the presence of those silent, drifting spheres.

Two Royal Engineer officers from Farnborough disturbed the customary Sunday calm of Penge by landing precipitately in their war balloon. Despite the quantity of ballast that was being thrown overboard, the balloon came down rapidly. Across the tops of the houses it swept, with crowds of people on that Sunday afternoon in May rushing wildly along the streets in pursuit, with the officers shouting directions to the crowd. A heavy bump, which carried away part of a chimney-stack, nearly pitched the officers from the small basket, which then descended into the centre of Padua Road, where it was grasped by willing hands. The officers climbed out, the balloon was deflated, packed upon a cart and sent to Aldershot, and Penge relapsed into its Sunday quietitude.

To put such domestic events as these into some perspective, two brothers, Orville and Wilbur Wright, were at that time making flying history at a lonely place called Kill Devil Hill in North Carolina. They flew 30 miles with certainty and ease in an aeroplane they themselves had made. Furthermore, they had had no problem in returning to their starting point. In Europe, Henry Farman and Santos-Dumont were flying their own aeroplanes in France, but the Wright brothers had obviously beaten them to smithereens.

Mr. Percival Spencer was still lumbering about in an airship. Starting from Wandsworth Gas Works, he set off to circle the elusive dome of St. Paul's, and then to go on to the Crystal Palace. He found he could not make St. Paul's, so he tried to make the Crystal Palace. He got to Balham and Brixton, and then the wind carried him to Croydon, where he made an unexpected descent near Factory Lane.

Mr. P. W. Bennett, the Penge grocer, was still inventing. His latest invention was alleged to be under consideration by the War Office. It had about it an old-world flavour. It was being described in the newspapers the day after the Wright brothers had set new fantastic records at Kill Devil Hill.

"The balloon", said Mr. Bennett, "is so constructed that friction and resistance to the wind in its progress through the air is largely prevented. In the event of an explosion, the balloon immediately turns into a parachute, and as such will descend steadily and gracefully to earth. The bag is inflated with refined atmosphere manufactured by an apparatus built in the structure, and which is capable of refining 100,000 cubic feet of air at a cost of £1. The propelling force is created by two screw propellers, which, when driven at the rate of 1,500 revolutions per minute, will displace 200,000 cubic feet of atmosphere and make 10,000 feet of progress in a short time. The airship is made to ascend and descend without the use of ballast or gas, and when not required for use, the bag can, in a few minutes, be converted into a tent to protect the machinery from exposure."

On 18th November, 1908 another serious attempt was made by *The Daily Graphic* balloon, *Mammoth,* to secure the world long distance record held by France. With Mr. A. E. Gaudron, accompanied by Mr. C. C. Tanner, and Captain Maitland of the Essex Regiment, who was a member of the Aero Club and an experienced balloonist, the giant aerostat crossed the North Sea to the Belgian coast at Ostend. It passed over northern Germany, and was finally driven down by snow after a flight of 31½ hours at Mateki Derevni, Novo Alexandrovsk, Russia. The distance from the Crystal Palace was 1,117 miles. This was 76 miles short of the 1900 record. It was, nevertheless, a very worthy and gallant attempt, beaten only by the weight of snow on the balloon. Captain Maitland made several remarkable and hair-raising balloon flights from the Crystal Palace, which invariably spoke for his coolness and courage in adversity.

In November, 1909 was published the first edition of *All the World's Airships, Aeroplanes and Dirigibles.* It was edited by F. T. Jane, of *Jane's Fighting Ships* fame. This new publication gave particulars of 24 German dirigibles, including, of course, the famous and sophisticated Zeppelin, and 19 French, all actually in use or building in the approved lines. The British record, on the other hand, was one Army airship, which was "purely experimental and much too small even for private pleasure", and one private dirigible belonging to a Mr. Willows living in Wales. There was no mention of any Spencers' airship.

It should be added here that Willows was the owner of the second airship he had built and flown with considerable flair. By 1910 the Crystal Palace was a powerful magnet of attraction to men of the air generally. Flying in all its forms was still largely a civilian pursuit, and thither Mr. Willows turned his young eyes. He was soon to come to the Palace, for things were moving. Bleriot had flown the Channel, and Grahame-White had emerged as a skilful and daring English aeroplane pilot, while the American Wright brothers had shown conclusively that they were the masters of heavier-than-air flight. A proposal had been put forward that there should be a flying way from Croydon to Brighton. The idea was to have a smooth grass course, from 200 to 300 feet broad, from Purley to Brighton, which would be open on certain days of the week to aeronauts, who would, of course, pay a fee for the privilege of using it. At each end there would be a number of sheds in which aeroplanes could be stored, and at different points along the airway repairing depots and refreshment chalets.

It was claimed that such an aeroplane way would encourage aviation and quickly put England ahead of any other country in the world as regards the science of flying. At present, it was argued, everything was against the British aeronaut, the skill and nerve required for manipulating a machine over open country being too great for the sport to become popular.

"But directly we have an airway, all this is changed. The aviator sets out with a definite journey before him, and if he does not at first succeed in actually flying the whole distance, he will be able to finish the journey on wheels, as an aeroplane will travel along the ground at 20 or 30 miles an hour."

In February, 1910 Frank Hedges Butler received an official intimation from the Home Office that the King had been pleased to signify his consent to the petition that the Aero Club of Great Britain should henceforth be known as the Royal Aero Club, which Mr. Butler was mainly instrumental in founding when accompanied by his daughter Vera and the Hon. C. S. Rolls on his historic balloon ascent from the Crystal Palace in September, 1901. By 1910 the club numbered nearly 1,500 members, which included Army Officers determined to become familiar with the medium of the air, whereby the efficiency of the Service had been improved in a way which would not otherwise have been possible. Captain Maitland of the Essex Regiment was such an officer, and had become an experienced aeronaut. He had accompanied Gaudron on his November, 1908 balloon voyage from the Crystal Palace to Russia.

Captain Maitland made a balloon trip from the Crystal Palace on a Saturday afternoon in April, 1910 that was a classic example of disaster coming out of a clear sky. It was a voyage which ended in the balloon being wrecked and the roofs of two houses damaged, but nobody hurt. Captain Maitland and a lady companion ascended from the Palace grounds at half past three with a gentle south-easterly breeze and brilliant sunshine. After about an hour they became becalmed over the Oval at an altitude of 2,000 feet. They threw out ballast to try to find a current of air higher up, but found none. Then they came down in search of ground currents, but still without success.

Then, while still becalmed, they got lost in clouds which were so dense that they could not see a yard in any direction. It was now bitterly cold, and they drifted into a storm. The rain poured down, then it hailed, and then it snowed. There was vivid lightning and crashes of thunder, with the thunder peals *below* them.

The weight of the balloon had become enormously increased by the rain and snow, and they were slowly falling; by now they had used up all their ballast. There was a sea anchor on board, and Maitland hoped to anchor in the Thames. But they could not see the Thames. Shortly after 5 o'clock, with the balloon falling rapidly, they dropped below the clouds and could see streets and houses.

"I had my hand on the ripping cord", said Maitland afterwards. "I hoped to make a descent in a fairly wide street, which was below us, but the wind caught the balloon and the car struck the corner of a house, and then rebounded on to the next house. The envelope caught on to the roof, leaving the car suspended about 5 feet from the ground."

"When we struck the second house", added his companion, "I saw a white-faced woman looking out. Naturally she was surprised to see us, and I shouted out, 'Don't be afraid, it's all right'. And as you see, it was all right. This was my first trip, but I hope to make many more ascents. It was the most exciting and certainly the most enjoyable experience I have ever gone through."

By a coincidence, Captain Maitland had a similar experience a few weeks later. After ascending from the Crystal Palace with two companions, a man and a woman, the balloon drifted at 8,000 feet into the heart of a thunder storm. The balloon swayed alarmingly, rain poured off the envelope, and vivid flashes of lightning seemed to threaten destruction. The peals of thunder were continuous, and to add to the dangers the party was almost in darkness.

The weight of water on the envelope caused a quick descent, and at 7,000 feet the aeronauts found themselves over the Thames at Northfleet. The wind was carrying the balloon eastward, and it continued rapidly to descend. It passed over the railway, uncomfortably close to a passing train. It was then carried on to the roof of one of a row of houses, and descended in the backyard of another, where the car narrowly missed knocking down a woman who was standing there. A number of bricks and tiles were dislodged, and the balloon occupants were considerably shaken. So rapidly did the balloon fall from the sky that a serious accident had been feared by the spectators. Captain Maitland reckoned they had dropped 7,000 feet in under two minutes.

Remarkably, both balloon and occupants were unhurt. It was duly packed and carted to the station and returned to the Crystal Palace.

With the death of King Edward VII on 6th May, 1910, and the impact of Court and national mourning, it became necessary to find an outstanding attraction to entice the public through the Crystal Palace turnstiles. Claude Grahame-White, the up-and-coming young aviator, who was then flying with quite spectacular success, was approached to make a series of exhibition flights. Arrangements were made, and in due course Grahame-White arrived at Norwood, towing his Farman aeroplane on a trailer. He stopped for refreshment at the *Rose and Crown,* which stands at the corner of Crown Lane and Beulah Hill.

Mr. J. E. Ryland, a Norwood builders' merchant, recalls the occasion; he was there himself as a boy. "When Grahame-White came out, a large crowd had already collected. We had never seen an aeroplane before, and it caused a deal of excitement. People were hurrying from all directions to have a look at it. A boy, I remember, was writing his name on the wing. Grahame-White saw him, and caught him a clip over the head that nearly sent him into the blacksmith's forge opposite, where a horse was being shod. Grahame-White examined the wing very carefully to see if it had been damaged. He then moved off to the Crystal Palace, with a wave of his hand to the crowd."

The flying ground earmarked by the Crystal Palace authorities was, in Grahame-White's opinion, quite unsuitable. He picked another piece of ground which had a tennis court on it. After a few trees were cut down, some flower beds levelled, and the wire netting removed, he had a total length of 80 yards in which to take-off and land. But it would be a tight squeeze. To make the take-off a practical proposition, his mechanics would have to hold on to the tail of the aeroplane whilst the engine was being revved up to its maximum. Then, on a signal, they were to let go, and it was hoped that the aeroplane would be almost catapulted off the ground well within the safety limits.

Landing was a greater problem. Grahame-White solved it by a method of his own devising which was, in principle, the same as that to be used in years to come on aircraft carriers. Half a dozen ropes were to be stretched across the runway at a height of two feet from the ground. They were to be parallel, about ten feet apart, and at right angles to the path of the incoming plane. At each end of the ropes heavy sandbags were attached. When coming in to land, the skids would hook onto the loaded ropes, and so be rapidly dragged to a standstill.

He planned to give a first demonstration on 14th May, but the wind was a strong following one down the runway – the worst possible quarter. The crowd expressed their disappointment when it was first rumoured that the flight would not take place. The definite announcement of the abandoning of the flight was made shortly after. The spectators in the enclosure were informed that they could witness the performance of *Pompeii,* a spectacle, without further payment, but the thousands who had paid admission to the Palace, and the hundreds who had paid a further 2s. 6d. for places in the stands had no compensation, and they swarmed into the enclosure in a somewhat threatening manner. Grahame-White seemed to be more disappointed than anybody else, and tried to make it clear that the strong following wind would render any attempt at take-off or landing extremely dangerous. The explanation was accepted, and he was cheered as the machine was wheeled back into its shed.

Next evening the wind was favourable, and Grahame-White delighted everybody with a display of flying before setting off to Brooklands, where he had an engagement. He rose from the Palace grounds at 7.5 p.m. and circled overhead, thus making his first appearance in the Norwood skies. To the people of Norwood outside the Palace, well accustomed to the drifting, silent globes, this fragile, buzzing thing, travelling through the air like a dragonfly, was a thrilling revelation of human flight.

After about 20 minutes, the aeroplane made a turn by the South Tower, and flew away at a height of between 200 and 300 feet, dwindling into the distance, and leaving Norwood and district vaguely aware, perhaps for the first time, that a new age had dawned. Neither Norwood nor anywhere else in the world would ever be quite the same again.

Demonstration flights by Grahame-White were planned to take place at the Crystal Palace every Tuesday evening during the months of June and July. They were to be conducted under the auspices of the Aerial League of the British Empire. The League had been founded by Colonel Massey, Chairman of the Crystal Palace Flying Ground Committee, and had been launched impressively at the Mansion House by the Lord Mayor of London. That was a year ago, and speakers had included Lord Montague of Beaulieu, Admiral Sir Percy Scott, Major Baden-Powell, and Sir Hiram Maxim. The object of the League was to foster and in every way encourage aviation in Britain by all means in its power. A resolution passed at the meeting was as follows:

"That this meeting of the citizens of London regards with considerable anxiety the rapid development of the science and practice of aerial navigation by other nations, and deplores the backwardness and apathy shown by this country regarding this new means of communication, which is of vital importance from a commercial, as well as from a national defence point of view, and pledges itself heartily to support the objects of the Aerial League of the British Empire."

The League was now appealing for £200,000 to train as aviators men who could not themselves afford to become owners of aeroplanes and pay for private instruction. The Grahame-White demonstrations at the Crystal Palace, Brooklands and elsewhere helped to put the appeal to the forefront.

A Crystal Palace flight was timed for 5.30 to 8 p.m. and special trains were run from Victoria, London Bridge and Ludgate Hill. When Grahame-White made his appearance in the Aerial League's enclosure, where his mechanics had already wheeled his aeroplane to the top of the slope, there was a sense of expectancy that was almost electric. Methodically, the young aviator pulled on a suit of brown overalls, and ordered the engine to be started. Then, satisfied that all was in order, he climbed into the seat, and after testing the controls, waved his hand as the signal for his mechanics to let go.

With the help of the down slope, the machine became airborne after covering about 30 yards. To the cheers of the spectators in the enclosure, and of the crowds on the terraces, the flimsy aeroplane climbed to a height of about 150 feet. Grahame-White described two large circles, and then landed neatly on the spot whence he had taken off, the drag-ropes now in position. His flight had lasted 3½ minutes.

After he had left his aeroplane, he was surrounded by an enthusiastic crowd, cheering and shaking him by the hand. He spent a long time signing cards for lady admirers. Among them was Miss Pauline Chase, the American actress who had taken London by storm, and had this year played Peter Pan. She was eager to fly with Grahame-White, both for the thrilling experience and for the publicity. This would have helped the funds of the Aerial League, but owing to the somewhat hazardous circumstances of the flying strip, Grahame-White had to refuse.

Grahame-White's next flight on that memorable day was just as successful as the first, and this time he rose into the air after a run of only 22 yards, the exact distance being measured by Colonel Massey. On this occasion the aviator flew low over the starting point, waving to the cheering crowd that lined the runway.

The Daily Telegraph in a review of Grahame-White's flying demonstrations at the Crystal Palace had this to say:

"Last evening Mr. Grahame-White gave another exhibition of his skill as an aerial pilot at the Crystal Palace. The Aerial League have a small grass lawn overlooking the running and football grounds there. It slopes downwards, and only gives a possible run of 80 yards and an actual one of 50. From this confined spot Mr. Grahame-White started, and successfully rising, flew for 8½ minutes over Norwood and Penge, and returning over the Palace itself at an altitude of about 600 feet. On all sides, the fences and trees presented obstacles of danger; but notwithstanding a south-west breeze of about 8 m.p.h. Mr. Grahame-White landed with his Farman biplane on the small lawn from which he started.

"This was an excellent testimony of his skill as a pilot, but made those onlookers who had experience of flying thankful he had landed safely. His first flight was made soon after half past six, and after an hour's delay he made a similar ascent for another eight minutes. It is to be hoped that these exhibitions will be free from accidents, as, should any weakness be shown by the engine soon after starting, there is no good landing spot available. The trees compel an aviator to rise quickly, and a following wind would prevent this. Last night the wind was across the starting-point, so all ended happily, but should the breeze be behind the aeroplane, it is to be hoped that no flights will be permitted, however many spectators may express their disappointment."

The flying displays at the Crystal Palace were an unqualified success, unmarred by any accident. On 7th July, however, when Grahame-White set off from the Palace to take part in the flying display that was to take place at Bournemouth during the centenary celebrations, he had not flown a mile and a half when a choked petrol feed pipe forced him to land in a field on South Norwood Hill, opposite the junction with White Horse Lane. All would have been well, but for the presence of one tree, which Grahame-White was unable to avoid due to loss of power. One wing struck the tree, and crippled the plane. Unfortunately, Grahame-White's mechanics had already left by train for Bournemouth. The damaged plane was therefore dismantled, taken to South Norwood Junction, and sent by train to Bournemouth.

That was not Grahame-White's lucky day, for only that morning he had been fined £10 for furiously driving a motor car on June 12th. A tram driver in evidence said that Grahame-White had covered two and a half miles in two minutes!

What may well be considered the last of the great aeronautical occasions at the Crystal Palace followed a telegram dispatched on 7th August, 1910. It was addressed to the Aerial Manufacturing Co., who owned the hangars on the aviation ground at the Palace. The telegram came from Cardiff, and was signed by E. T. Willows, a young man of genius and daring, who had built two eminently airworthy airships. The telegram advised the Aerial Manufacturing Co. of his imminent departure, by his airship, *Willows II,* from Cardiff to the Crystal Palace. His intention was to travel that night. He completed the 150 miles flight in 10 hours.

"It was", he said afterwards, "comparatively easy to make the journey – there are well-lighted towns situated about 20 miles apart, all along the route."

He occasionally shouted down in the darkness to check where he was. "It was peculiar to hear the sound of your own voice when aloft – flying in the dark is somewhat eerie. One very curious thing I noticed was the echo of my own voice. I would call out, 'Anybody below there?' and the echo came clear and loud two or three seconds later."

His intention was to land in the Crystal Palace grounds, but as he was passing over the Crystal Palace his supply of petrol ran out. He was obliged to pass the Palace, and to descend by opening the gas valve of the balloonette, thus getting near enough to earth to enable him to lower a trail rope on an estate at Mottisham. A gardener caught hold of the rope and guided the aeronaut to a safe landing place.

During the day Willows busied himself with repairing a leaky patch on the balloonette. 10,000 cubic feet of hydrogen was needed to restore full buoyancy. Late in the afternoon, he started on his 5-mile trip to the Crystal Palace. His progress was watched by thousands of people as he passed over Catford and Lower Sydenham, arriving at his destination at seven o'clock. There were large crowds assembled on the terraces and, amid general excitement, he circled the grounds several times before landing on the lawn of the Aerial League enclosure.

By his flight from Cardiff to London he had achieved a national reputation, and had accomplished not only one of the longest flights ever made in this country by any form of self-propelled aircraft, but absolutely the longest flight by a dirigible balloon. Previous efforts of this character had been confined to the Army, but Willows's achievement had put all those into the shade.

During the following days he delighted huge audiences with his handling of the airship. He capped it by achieving that which was dear to the heart of Londoners – the circling of the dome of St. Paul's.

On his way to St. Paul's he was sailing directly into a light gusty breeze, which caused the dirigible "to look ludicrously like a baby elephant gambolling in the sky!" After hovering over St. Paul's, having made his circle of the dome, Willows then followed the line of Fleet Street and the Strand to Westminster. He then turned due south back to the Crystal Palace. The total journey was accomplished in just one hour and a half.

It was while he was at the Crystal Palace that Willows constructed a third airship, and later flew in it to France.

While Willows was at the Crystal Palace, an American aviator named John B. Moisant became the first to fly from Paris to London, making the Crystal Palace his terminal objective. He was dogged the whole way by bad luck. Having made the flight from Paris to Dover without a hitch, he found the last 35 miles frought with mishaps and bad weather conditions, so that it took him 21 days to fly from Paris to the Crystal Palace. He reached the Palace on 6th September, where he circled the two towers as a gesture of victory. He then circled the grounds, looking for a convenient place in which to land.

Grahame-White, who was then dazzling America with his impeccable flying, could have told Mr. Moisant of the inhospitable nature of the landing facilities for aeroplanes at the Palace. Seemingly, Mr. Moisant had not been warned about this, and after a fruitless search, had to turn away. He alighted on the cricket field of the Beckenham Cricket Club, but there was a jinx on him. In his descent he struck a fence, smashed his propeller, two front wheels of his machine, and damaged the fore-carriage.

Moisant immediately telegraphed Paris: "I have reached London, and accomplished my object."

Its unsuitability for aeroplane landings and take-offs largely accounted for the fading out of the Crystal Palace as an aerial centre. Flying was advancing with such speed that this was, in any case, inevitable. But it must always be given an honoured place in the history of aeronautics, from Glaisher to Grahame-White and E. T. Willows, from the origins of the Royal Aeronautical Society to the formation of the Royal Aero Club, and the awakening of a national spirit in the concept and founding of the Aerial League of the British Empire. It played its part.

Chapter Fourteen

Pyre

Paxton believed that what people wanted in the way of relaxation and entertainment were scientific amusements, gardens, fountains, and works of art, preferably statues. His own tastes had been conditioned in the expansive surroundings of Chatsworth, stately home of his patron the Duke of Devonshire. Much of Paxton's experience in such matters had been gained on the grand, but expensive, Chatsworth scale.

The outcome of this was that Paxton had shown himself incredibly extravagant when it came to building the Crystal Palace at Norwood. Because of his grandiose schemes of enlarging the new Palace out of all proportion to the original version in Hyde Park, the final cost was so high that the shareholders' hopes of their shares increasing in value were soon rudely dashed. Income was low in proportion to the capital expenditure. This state of affairs was aggravated by pressures that saw to it that the Crystal Palace and grounds were rigidly closed on the one day of the week when the working people would have been able to take advantage of it.

On gala occasions there were undoubtedly vast numbers of visitors – as many as eighty thousand in one day – but such occasions were relatively few. For the rest of the time the money taken was well below the profit level. The railway companies' dreams of a perpetual Derby-day type of traffic were not realised.

Because of lack of funds the Palace was grossly under-insured, and when the North Transept was burnt down in 1866 there was not the money to rebuild it. For its subsequent 70 years of existence the building remained truncated at the north end. Neglect of the fabric became evident in later years. The roof leaked and the paint peeled. The early splendour of the gardens took on a less cared-for aspect.

Despite this, the fountains still played and the grounds had their moments of effulgence. Brock's fireworks rendered great service in popularising the Crystal Palace. Alan Brock declared that from 1865, when the fireworks started there, until the end of the century, the history of pyrotechnics in this country was practically the history of pyrotechny at the Crystal Palace.

The idea of presenting fireworks at the Crystal Palace occurred to Charles Thomas Brock. He saw in the terraces, fountains and masses of foliage unrivalled advantages for the display of fireworks on a grand scale that would be worthy of Handelian music. The Crystal Palace directors, on the other hand, were not so enthusiastic. They considered that fireworks would lower the tone of the place and bring it down to the level of Cremorne. The Crystal Palace felt itself to be superior to a mere pleasure garden.

Brock pointed out that at the Crystal Palace exhibition of 1862, though every other type of manufacture had been on show, and thereby could compete with its rivals, there had been no such opportunity for firework manufacturers. With the Palace's magnificent and spacious grounds such a contest might reason-ably be held between rival pyrotechnics manufacturers. The directors conceded the point, and the first firework display took place on July 12th, 1865. Twenty thousand people paid to watch the fireworks, and after that all doubts about the propriety of fire-works at the Palace vanished. From then on firework displays continued up to 1910, when the Crystal Palace was taken over by the Festival of Empire promoters. Brock's fireworks were resumed in 1920 at the conclusion of the Great War.

Such was the success of the fireworks at the Palace that they became generally fashionable, this being helped by the Royal

Patronage of the displays. Gigantic effects were achieved in the form of pictorial pieces. These were first introduced in 1875, continually increasing in size until Brocks were exhibiting firework pictures 90 feet high and 200 feet long.

With the technique and such a canvas as this, almost anything was possible. Sea battles were a favourite subject for display. On the occasion of the Duke of Edinburgh's return from a voyage around the world in H.M.S. *Galatea,* a full-sized representation of the ship under full sail was carried out in brilliant fire. It was considered a masterpiece of pyrotechnic art.

A still more ambitious effect was produced on the occasion of the Railway Conference in 1895, when a life-size representation of Stephenson's *Rocket* and the latest type of express locomotive were presented in near-exact detail with all moving parts working.

Effects were endless. Blondin walked on a tightrope on the terrace, his performance silhouetted against a background of fireworks. A man in a suit of reflecting metal mirrors and framed in fireworks dramatically slid down a cable stretched from the north tower to the terrace. He was supposed to represent Zeus, the Father of the Gods. On about the second occasion the Father of the Gods – in fact, a Brock employee – stuck half way down, and there remained until the end of the performance.

Doubts had been expressed concerning the advisability of continuing this particular performance, not on grounds of safety to the man employed, but as regards the safety of the tower itself. The strain on the cable to keep it taut was enormous, and it was feared that the stress on the tower might be dangerous. Accordingly the plan was abandoned.

The legend, which has survived to this day, that Blondin walked on a tightrope stretched between the two Crystal Palace towers no doubt grew out of the firework displays. In fact, Blondin never made such a walk. Reflection shows that were such a heavy cable stretched between the two towers, the tension that would have to be applied would be more than the towers could stand.

A popular feature of the golden days of Crystal Palace fireworks was portraits in fire. By that means distinguished visitors were honoured, as for example the Shah of Persia and Lord Roberts. Such an honour was not invariably a success. When the King of the Zulus, Cetewayo, visited the Crystal Palace in his royal capacity, he was persuaded to press the button which would ignite the portrait by electricity. Cetewayo, unfortunately, was quite unable to recognise his portrait, which was outlined in white fire; he thought it ought to have been in black fire!

On another occasion, the King of the Maoris objected to the complicated tattoo marks on the face of the portrait. The colours were wrong. It had not proved for him a very satisfactory day. He had been decked out in a frock coat, silk hat and patent leather boots for the ceremonial occasion. Unfortunately, the boots pinched and hurt his feet. The Maori king suddenly sat down on a bench during his official tour, wrenched off his boots and cast them disdainfully on one side. Not until a pair of carpet slippers had been produced from somewhere did the Maori king continue his tour.

The weekly fireworks with the rockets ascending into the sky and bursting into many coloured stars were indeed a part of life in the Crystal Palace district. On Thursday evenings in the summer months windows would be opened while the family gathered there to watch what they could see of the spectacle. Suburbanites conditioned to the dramatic bangs and flashes and patterns of light in the sky shared the frivolity wholeheartedly. Children were brought up from babyhood to enjoy the thrill of fireworks, and regarded these friendly explosions as part of the way of Norwood life.

The term "Brock's Benefit" has passed into the language, as denoting brilliant spectacle and pictorial exuberance. The first time the term was used was in 1869, when the Crystal Palace directors granted C. T. Brock a benefit "as a mark of their appreciation of his unfailing efforts and outstanding achievements in the field of pyrotechny during the last five seasons." The Brock's Benefit was repeated at the Crystal Palace a number of times.

In the year 1909 Bleriot flew the Channel, and the Press were not slow to see what this could portend. There were grim cartoons of night flyers dropping death from the skies on civilian populations. "As might be expected," said *The Sketch,* "M. Bleriot's flight across the Channel has resulted in a revival of those invasion scares that were so prevalent recently in connection with dirigibles, and there seem to be a good many people who cannot sleep o' nights for fear that enemies skimming into England like a flight of all-devouring locusts, drop bombs outside their doors."

The actor-manager and impresario, John M. East, who had put on many shows at the Crystal Palace, was quick to fasten on to this trend of thinking. In collaboration with Brock's Fireworks, he mounted a grand spectacle on the Crystal Palace football ground to dramatise the warlike theme. A complete village constructed of canvas and wooden framework was "bombed" nightly by aircraft picked out in searchlight beams. These dummy aeroplanes would sweep across the scene, borne on invisible wires, and drop their firework bombs, while on the ground a contingent of territorials resisted with a formidable display of extemporised ack-ack gunfire. This proved an immensely popular feature and brought the crowds to the Palace to enjoy all the thrill of air attack with a village being devastated before their very eyes.

The Crystal Palace itself was by now in a state of penury. By 1911 it was bankrupt and in the hands of a receiver. On 28th November it was to be sold by auction, to be offered in one lot as a going concern. This was a fateful period in its history. There was grave danger that it would pass into the hands of the developers. In fact, a member of the London County Council proposed that a town planning scheme be drawn up to apply for the grounds and convert them into streets and rows of houses. Every jerry builder within striking distance was eager for the moment when he might be in a position to swoop down on the beautiful grounds and reduce them to terms of bricks and mortar.

But that ultimate indignity was not to be. The Earl of Plymouth produced £230,000 to buy the Palace as a going concern; at the same time the Lord Mayor of London opened a fund to purchase the Crystal Palace for the nation, and to reimburse Lord Plymouth. This was completed in 1913, and the Crystal Palace was saved.

With the coming of the Great War the Government commandeered the Palace and constituted it a Navy landship, H.M.S. *Victory VI,* and it was occupied by the Royal Naval Division. At the end of the war it became a demobilization centre. In June 1920 it was officially opened by King George V as the first home of the Imperial War Museum. The Victorian Palace of Pleasure, with its fishponds and fountains, its statuary, its historic art courts, its Handel organ, somehow looked strangely dejected and forlorn with its clutter of Big Berthas, tanks, naval guns, dummy soldiers dangling below suspended open parachutes, and all the drab bric-a-brac of modern war.

There was a sigh of relief when the Imperial War Museum left the glass building. But what should be done with the Palace itself? Sir Edward Lutyens suggested that it should be preserved under glass as a monument to the vanished Victorian age! The Handel Festivals were things of the past. There were, however, more modern innovations such as dirt-track racing, with new-type heroes like Roger Frogley throwing up showers of cinders as they broadsided round the sharp corners. There were resumed brass band festivals, dog shows, cat shows, dancing, and, of course, fireworks.

Sir Henry Buckland, General Manager of the Crystal Palace, laboured ceaselessly and worked wonders towards restoring the building and bringing the grounds back into a trim condition. The crowds began to return and achieved nearly a million visitors in one year. Logie Baird, the pioneer television inventor, broadcast programmes from the South Tower, the antennae for which projected from the top platform. A motor racing track was laid out in the grounds. The Crystal Palace was being geared to compete with the brave new world.

On 30th November, 1936 a fire broke out in the building at about 7 o'clock in the evening. People outside saw a red glow increasing in brightness within the glass walls. Sir Henry Buckland saw it too. He hurried to the Palace and found members of the staff attempting to deal with a fire that had broken out not far from the Handel organ. But already it was too late.

There was just about time to warn a group of members of the Crystal Palace Amateur Orchestra. They had been practising in the Garden Hall, and were unaware of the fiery dagger which had been plunged into the heart of the Palace. As it was, the flames spread so swiftly that the orchestra was in danger of being trapped, such was the tinder dryness of the massive woodwork that made up the floors and so much else.

The floor was composed of heavy planks separated from each other by a quarter-inch gap, and supported on wooden joists. The quarter-inch gap had been Paxton's idea to aid cleaning. When the crowds were gone the floors had only to be sprinkled and swept, and all the dust of the day would fall between the planks. As the years went by this layer of dust below grew into a highly inflammable–even explosive–mixture that required only to be ignited by a chance cigarette-end and, fanned by a draught, to glow more strongly and build up heat in the surrounding dust. Something of that nature had now taken place, and had only manifested itself when the accumulated heat had burst into swift crackling flame.

Miss Roper-Norrish, a violinist in the orchestra, and an old Norwood resident, said afterwards: "I had barely time to gather up some money that was the property of the orchestra and run for the exit. Already the flames were blazing terrifyingly in the centre transept, where there were piles of chairs. The Handel organ was near the flames and from it were coming the most strange groans, like some person in terrible pain. It was afterwards said that the sounds were produced by the violent heat forcing air through the organ pipes. But I shall never forget those ghastly groans."

When the flames broke through the glass roof they rose to a height of 300 feet. Sparks fell as far away as Beckenham. At

8.35 p.m. the great transept fell with a thunderous crash. The south transept was the next to go. The end wall fell out at 8.55 p.m., and the transept crashed to the ground at 9 o'clock.

It was quite impossible to save the building, and the firemen concentrated on the South Tower, which was in imminent danger. The lower floors contained the works and offices of the Baird Television Company. Some of the valuable equipment was saved, but the greater part was ruined.

Among those who watched the spectacle from the Crystal Palace Parade was Winston Churchill, who was on his way home from the House of Commons to Chartwell. He stood there among the great awe-struck crowd, tears on his face. "This is the end of an age" he was heard to say, and repeated the words, "This is the end of an age." Thus, eighty-two years after the Inauguration by Queen Victoria, the Crystal Palace perished in the greatest individual fire London had ever known, but without the loss of a single life. Its fiery passing was attended by 500 firemen, 90 engines, and the greatest concourse of people that had ever been drawn to that high Norwood hill. Thousands of birds in the Crystal Palace aviary were released, and many escaped, rising in flocks through the smoke and flame.

There was also another army that escaped. It came racing across the smooth lawns, a vast grey army of rats. To the startled onlookers, the thousands of rodents racing shoulder to shoulder from the flames were like some monstrous grey, moving carpet.

The destruction was complete, but a still greater damage was done to the district. Its very heart was torn out, and the neighbourhood has never recovered from the loss of its centre-piece. It is unlikely that anything comparable with the old Crystal Palace will ever take its place, but so long as that vacuum persists damage is being perpetuated within the surburban community.

The Crystal Palace has passed into limbo, but the tradition of the Palace of the People remains. In 1951 the *London County Council (Crystal Palace) Act 1951* was passed, and under that Act the L.C.C. was given the duties and responsibilities of the

Trustees to use the Crystal Palace for the purposes of education and recreation and the furthering of commerce, art and industry. This was, in effect, a reaffirmation of the original rôle and purpose of the Crystal Palace. The L.C.C. had indicated its willingness to assume the position of controlling body, subsequently to be vested in the Greater London Council.

What has emerged to date has been the Crystal Palace National Recreation Centre. It flourishes, though isolated and detached from the life of the surrounding community. There seems to be little social contact between the two, which is a fundamental difference between the old and the new Crystal Palace to date.

Concerning the Crystal Palace National Recreation Centre, Sir Gerald Barry said: "It may perhaps seem remarkable that the British nation, which invented and bequeathed to others most forms of sport which are now enjoyed throughout the western world, should have no central home for sport of their own to which their own athletes and those of other nations can look on as a focal point."

The National Recreation Centre was designed to make good this deficiency, and its main purpose has been to provide facilities for the training of coaches and players which will compare with any presently available at home or abroad.

Important though this is, it nevertheless is but one facet of the many possessed by the earlier Crystal Palace in its service to the public. The present Crystal Palace, too, has regrettably hidden its face for far too long from the broad roadway that once set it off. The blank and enigmatical desert strip that skylines the length of the Crystal Palace Parade appears indifferent–even faintly hostile–to the district that once was closely integrated with its life and purpose.

Aunt Crystal Palace was a term of affection used by some local residents. To many who lived about, the Crystal Palace was a benign and friendly presence, all things to all people, particularly so to those who lived near to her voluminous, though somewhat faded, Victorian petticoats.

Chapter Fifteen

To Preserve, Protect and Improve

Towards the latter end of 1959 Norwood residents were becoming increasingly disturbed at the changing face of the suburb in which they lived. Letters appearing in the local Press showed concern at the growing number of derelict houses, neglected open spaces, and the appearance of new and unsightly development.

The whole district had suffered much from wartime air raids, and there had been many flying bombs and rockets. In those long-range attacks Norwood was part of what was called Doodle-bug Alley. The vast amount of damage and neglect of property caused by the war had been followed by years of inertia. But new developments were now appearing, and some of these left much to be desired. There was an enormous back-log of leasehold property more than 100 years old that would sooner or later be pulled down and the land used for re-development.

There were, however, to be seen some distinguished relics of an earlier Norwood. Thus, in those post-war years there stood on Beulah Hill a somewhat delapidated but imposing house that had known better days. The house was Little Menlo, which today is commemorated in Menlo Gardens, the name of a housing estate close by.

Little Menlo possessed interesting historical associations dating from the 1870s, when an American business man,

Colonel George Gouraud, lived there. He was a man with great drive, and, among other things, was the lively and active promoter in England of the products of the famous American inventor, Thomas Edison.

Edison had been living and working in the tiny New Jersey village of Menlo Park, where he had his huge laboratory and team of specialists. Colonel Gouraud took the name of Little Menlo for his Beulah Hill house.

Two of Edison's many inventions were the telephone transmitter and the phonograph. Both of these were demonstrated at Little Menlo. Furthermore, Gouraud arranged the installation of a demonstration telephone exchange at the Crystal Palace.

There was an historic occasion when Edison perfected his phonograph and dispatched it to Gouraud at Beulah Hill, who played it before an invited audience at Little Menlo. The voice of Edison and the baby cries of his new born daughter were heard with startling clarity and made a tremendous impression. The wax cylinder which held the sound-track was verbally addressed to "Friend Gouraud". The voice of Edison said "This is my first mailing phonogram", and went on to say that "Mrs Edison and the baby are doing well. The baby's articulation is quite loud enough but a trifle indistinct. It can be improved, but it is not bad for a first experiment."

Blank cylinders were also sent to Gouraud so that he could make his own demonstration recordings. Famous people were invited to have their voices recorded. These included Robert Browning reciting his own verses, the silvery voice of Gladstone, and Arthur Sullivan. Arthur Sullivan was recorded saying, "I am astonished and somewhat terrified at the results of this evening's experiments – astonished at the wonderful power you have developed, and terrified at the thought that so much hideous and bad music may be put on record for ever."

That was Little Menlo, which drew so many distinguished visitors, and famous as the herald of the now familiar sound track and all it stands for. At the same period there was another Norwood house with unusual historical associations, and possessing a name possibly even more individual than Little Menlo.

Ly-ee-Moon was a large Victorian mansion that stood a hundred yards or so back from Church Road. It had been named Ly-ee-Moon by its first owner, Captain Norman Hill, who had been skipper of the *Ly-ee-Moon*, one of the great racing steamers that in the late 1850s had been replacing the clipper ships built specially for the opium traffic between India and China.

The *Ly-ee-Moon* was a true greyhound of the sea, and almost a sister ship to the Royal yacht, *Victoria and Albert*. The *Ly-ee-Moon*, which took her name from the Ly-ee-Moon Strait off the coast of China, was built specifically for the opium trade in 1860, and for some time held the record for the fastest opium runner afloat. She actually began her career as a blockade runner, and saw service off Charleston in the American war between the States. The *Ly-ee-Moon* then went into active participation on the opium run, where her great speed of 17 knots enabled her to out-distance any vessels commissioned by the Mandarins to oppose this nefarious trade.

The history of the *Ly-ee-Moon* was a chequered one. In 1872 she was rammed in Hong Kong harbour and sunk. She was raised and brought to England where she was reconditioned and then placed on the trade run between England and Singapore. After five years of this the *Ly-ee-Moon* was sailed to Australia and sold to the Australian Steamship Navigation Co. The ship lived up to the legend that no luck ever came to an opium runner. In 1878 she was gutted by fire in Sydney Harbour. She was restored, and then in 1886 the ship crashed on the rocks at Cape Green. She broke in two with the loss of 80 lives, and was a total wreck.

Captain Hill, the first master of the *Ly-ee-Moon*, placed in the hall of his house in Norwood a plate-glass window which bore a cut-glass outline of the ship under full steam and full sail. The glass window had a sea-blue surface, against which the crystal outline of the ship and waves gleamed white.

This handsome window was shattered by the blast of an enemy bomb during the war. Ly-ee-Moon House was demolished in the early 1960s, and a housing estate now exists in its place. Most regrettably, the name Ly-ee-Moon has not been commemorated, the authorities having settled for the more pedestrian name of Homelands for the redeveloped land, under the impression that the fire authorities, who are apparently considered in these matters, would find Homelands easier to understand and locate than Ly-ee-Moon!

There is a third house, however, that has yet survived the passing of the years. The Sycamores on Beulah Hill, and home of the author, dates back to 1690. In its beginnings it was a four-square building, with the present kitchen door the original front door. The 1690 cellars were wine and beer cellars, for the house was a house of call for travellers, and was also a tea garden. It is said that the extensive cellars were not unacquainted with the 18th century contraband spirits that passed through Norwood.

The house was enlarged in Regency times, and a photograph taken in the 1860s shows it with the fashionable belvedere of the period.

In the main, however, Norwood was going through a period of great change.

A Norwood resident, Mr. F. Amphlett Micklewright, wrote to the local press proposing that residents who were concerned about the state of affairs should meet together to discuss the formation of a society to watch and, where possible, influence the changes that were taking place.

On 5th February, 1960, thirty-six residents, including two local Borough Councillors, met in the All Saints School on Beulah Hill, and formed the Society for the Preservation of Upper Norwood and District. A provisional constitution was approved, with Mr. Micklewright as first Chairman, and Mrs. Hamilton Flint as first Hon. Secretary. It was generally agreed that the aims of the Society were to seek to preserve and protect existing local amenities, and to have a voice in the future developments affecting the district.

The preservation of local amenities largely meant protecting the wooded hills of Norwood, the skylines, and surroundings from bad and unsightly development, and to seek to prevent buildings of quality and character being needlessly destroyed.

Future building should, as far as possible, enhance natural beauties. As to how far a group of private citizens could exercise such an influence remained to be seen,.

The meeting made the headlines in the local papers. At a second meeting on 19th February, about 60 residents turned up, and discussed more fully the future work of the Society. The detailed aims were drawn up. They were:

"To influence public opinion and assure local authorities of the Society's interest.

"To preserve, protect, and improve the amenities of the district.

"To ensure that unoccupied land be kept in good order.

"Gradually to build up cultural activities.

"To issue publications bearing upon the aims and activities of the Society."

The official name for the Society was to be "The Society for the Preservation of Upper Norwood and District", but for general use a shortened version would be "Norwood Preservation Society."

Sir Ninian Comper, the distinguished church architect and stained and painted glass artist, was the Society's first President. He had come to live in Norwood in the early years of the century and had set up his studio at the top of Knight's Hill at Crown Point. It was there that many of his architectural plans were prepared, and where many of his famous church windows were painted and fired and pieced together in their traceries of lead. He later moved to The Priory on Beulah Hill, a large rambling house built in 1836, and to there he transferred his studio and glass ovens in 1948.

Sir John Betjeman, the present Poet Laureate, wrote of Ninian Comper: "No English architect is better known in cathedral close and distant rectory than J. N. Comper. Comper is, in the opinion of many, the only considerable living architect of churches, with the exception of one or two."

After the first year, in which it was growing in numbers and experience, the Society decided to change its name to "The Norwood Society". The word "Preservation" was not a complete success. "What is there to preserve?" was the facetious comment of some as they surveyed the post-war desolation. That the Society was really seeking to preserve the opportunity for enabling a new Norwood to emerge from the ashes of the old, so that it should compare favourably with its earlier charm, was perhaps too obscure. Preservation of trees, so distinctive a feature of Norwood, and their replacement when lost, was a first priority. Protection of skylines was another urgent matter. Preservation of semi-derelict Victorian houses that could not be adapted to modern requirements was not in the master plan. Accordingly, the word "Preservation", because it was open to so many inter-pretations, was abandoned.

In the Court Circular of 13th November, 1961, appeared the following paragraph:

"The Duke of Edinburgh has consented to become patron of the Crystal Palace Exhibition, which the Norwood Society will hold next May."

That was indeed an honour and a considerable feather in the cap of an amenity society not yet two years old, but which had grown then to be the largest of its kind, with a membership of over 400 people all deeply interested in the environment in which they lived.

The purpose of the exhibition was to bring to South Londoners a reminder of the forgotten glories of the Crystal Palace district. Thereby, it was hoped, people would be stirred to try to recover something of that which had been lost from an essentially residential district. The district had evolved spontaneously, with the Crystal Palace as its focus point, much as a seaside resort evolves from its own sea front. Take the inspiration away and the effect can be disastrous.

To a great extent the planning of the Norwood Society Exhibition was an act of faith. Its cost could have bankrupted the Society, but members themselves guaranteed the cost of the whole project. As it turned out, the guaranteed money was never called upon. The exhibition consisted largely of a massive display of photographs and drawings of the Crystal Palace–its inception, its life and death and the aftermath. The creation of the National Sports Centre was shown in models and drawings, and there were plans for a new Crystal Palace Exhibition Hall. (The Exhibition Hall idea was subsequently abandoned.)

The London County Council, after consulting with the Norwood Society, provided all the screens for the display, and also sent their own exhibition staff to set up the screens to the Norwood Society's plan, and connected up the electric lighting for the display. The exhibition was staged in the ballroom of the Crystal Palace Hotel.

Photographic expenses were heavy, many old and rare photographs and drawings being copied and then greatly enlarged. Here again the Society was spared expense. The great steel firm of Guest, Keen and Nettlefold, lineal descendents and successors of Fox and Henderson who built the Crystal Palace, paid all the cost of the photography. *The Illustrated London News* provided enlarged photographic reproductions of illustrations of historic Crystal Palace events. This, too, was done free of charge.

The name given to the exhibition was "The Crystal Palace Story". It was formally opened by Lord Bossom of Maidstone in the presence of the Mayor of Croydon, the Mayor of Camberwell, and the Member of Parliament for Norwood, Mr. John Fraser.

The exhibition was open to the public for 10 days, and during that time more than 3,000 people paid to see it. A television programme was made of it, the national press reviewed it favourably, while many overseas visitors, particularly from Canada and the United States, made the journey out to Norwood just to see pictures of a famous building which they had never seen but had always known about.

Not long after this the Town of Norwood, Massachusetts presented the Norwood Society with a banner brought over especially by Mr. George T. Mahoney, City Treasurer of Norwood, Mass. The banner was designed to commemorate the Incorporation of Norwood, Mass. as a township in 1872. The device on the banner is that of a young volunteer in a red coat with his musket on his shoulder, Aaron Guild, a Norwood, Mass. patriot. He is depicted leaving his oxen and plough behind to fight in the American War of Independence. The date of Aaron's departure to fight is given as April 19, 1775.

That Aaron Guild is shown leaving his oxen and plough to fight the English in no way diminishes the regard the English and American Norwoods hold for each other. George Mahoney became a member of the Norwood Society, and on February 23rd, 1972, a cablegram of congratulation was sent from Norwood, London to Norwood, Massachusetts on achieving its Centenary. The tradition in Norwood, Massachusetts is that it was so named by an original settler from Norwood, Surrey.

Much of the work of a local amenity society is somewhat that of a vigilante, watching for any signs of attempted erosion of amenities, and taking prompt counter-action.

Towards the end of 1963 it became known that an application had been made to the Council for permission to erect large advertising hoardings along a tree-clad frontage of a section of Beulah Hill. Behind the fringe of trees and bushes flats were being put up. The prospect of hoardings standing close to the pavement on an essentially residential road was strongly resisted by the residents. The Norwood Society also entered a formal objection, and in due course a letter was received in which it was stated that in view of the local residents' views the application for hoardings had been rejected.

This looked like success, but later the Council quite inexplicably reversed its decision and the advertisement hoardings were licensed to go up against their leafy background of forest trees. This produced a storm of indignation, so much so that when the time came for the contractors to apply for an extension of their licence it was refused. But the eyesore remained while the contractors appealed to the Ministry of Housing and Local Government. At the same time Croydon

Corporation submitted their objection to a renewal of the licence together with the objections made by the Norwood Society and local residents.

The Minister's decision, made on 4th April 1966, makes interesting reading to those who are concerned in preserving the amenities of the environment. It was as follows:

"Advertisements on temporary hoardings screening re-development operations are often acceptable on sites which would be unsuitable for a permanent display of posters. This is true especially when amenities are affected by the demolition and excavation works which precede the construction of new buildings. In the present case, the rebuilding is well advanced and any advantage which may be gained by the screening effect of the posters is outweighed by their incongruous appearance in this attractive street. The panels are completely out of character with the residential nature of the surroundings and they form an incongruous and over-obtrusive commercial intrusion in a pleasant road scene and the view from nearby residences. Although express consent is required for a limited period until the flats under construction are completed, it is thought that the display is so alien to the area and injurious to amenity that it ought not to remain in position. Accordingly the Minister dismisses the appeal."

Three important points emerged. The Minister agreed almost completely with the views put forward by the Norwood Society. The second point was that the approval for the poster displays and hoardings expired in October, but they were not removed until the following May, thus giving the advertising contractor an additional seven months use – seven months which clearly on the Minister's decision should not have been allowed. Thirdly, the incident remained an elementary lesson in public relations, not unnoticed by the Civic Trust, and became an example of where an amenity society had success-fully taken on Big Brother and shown positive results.

The Norwood Society kept in touch with the four local government authorities whose ancient boundaries met at the top of Anerley Hill, namely Croydon, Lambeth, Camberwell and Penge. The Society also maintained friendly relations with the London County Council.

A problem for the Norwood Society had been the apparent lack of co-operation on boundary matters existing between the various local authorities. They seemed to be oddly out of touch with Upper Norwood's needs. What to the Norwood community was a unified social group with complete community of interests was from the local government level almost as though each separate area was being as jealously guarded as in the days when the Archbishop's men confronted the King's men when beating the bounds.

An entertaining example of this boundary mentality was displayed in 1964 when the Norwood Society Planning Committee had talks with the Chairman of a Council Planning Committee on Triangle matters. A Norwood Society member observed that if the Crystal Palace was redeveloped it would have considerable impact on the Triangle, and that would affect the subject of the present discussion. The reply to that was that the Crystal Palace was not in this particular Council's area. It seemed almost to imply that so far as that Council was concerned, the Crystal Palace did not exist. Indeed, a plan of the borough hanging on the wall was shown to be surrounded by an inscrutable blankness of white!

One hastens to add that much water has flowed under the bridge since then, and such a remark would never be made today.

The year 1965 saw changes in matters of local government affecting Upper Norwood. Croydon ceased to be a County Borough and became the London Borough of Croydon. Lambeth, so far as Upper Norwood was concerned, remained unaffected. On the other hand, the Borough of Camberwell totally disappeared, being absorbed into the London Borough of Southwark, which for the first time so to speak, met its neighbours at the Vicar's Oak. The tiny Urban District of Penge, which had gained autonomy in 1904, was likewise swallowed up, to become part of the huge London Borough of Bromley.

The London County Council disappeared into the Greater London Council. This was important to the whole Norwood question. As the L.C.C., its interests in Upper Norwood had extended only as far as the Lambeth-Croydon boundary, and the Camberwell southern boundary plus the area of the Crystal Palace Park. Now for the first time in a thousand years of Norwood history a unifying force had come into being which might be of benefit to a sadly dilapidated and divided suburb.

In July 1966 the Norwood Society launched its second exhibition, "Living With the Palace". In addition to showing something of the historical past, it high-lighted the new National Recreation Centre, the shopping centre, the open spaces, trees and views and local industry. The exhibition also showed the chaos and confusion existing in the form of traffic problems and run-down property, and indicated how it could be dealt with by proper co-ordinated development.

H.R.H. the Duke of Edinburgh again honoured the Norwood Society by becoming Patron of the exhibition. Lord Kennet, Parliamentary Secretary to the Ministry of Housing and Local Government, performed the opening ceremony. The exhibition was held in the Crystal Palace Hotel ballroom, and the Greater London Council provided modern display screens and lighting.

In his opening address, Lord Kennet said: "Everybody who cares for the quality of his surroundings ought to welcome the growth of local amenity societies like the Norwood Society. It is excellent that the Norwood Society should stimulate public interest in the problem of urban planning and help to understand both the need for change and the ways in which change might be controlled for the common good. Our towns are being transformed rapidly under pressure of various kinds, traffic, decay, new economic and social needs. Norwood with its fine hillside site is no exception. Such amenity societies as the Norwood Society have a greater power than they sometimes realise. It is up to people like the Norwood Society to help improve what is bad and keep what is good."

The occasion was marked by the presence of the Mayors of Lambeth and Croydon, Mr. Gabriel White, Art Director of the Arts Council of Great Britain, and Mr. John Frazer, Member of Parliament for Norwood. The Press was there in strength. The *Crystal Palace Advertiser* said in its next issue: "It is very heartening to see such a public-spirited body of men and women who obviously have the welfare of Norwood very much at heart. Certainly they are proud of the area's past, but they are also very much concerned with its future. And far from being just concerned, they do something about it– something like the exhibition which has entailed a very great deal of hard work and research on the part of the members."

The Architect and Building News was blunt in its review. "There are some towns–like Richmond-on-Thames–where anyone can see there is a handful of things still worth preserving, but it is the hell-holes like Norwood that need loving defenders. It would be too easy for the G.L.C. to think–as many of us would be tempted to think–that Norwood couldn't possibly be harmed by a few more large-scale traffic jams. It is this kind of attitude that eventually makes a town so awful that no-one wants to revive it. So good luck to the society."

The Press generally supported the exhibition, and stressed the point the Society was making, that to live comfortably and well in the precincts of the shattered Crystal Palace depends on wise planning. It was an exercise in suburban development and suburban living which, if carried out with wisdom and generosity, would create a pattern for human relations which would last a hundred years.

Turning to the matter of trees in urban surroundings, it seemed to the Norwood Society that Lambeth Council was reasonably tree-conscious. Looking southward to the Norwood hills, Lambeth obviously valued its share of trees that abounded there.

So many lovely trees, beeches in particular, had been felled because it suited the developer to cut them down, that the Society established a Trees Sub-committee. Its first duty was to record all trees in the district, both singly and in clumps, that seemed worthy of protection, and apply to the authority concerned for them to be considered eligible for official preservation. By this means it was hoped to put a check to some of the tree slaughter that was going on.

The Trees Sub-committee was so successful and explicit in its work that Lambeth Council asked for an expert assessment by the Sub-committee's Chairman, Mr. R. Roxburgh, of the tree population in the Leigham Court Road area. As an outcome of this the Council put a preservation order on 297 trees. Croydon, too, had become tree-conscious in the Norwood area and had begun to put protection notices on selected trees and clumps of trees that could be seen from the road.

Preserving trees is no easy matter; preserving architectural relics in Norwood is equally difficult. The old All Saints School building, containing the headmaster's house, became a sad example of this.

The building stood next to All Saints Church on Beulah Hill. Both church and schoolhouse were architectured by James Savage, the well-known early Victorian architect. All Saints Church was built in 1829; the schoolhouse was finished in 1838. The two were complementary to each other and made a delightful corner of old Norwood. The school itself had been in continuous use as a school until 1968. It was also used as a church hall. Successive headmasters had lived there, and Archbishops in turn had met parishioners there when visiting All Saints Church. The history and fabric of the village schoolhouse was as much a part of the fabric of Norwood history for over a hundred years, as was the parish church itself.

When the new All Saints Schools were completed in 1967, the old schoolhouse and another school building of no architectural importance were made redundant. The intention of the Croydon Education Department was then to pull down the old buildings and increase thereby the already extensive playing space.

The Norwood Society protested at the proposed destruction of the original schoolhouse on the grounds of its historical background, that it was one of the nicest examples of early Victorian architecture, and, finally, that it could be usefully employed, and so fully justify its continued existence. The headmaster's house could be lived in by a family, and the two schoolrooms made into public rooms.

Meanwhile, the building was left unoccupied and quite unprotected. It suffered from vandals who did great damage. The All Saints Church Council considered the possibility of merely restoring the south wing and turning it into a parish hall while the rest of the building should be demolished. After adverse reports from a surveyor, the church abandoned the whole idea in favour of a plan for putting up a prefabricated building in the churchyard. This plan was objected to by the Norwood Society and others on the grounds that it would spoil the charm of the churchyard which gives a beautiful setting to the parish church, and which should be made a protected area for conservation.

In 1971 the Norwood Society made urgent representation to Croydon that the old schoolhouse should be preserved. The Education Committee replied by asking what the Society would be prepared to do to assist in the preservation. Accordingly, the Society arranged a professional survey of the building and prepared a detailed estimate of the cost of repairs. The plan was to reinstate the house as a dwelling and for that part to be let to a suitable person who would be able to act as caretaker of the two wings which had formerly been the classrooms. These could be put to use as meeting rooms, a local museum, a junior library, and even perhaps as auxiliary class rooms to the new school. It was also hoped that after such a renovation the parish church would be prepared to use the wing nearest to them as a church hall once more.

The Society's outline proposal announced that it was prepared to spend £5,000 or so on putting the house in good order, while there would be also other sources of funds to aid the restoration of an historic and useful building. It remains only to be said that the Education Authority rejected the Society's proposal and decided on demolition, which was afterwards carried out, whereby Norwood lost one of its few historic buildings.

The lesson to be learnt from this unhappy case and the Philistine attitude which grew up against retaining the building is that the Norwood Society should have stepped in strongly at the very beginning when the schoolhouse had been lately occupied and was still in good shape. In the preservation of amenities a continual vigilance and early anticipation of what others may do is an essential. In the case of the All Saints Schoolhouse, the Norwood Society might have won the day had it been quicker off the mark. The moral here in the matter of amenity and preservation is always to try to be one jump ahead.

In the latter part of 1969 the Society decided to launch its third exhibition. Attention at the time was being firmly directed on the Upper Norwood Triangle, sometimes derisively called the Eternal Triangle. Due to a deadly mixture of inertia, of waiting for somebody else to make the first move, and of conflicting interests, the Triangle was in an advanced state of physical and moral decline. Shops were becoming empty and a general depression among the tradesmen was becoming more and more evident.

The Norwood Society took the view that if a practical road scheme could be agreed by all parties there was no reason why the Triangle should not be revitalised forthwith. Tradesmen whose premises would not be affected by any road changes would be able to bring their premises up-to-date with confidence. Where leases were short they should be extended so as to make improvement of premises financially worth while.

The Triangle being essentially a Victorian village shopping centre, the style should be retained, and where possible existing buildings restored. As such it should be treated as a conservation area within broad limits. The Society set its face firmly against any grandiose scheme for total rebuilding.

This was the basic concept for the third exhibition, which bore the somewhat macabre name of "The Triangle – Dead or Alive!" Croydon and Lambeth, who were at the time involved in proposals for solving traffic problems and reconditioning the Triangle, held practically diametrically opposing views on how to go about it. The hope now was to try to bring them together. Accordingly, the Norwood Society invited both Councils to exhibit at the exhibition and display their respective theories on Triangle restoration. Various local groups and organisations, including the Rotary Club, the local Chamber of Commerce, and the newly formed Crystal Palace Triangle Community Association all offered their contributions.

The principal exhibit of the Norwood Society was its plan for a diversionary road to clear the main stream of through traffic out of Westow Hill, and thereby provide a formula for a future revitalisation of the Triangle. This was the brain child of the Society's Planning Chairman, Mr. Leo Held, and consisted of an underpass, or cut-and-cover road, on the south side of Westow Hill, and roughly parallel with it. The special advantages claimed was that Westow Hill could then be converted into a shopping precinct, while the cover of the underpass could be turned into gardens and a walkway.

Mr. Arthur Skeffington, M.P., Joint Parliamentary Secretary for the Ministry of Housing and Local Government, had accepted the Norwood Society's invitation to open the Exhibition. Mr. Skeffington was, in the opinion of the Norwood Society, the ideal man for the job. He was the champion of the grand conception that local people and local bodies should be encouraged to co-operate and participate with local government in all matters that concerned them. To gild the lily, Mr. Skeffington had himself lived in Norwood and was gratifyingly familiar with local problems.

In his speech, the Joint Parliamentary Secretary said: "People should be able to say what kind of community they want and how it should develop. It is everyone's right to be allowed to have a say in how their environment should be developed. I can see an intense feeling of frustration if people are not given the opportunity to help in their community, and I would congratulate the Norwood Society for blazing the trail with their exhibition."

Three thousand people visited the exhibition, which was open from 20th to 31st January, 1970. In conjunction with it a public meeting was arranged by the Society for January 30th. This was a very full meeting, and a great many people showed that they were very tired of the years of stagnation, as well as deploring the spectacle of two local government authorities confessing themselves unable to agree on what should be done to put the Triangle back on its feet. A resolution was adopted by the 250 or so Norwood residents from both the Lambeth side and the Croydon side who were present at the meeting. It was as follows:

"That this meeting urges the Councils of the London Boroughs of Croydon and Lambeth to instruct their officers to construct together an agreed plan for the revitalisation of the Triangle, to be endorsed by the respective Councils in time for presentation at a further public meeting in the autumn of this year."

This was local history in the making, something which had never quite happened before. It indicated the growing influence of an amenity society in matters concerning local government.

News of the fantastic Triangle situation got around. In June 1970 an article appeared in *Architectural Design* by Mr. L. Hansen. "For years one of South London's most unusual centres – the Westow Hill Triangle, Norwood – has slowly lingered into an advanced stage of neglect, except for the passing vehicles which clog its main street. Fading memories still recall the prosperous times when folks came from miles around just to be in the amazing Crystal Palace standing next door.

"The centre itself is an extraordinary enough place. The principal shopping street (Westow Hill) runs East-West on a ridge top which defines the southern edge of the Thames Valley, with sharp falls and panoramas. This is a narrow, delightfully scaled street full of Victorian eccentricity, also serving as 'metropolitan road' carrying through traffic for which it is inadequate. The street forms the base of the Triangle, the other two sides leading down the southern slope and housing miscellaneous shops, some derelict, and businesses. In the centre of it all in an obsolete warren of industrial activity.

"The Triangle has long awaited planning action, the lack of which is mainly responsible for the decay. After years of campaigning, the traders and the Norwood Society evoked quite contrary schemes from the two local councils concerned. . . In January the Society's exhibition, 'The Triangle – Dead or Alive!' exhibited the boroughs' schemes alongside plans prepared by private individuals including Owen Luder, and Leo Held, Norwood Society's Planning Chairman.

"It was an adroit move, because goodies and baddies stood out in clear relief. . . . A scheme could have been presented years ago."

As it turned out, no agreed plan was forthcoming at the public meeting which took place in the following October. The contending local government officials had not found a formula acceptable to both sides for getting the Triangle out of the doldrums, and it was only too evident that they were quite unable to come to terms. Both sides had dug their heels in. The ordinary Norwood people who had come to hear something tangible at long last were not at all pleased.

Then it was that a new factor appeared on the embattled scene in the person of the Chairman of the South East Board of the Greater London Council Environmental Committee. No one had expected him, nor for that matter had anybody been expected from the G.L.C., as none had turned up at the previous meeting. His arrival, therefore, was in the nature of the God from the Machine.

He listened with great attention to the observations which had been coming across from the frustrated and quietly angry Norwood people. The climax came when he rose to his feet and said how deeply impressed he was with the arguments he had heard put forward by Norwood residents, *and promised that something would be done!*

That indeed appeared to be the thaw for which the Society had been working for so long. The Norwood Society's Chairman, John Yaxley, said: "If we discovered any hope to be extracted from the meeting it was this assurance that the South East Board would now be moving to break the deadlock which had so far frustrated all local efforts concerning the Triangle. Furthermore, he gave his undertaking to advise the Norwood Society of the Greater London Council's plans and deliberations on the Triangle *at the same* time as the Councils concerned are advised."

Certainly some sort of break-through had at last been achieved after years of frustration. The tired old static state of affairs would never be quite the same again. An amenity society had at last been able to force local government attention on the domestic problems that had so beset the neighbourhood.

The proposed G.L.C. plan made its appearance in August, 1971. It was a provisional plan, presented to the Councils involved, and to the Norwood Society, for criticism and amendments, but it was the first tangible step towards breaking the Triangle deadlock. Once it was accepted, in any modified form which might emerge, or, for that matter, an agreed alternative road scheme, it would release the brake that had been holding up revitalisation in its iron grasp. Fresh life could be injected into a suburban shopping area that had been dying on its feet for more than a decade.

The appearance of the G.L.C. plan was followed in September by a visit to the Triangle of the Chairman of the Croydon Planning Committee, on a fact-finding tour. He was conducted on this intricate tour by officials of the Norwood Society and other Norwood associations invited for the occasion.

One may ask where all this stirring of the pot by the Norwood Society was leading, and what was the impact. Its basic importance was a moral one. In place of laissez-faire and frustrating inertia, it built up interest in the neighbourhood, developed pride in local citizenship, and demanded that surroundings should be improved for the direct benefit of those who live there. If an amenity society succeeds in prodding a local council into becoming aware that local residents are not mere cyphers to be pushed around to suit their convenience, then it has achieved something.

At long last, but only after the Norwood Society had played its ace, "The Triangle – Dead or Alive!", and followed it up with the sound and the fury of public meetings, has thinking on the shopping centre taken a turn which may lead to some constructive results. As a positive indication the Triangle has now been considered as an area suitable for conservation. A Conservation Area under the Town and Country Planning Act, 1971, is defined as "an area of special architectural or historical interest, the character or appearance of which it is desirable to preserve or enhance."

When only a few years ago all that the planners seemed to want to do was to pull down the Triangle and build something new and ultra-modern, to be talking now in terms of conserving its Victorian charm is enlightened thinking indeed. There is hope for the Triangle yet.

That for the moment is where the history of Norwood pauses. But there is a stirring in the ashes.

Bibliography

This bibliography has been arranged in order of publication dates.

History of Croydon, G. Steinman Steinman, Longman, Rees, Orme, Brown, Green, & Longman, 1834

A Guide to The Beulah Spa, Norwood, J. Wyld, 1834

The Removal of the Crystal Palace, Lord's Day Observance Tract, 1852

The Crystal Palace and Park, Samuel Phillips, Crystal Palace Library, 1854

English Hearts and English Hands, or The Railway and the Trenches, James Nisbet & Co., 1858

Aerostatic Magazine, edited by Henry Coxwell, 1869

The Life of Isambard Kingdom Brunel, Civil Engineer, Isambard Brunel, Longmans, Green & Co., 1870

Travels in the Air, James Glaisher, F.R.S., Richard Bentley, (Second Edition) 1871

Ye Parish of Camerwell, William Harnett Blanch, E. W. Allen, 1875

Sydenham, Dulwich and Norwood, T. Fisher Unwin, 1881

Chronicle of the Parish of Croydon, J. Corbet Anderson, Reeves and Turner, 1882

Croydon in the Past, Jesse W. Ward, "Croydon Advertiser" Offices, 1883

History of Streatham, J. R. Nicholl, Elliot Stock, 1886

Reminiscences of a Country Journalist, Thomas Frost, Ward & Downey, 1886

Life of Ann Catley, London, 1888

Platt's Handbook to the Crystal Palace District, J. Platt, 1888

The Life of Sims Reeves, by himself, Simpkin Marshall, 1888

Croydon Inclosure, J. Corbet Anderson, Printed for the Subscribers, 1889

My Life and Balloon Experiences, Henry Coxwell, W. H. Allen & Co., 1889

Norwood and Dulwich, Allan M. Galer, Truslove and Shirley, 1890

The Light of Other Days, Willert Beale, Richard Bentley & Son, 1890

Upper, West and South Norwood, J. Corbet Anderson, Printed for the Subscribers, 1898

South London, Walter Besant, Chatto & Windus, 1899

The Early Married Life of Maria Josepha Lady Stanley, with Extracts from Sir John Stanley's 'Praeterita', edited by Jane H. Adeane, Longmans, Green & Co., 1899

Picturesque Norwood, J. A. Squire, 1899, 1902 and 1906

C. H. Spurgeon's Autobiography, compiled by his wife, Passmore and Alabaster, 1897–1900

Historic Souvenir of The Crystal Palace, Austin Freyers, Daily Express, 1900

Croydon, New and Old, Edward A. Martin, Homeland Association, 1901

Memories of Norwood Since 1852, Mrs. Elizabeth Louisa Dee, G. Lucas

Life and Letters of Sir George Grove, Charles L. Graves, Macmillan & Co., 1903

"Borough" Guide to Sydenham, Forest Hill and District, 1909

August Manns and the Saturday Concerts, H. Saxe Wyndham, The Walter Scott Publishing Co. Ltd., 1909

Springs, Streams and Spas of London, Alfred Stanley Foord, T. Fisher Unwin, 1910

Aerial Navigation of Today, Charles C. Turner, Seeley & Co., 1910

The Amazing Duchess, Charles E. Pearce, Stanley Paul & Co., 1911

The Crystal Palace, Sydenham, Auction Catalogue, 1911

The Romance and History of the Crystal Palace, J. E. Preston Muddock, Official Souvenir Edition, 1911

Norwood in Days of Old, W. T. Phillips, Truslove & Bray, Ltd., 1912

Journal of the Aeronautical Society of Great Britain, 1912

Old London's Spas, Baths, and Wells, Septimus Sunderland, John Bale, Sons and Danielsson, Ltd., 1915

Life and Friendships of Catherine Marsh, L. E. O'Rorke, Longmans, Green & Co., 1917

Birthplace of Aerial Power, published by the Grahame-White Co. Ltd., 1919

Pyrotechnics, Alan St. H. Brock, Daniel O'Connor, 1923

Sims Reeves, Charles E. Pearce, Stanley Paul & Co., 1924

Arthur Seymour Sullivan, Henry Saxe Wyndham, Kegan Paul, 1926

Hamlet of Penge with Anerley, Sidney Hodgson, The Public Library, Penge, 1927

Steamships in Australia, Dickson Gregory, Richards Press, 1928

By-Ways in the History of Croydon, Clarence G. Paget, The Central Library, Croydon, 1929

Henson and Stringfellow, J. B. Davy, H.M. Stationery Office, 1931

The Grand Surrey Iron Railway, F. G. Bing, Croydon Public Libraries, 1931

Forgotten Croydon, Ronald Bannerman, Croydon Times, 1933

The Opium Clippers, Basil Lubbock, Brown, Son & Ferguson Ltd., 1933

C. H. Spurgeon, J. C. Carlile, Religious Tract Society, 1933

Paxton and the Bachelor Duke, Violet R. Markham, Hodder & Stoughton, 1935

A Blind Musician Looks Back, Alfred Hollins, William Blackwood & Sons Ltd., 1936

Early Railways in Surrey, Charles E. Lee, The Railway Gazette, 1944

Journal of the Royal Aeronautical Society, 1946 and 1966

Fireworks and Fetes, Alan St. H. Brock and Webster Murray, 1947

A History of Fireworks, Alan St. H. Brock, Harrap, 1949

Sir Arthur Sullivan, Herbert Sullivan and Newman Flower, Cassell, 1950

London County Council (Crystal Palace) Act, 1951, H.M. Stationery Office.

Augustus Hervey's Journal, edited by David Erskine, William Kimber, 1953

The Railway Engineers, O. S. Nock, B. T. Batsford Ltd., 1955

Survey of London: The Parish of St. Mary Lambeth, Part Two, Southern Area, London County Council, 1956

Unusual Railways, John R. Ray and B. G. Wilson, Frederick Muller, 1957

In the Footsteps of Sherlock Holmes, Michael Harrison, Cassell, 1958

Flying Witness: Harry Harper, Grahame Wallace, Putnam, 1958

Claude Grahame-White, Grahame Wallace, Putnam, 1960

Edison: A Biography, Matthew Josephson, Eyre & Spottiswoode, 1961

The Works of Sir Joseph Paxton, George F. Chadwick, The Architectural Press, 1961

Santos-Dumont, Peter Wykeham, Putnam, 1962

Atmospheric Railways, Charles Hadfield, David & Charles, 1967

'Neath the Mask, John M. East, George Allen & Unwin Ltd., 1967

The Canals of South and South East England, Charles Hadfield, David & Charles, 1969

Index